The making and unmaking of an evangelical mind

Edward John Carnell

The making and unmaking of an evangelical mind

The case of Edward Carnell

RUDOLPH NELSON
State University of New York at Albany

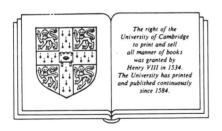

The right of the
University of Cambridge
to print and sell
all manner of books
was granted by
Henry VIII in 1534.
The University has printed
and published continuously
since 1584.

CAMBRIDGE UNIVERSITY PRESS
Cambridge
New York   New Rochelle   Melbourne   Sydney

Published by the Press Syndicate of the University of Cambridge
The Pitt Building, Trumpington Street, Cambridge CB2 1RP
32 East 57th Street, New York, NY 10022, USA
10 Stamford Road, Oakleigh, Melbourne 3166, Australia

First published 1987

Printed in the United States of America

Library of Congress Cataloging-in-Publication Data
Nelson, Rudolph, 1928–
The making and unmaking of an evangelical mind.
Includes index.
1. Carnell, Edward John, 1919–1967. 2. Evangelicalism
–United States–History–20th century. 3. Theology,
Doctrinal–United States–History–20th century.
I. Title.
BR1643.C37N45   1988   230'.044'0924 [B]   87-12079
ISBN 0 521 34263 5

British Library Cataloguing in Publication Data applied for

For Shirley White Nelson

Contents

Let me say a word about that anxious breed of younger men who are conservative in theology but are less than happy when they are called "fundamentalists." These men are both the cause and the effect of a radical atmospheric change within American orthodoxy.[1]

Edward Carnell

Man's anxiety in leaving embeddedness is the one most powerful antagonist of his world-openness.[2]

Ernest G. Schachtel

Preface

In an attempt to explain the cluster of influences and circumstances that led him to write a biography of Harry Crosby, an obscure American expatriate of the 1920s, Geoffrey Wolff said: "It seemed to me . . . that any story that had stuck to my memory fifteen years was trying to tell me something."[1]

Edward Carnell is surely just as obscure a figure as Harry Crosby, except to Protestant evangelical Christians of a certain vintage, and this preface would normally be the appropriate place for me to explain who he was, how I finally decided his story had been trying to tell *me* something for years, and why readers today – even those who feel no kinship whatsoever with evangelicals or fundamentalists – ought to be interested in a book about him.

However, since those questions are an integral part of what I have tried to do in the first chapter, I will not discuss them here. What I will do instead is offer my thanks to a number of people.

One of the first and most discouraging discoveries I made when I actually began working on this project, rather than merely thinking about doing it sometime, was that no collection of Carnell papers existed. Shortly after Edward Carnell died, his widow sold the family home, gave away his books and his opera recordings, and (with one or two exceptions) destroyed all his correspondence and personal papers – not for any dark, conspiratorial reason but simply because she assumed they were of no value to anyone. I was astonished to find out that Fuller Theological Seminary had no files of correspondence and papers covering Carnell's five-year presidency – again with a few notable exceptions that I found scattered in cardboard boxes in a seminary basement storeroom. I had his published books and articles, of course, and official personnel files, but in the absence of these other primary source materials, I had to depend heavily on Carnell's family, friends, colleagues, college classmates, and former students for the enriching details that are the lifeblood of this kind of book.

I am grateful most of all to Shirley Carnell, Edward Carnell's widow (now Mrs. John Duvall), without whose gracious cooperation the project would never have gotten off the ground. Carnell's older brother and sister (Paul Carnell and Dorothy Carnell Campbell) provided invaluable information and insights about their family life in the Midwest during the 1920s and 1930s. Donald Weber, Carnell's brother-in-law, provided a uniquely valuable perspective, both as a member of the family and as Carnell's intimate colleague in the administration at Fuller Seminary.

Gradually, as I interviewed and corresponded with scores of people, the informational lacunae began to fill up with facts, anecdotes, and reminiscences. Whereas it would be folly to try to list all the contributors, a few deserve special mention: John Graybill, the late Carlton Gregory, James Tompkins, the late Joseph Bayly, James Mignard, Paul Jewett, William Buehler, Bernard Ramm, Dan Fuller, Lars Granberg, David Hubbard, Joe Cosgrove, Lloyd Dean, and the late Glenn Barker.

Three members of the fraternity of historians (in whose territory I am something of an interloper) gave me considerable guidance and encouragement. Professor William McLoughlin of Brown University, mentor and model, planted a new thought in my mind one afternoon in 1968 when he challenged me to make a serious study of my evangelical heritage. Later he did a thorough and penetrating critique of an early version of one of this book's chapters, which subsequently became a journal article on the Harvard fundamentalists. That article brought me in touch with Professor George Marsden, whose published work on American fundamentalism I had already read with respect and admiration. At the same time that I was completing this book, George was working on his forthcoming history of Fuller Seminary.[2] It was his discovery of an entire file of Carnell–Ockenga correspondence in the attic of the Ockenga house in Hamilton, Massachusetts, that filled in the biggest and most significant gap in the missing primary sources. Without his generous sharing of that find – and without his later comments and suggestions on a draft of the entire manuscript – this would have been a far less valuable book. Several years ago, Warren Roberts, professor of history at the State University of New York at Albany, asked me a leading question about my Carnell project on a drive down the interstate from Lake George. He listened intently and asked further questions for sixty miles, and has been an active source of support ever since.

Although Professor Hyatt Waggoner, former chair of the American Civilization program at Brown University, played only an indirect role in the evolution of this book, his influence for good on my life and career at a crucial stage was incalculable and I am greatly in his debt.

I wish to thank also for their timely and generous assistance the staffs of various educational institutions and libraries: Wheaton College, Westminster Seminary, Harvard Divinity School, Boston University, Fuller Theological Seminary, Gordon-Conwell Theological Seminary, the Billy Graham Center at Wheaton College, and the State University of New York at Albany. Two sabbatical leaves of absence from my responsibilities at SUNY–Albany enabled me to work full time on the project at two different stages. A grant from the SUNY–Albany Small Grants Program eased the financial pressure during the second of those leaves in the 1984–5 academic year.

Of the many people at Cambridge University Press who have made important contributions to this book, I have known only a few by name. In thanking David Emblidge, Katharita Lamoza, Susan Conn, and Joyce Blanchette, I intend also to express my sincere appreciation to all of their colleagues. As my manuscript made its way through the publication process, the skill and thoughtfulness of the Cambridge personnel lent credibility to my illusion that mine was the only book on their production schedule.

Finally, there is nothing quite like the experience of sharing married life with another writer who is just as deeply involved in her own creative projects. Let the dedication of this book to Shirley Nelson stand as a grateful recognition of the manifold ways in which she contributed to it, as a joyful affirmation of her central importance to everything I do, and as a witness to my love and affection.

Albany, New York   *Rudolph Nelson*
May 1987

Acknowledgments

A shorter version of Chapter V appeared under the title "Fundamentalism at Harvard: The Case of Edward John Carnell." Reprinted from *Quarterly Review: A Scholarly Journal for Reflection on Ministry*, summer, 1982, with permission of The United Methodist Publishing House and The United Methodist Board of Higher Education and Ministry, copyright © 1982.

Emily Dickinson, "Lad of Athens, faithful be," reprinted by permission of the publishers and the Trustees of Amherst College from *The Poems of Emily Dickinson*, edited by Thomas J. Johnson, Cambridge, Mass.: The Belknap Press of Harvard University Press, Copyright © 1951, 1955, 1979, 1983 by The President and Fellows of Harvard College.

Excerpts from Chad Walsh, "Ode on the First Ape that Became a Man," reprinted with the permission of Ohio University Press from *The End of Nature* by Chad Walsh, Swallow Press, 1969.

Robert Frost, "The Armful," from *The Poetry of Robert Frost*, edited by Edward Connery Lathem. Copyright © 1928, 1969 by Holt, Rinehart and Winston. Copyright © 1956 by Robert Frost. Reprinted by permission of Henry Holt and Company.

Robert Frost, "The Armful," from *The Poetry of Robert Frost* edited by Edward Connery Lathem. Reprinted by permission of Jonathan Cape Ltd.

Part one

CHAPTER I

The narrow ridge and the cognitive bargain

On a warm December afternoon in 1977, I parked my rented car outside the Alameda County Courthouse in Oakland, California, and sat for a few minutes before keeping my appointment with the County Medical Examiner. I had gone first to the palatial Claremont Hotel, in the hills between Oakland and Berkeley, overlooking the bay. Ten years earlier, the body of Edward Carnell had been found in his room at the hotel, an hour before he was scheduled to deliver a luncheon address to the delegates of a Roman Catholic ecumenical congress. He had been dead since the previous evening. Now I was about to read the coroner's report, which the present Medical Examiner had promised to pull for me.

As I entered his office, I saw that he had been studying the contents of the file. He found, he said, something rather strange about it. I assumed he must be referring to the fact that a theological seminary professor had died in circumstances that raised the question of suicide. But that was not what had caught his attention. He pointed out that whereas the office usually received a half-dozen or so requests for copies of the coroner's report on such cases, this file had an entire second envelope filled with requests, dozens of them, from all over the country. He could not figure it out. It did not take long to solve the mystery. Shuffling quickly through the letters, I recognized some of the names: the nationally famous pastor of a large Southern Baptist church, a right-wing fundamentalist college president, a writer of militant religious pamphlets, an executive of a hyperconservative separatist denomination. Even the unfamiliar names – some of them – were easily classifiable: pastors of independent fundamentalist churches in the Bible Belt, or laypersons whose very words betrayed unintentionally and not very subtly the thirst for damaging information. An Indiana minister had requested several copies.

It was all too clear what had happened. Edward Carnell, with a background himself of impeccable fundamentalist credentials, had become an object of intense criticism in the last decade of his life because of what some considered dangerous ideas. Now, having heard that he had died mysteriously in a hotel room, 400 miles from home, the guardians of the true faith had gathered around the body, hoping to find evidence of a tarnished reputation that would invalidate his unacceptable ideas.

For reasons I will explain, by this time I was already firmly committed to writing a biographical study of Carnell. If I needed further confirmation of my decision, I found it that morning in Oakland. I sensed anew that in the life and death of Edward Carnell there was a *story* to tell, an important story that might touch a nerve in the human spirit.

My own interest in Carnell goes all the way back to 1948 when I was a student at Providence Bible Institute in Rhode Island. As a graduation gift, an ex-roommate gave me a copy of Carnell's first book, *Introduction to Christian Apologetics,* winner of a $5,000 prize in a contest sponsored by a religious publishing house. As more of his books appeared – *A Philosophy of the Christian Religion, The Theology of Reinhold Niebuhr* – I bought them for my own growing library, where for years (I admit with some embarrassment) they remained unread. There was one Carnell book I did read: *Television: Servant or Master* (1951), a balanced approach to this rambunctious new medium of communication and a refreshing recognition that the rigid fundamentalist stand against Hollywood motion pictures had suddenly been rendered defunct. During this time I also began meeting young men and women who had studied under Carnell at either Gordon College or Fuller Seminary. Invariably they remembered him as the best teacher they had ever had, a man who perpetually agonized over whether or not he was communicating clearly to his students the profound complexities of his philosophical and theological material.

My interest in Carnell deepened significantly in the early 1960s, shortly after I had joined the faculty of a Christian liberal arts college – the same institution from which I had been graduated in 1948. Then, as Providence Bible Institute, it had still been reasonably content to be identified as *fundamentalist.* Now it had changed its name to Barrington College and – like Carnell, like a whole generation of restless erstwhile fundamentalists, myself included – much preferred to be known as evangelical. For some the shift brought traumatic complications over the years. Sometime early in the 1960s I heard that Carnell had suffered a breakdown and that his psychological troubles were related to merciless criticism leveled against him by those who disapproved of what they interpreted as defection from a conservative theological position. When the news came in 1967 that Carnell had died, and when the rumor began circulating that he may have committed suicide, some of us who by then had drifted to the outer margins of evangelical acceptance (and had begun ourselves to hear criticism from those more theologically orthodox) felt toward him a deep and genuine kinship.

I do not mean to say that I think of myself as a spiritual and psychological blood brother to Edward Carnell. I could never live the kind of life he chose, and my personality, tastes, and inclinations are so vastly different from his that I have had trouble imaginatively projecting myself into his experience. But my life and Carnell's have occupied at least one significant area of common ground: a persistent concern with the foundational problem of Christianity's credibility. I had had difficulties with Christian belief almost as far back as I can remember, although for long periods of time I buried them. Carnell was important to me because he had developed an apologetic for Christian orthodoxy that refused to turn its back on modern threats to belief.

But, you recall, I had not even read Carnell's books. They remained as dust collectors on the shelf. Precisely. If Edward Carnell played a role in preserving my faith, at least for a time, it was surely in a way he never intended. He was a talismanic figure who had read Kant and Hegel and Hume and Nietzsche, who had dealt also with those more problematic and perhaps more subtly dangerous thinkers, Kierkegaard and Reinhold Niebuhr, and who had ventured into the labyrinthine lair of the unbelieving Beast and emerged safely orthodox with not one but two doctoral degrees to hang as trophies in his study: a Th.D. from Harvard Divinity School and a Ph.D. from Boston University in successive years. Knowing he had those credentials, who needed actually to *read* his books?

By the time Carnell died in 1967, I was beyond the point where his books, read or unread, could have changed the course of my life. For about this time I was forced to acknowledge that for some twenty years my own faith had been suffering a steady process of erosion. The word erosion almost always carries pejorative connotations, and I certainly did not use it in those years to describe what was happening to me. I would have been much more pleased with the self-congratulatory notion that I was a sculptor chipping off superfluous matter in the effort to uncover a beautiful work of art. In the sculpture metaphor, what I was losing was not worth keeping anyway, and I would be left with a smaller core of Christian affirmations in which I *really* believed. But then parts of the core started to chip away too. I wondered if there was enough stone left to make a work of art. The erosion metaphor was the right one after all. It is one thing, though, to lose a few inches a year off the Atlantic shoreline. It is quite another thing to feel ominous subterranean rumblings and discover that the river of doubt has been eating away under the ground and that one's whole house of faith inevitably will soon be poised on the edge of the abyss.

Having glimpsed this much of the future, I knew that I could not merely sit back and watch faith erode. I concluded that I must sink a column of steel into solid rock – into some foundation that would not erode – and build a new house, however modest and unimpressive it might be. The solid rock had to be a complete honesty (as much honesty as I was capable of, at least) about my religious beliefs. If necessary I would think the unthinkable – and not in any dilettantish or merely academic way. I was through playing intellectual games.

The break with the past was not easy – not for one brought up in strict Protestant fundamentalism, trained for "full-time Christian service" in a Bible Institute, and spiritually nurtured throughout four undergraduate years at Brown University by Inter-Varsity Christian Fellowship. Add to that a liberal seminary education at Boston University School of Theology, a two-year stint as part-time pastor of a small-town church, and a decade on the faculty of an evangelical Christian college. I do not wish to attach more importance to all this than it deserves; I am simply making the point that I was solidly and actively entrenched in the conservative Christian tradition.

I might very well have stayed where I was. Some in my position could legitimately have done so. I could not. I resigned from the college faculty for several reasons, the most important of which was the annual requirement of signing a "Statement of Faith." At this point in my evolving faith journey, my adherence to several items in the institution's creed was so problematic as to raise in my own mind a serious question of personal integrity. Whatever resentment I felt over the conviction that I had to leave was soon far outweighed by the inner freedom to find out who I really was under all those layers of ill-fitting loyalties.

In order to bring Carnell back into the picture, I must explain briefly what I did for the next four years after resigning from the Barrington College faculty. Having sneaked into the teaching profession through the back door without completing requirements for a doctoral degree in literature, the field in which I was teaching, I realized that if I decided to stay in higher education there was only one road to take. I enrolled in the American Civilization doctoral program at Brown University. It is difficult for me to identify with the horror stories others tell about graduate school. I was a starving man at a feast. I also enjoyed an unexpected bonus: course work in my three fields (American literature, social and intellectual history, and religion) as well as my dissertation project seemed to fall into place to help make sense of my own experience and of the religious tradition in which I had grown up. Ironically (it *seemed* ironic to me at the time, much less so now), recognizing and accepting the fact that I had cut all my ties with creedal and institutional Christianity freed me to appreciate the values, as well as to see more clearly the shortcomings, of that background. The more deeply I probed, the more I saw to explore. With graduate work behind me and an appointment to the English department of the State University of New York at Albany, I knew that in addition to scholarly writing in my primary discipline, I would be continuing my research into American religious history. On reflection, it occurred to me that Edward Carnell, with his background in and deep commitment to both fundamentalism and evangelicalism, might provide a useful focal point for my interests and concerns.

I have already used the terms "fundamentalist" and "evangelical" as if there were general agreement on what they mean. Of course there is not. Each term activates different sets of conditioned responses that jeopardize meaningful discussion. "Fundamentalism," having become part of the common lexicon, is especially troublesome. We *think* we know who the fundamentalists are: They are the benighted others. For eighteen months, while Iranians held American diplomatic personnel hostage in the Teheran embassy, nightly television shows reported the actions of their "Shiite fundamentalist captors." The media thereby reinforced an already existing tendency to identify fundamentalism with religiously based fanaticism anywhere in the world, adamantly resistant to rational persuasion, intellectually out of touch with modernity. However vague we might be about our own religious commitments (if any), it is reassuring to know we are not fundamentalists. Our actual knowledge about fundamentalism, though, is often just a notch or two above absolute zero.

"Evangelicalism" evokes a different response. Americans have learned that former President Jimmy Carter is an evangelical but are not quite sure about President Reagan. We know that Billy Graham is an evangelical but wonder whether Jerry Falwell might be more accurately classified a fundamentalist. Whereas virtually everyone confidently presumes to know what fundamentalism is, the term *evangelicalism* is more likely to elicit either a blank look or an unexamined assumption that it must be merely another name for fundamentalism. Even in supposedly informed discourse, both terms are used with a minimum of precision and with little historical awareness of the connections between them.

Here is what I mean when I use the terms in this book. When American Protestantism faced intellectual crises in the late nineteenth century, precipitated chiefly by Darwinism and higher criticism of the Bible, a long struggle began between factions that supported conflicting strategies. The conservative wing argued that the liberal receptivity to modern learning undermined essential Christian doctrines. Between 1910 and 1915, some in this group published a series of pamphlets collectively called "The Fundamentals," written by a number of British and American scholars and popular religious figures, presenting the conservative arguments against modernism on a range of controversial issues. By the time the battle heated up in the 1920s, the antimodernists had been given the name fundamentalists. After they were put to rout in the 1925 Scopes trial in Dayton, Tennessee (over the evolution issue), they retreated behind the impenetrable walls of antimodernist ideology. Some fundamentalists followed the strategy of remaining within the major denominations as a leavening influence; others gave up the struggle and became separatists with varying degrees of militancy. For a number of reasons, the dividing line between these two groups was often indistinct. Whatever the ecclesiastical strategy, though, to be a fundamentalist was to be an enemy of modernism. Carnell was nurtured in this tradition.[1]

Twentieth-century evangelicalism was a later development, although it has nineteenth-century roots. When fundamentalism hardened its resistance to modernity after 1925, it did not by any means give up the fight. It changed the battle strategy. At the same time as the liberal denominations were going through a religious depression (parallel to the nation's economic depression), the fundamentalists were thriving.[2] They developed their own institutional network of churches, denominations, mission boards, Bible institutes and colleges, summer conferences, and radio programs. Although still a despised minority in the culture as a whole, by the late 1930s they found several reasons for thinking that a national religious revival might be on the way. Consistent with this new optimistic outlook, in the 1940s a new generation of fundamentalists decided it was time to reenter the modern world. Forsaking what they judged to be the much too negative orientation of an older fundamentalism, which established its identity by what the group opposed, they began to move positively in a number of directions. Most significantly for our purposes, many of their young scholars who were interested in the fields of philosophy, theology, and biblical studies enrolled in the top graduate schools of the country and emerged to take important academic positions within the fundamentalist educational network. At first they were not at pains to slough off the label fundamentalist, but as the 1940s progressed they showed an increasing preference to be known as evangelicals. When I use the term *evangelical* in this book, I am referring to these heirs of the 1920s fundamentalists. They have also been called "new evangelicals" and "post-fundamentalists."[3] Whereas they differed hardly at all from the fundamentalists in their theology, they affirmed the necessity of answering the threat of modernity by a response more effective than a retreat behind the fortress walls of militant ignorance.

This was the evangelicalism for which Carnell was a sort of intellectual bellwether from the time he emerged from his graduate study at Harvard Divinity School and Boston University, through his career at Fuller Theological Seminary (the movement's premier educational institution) as professor and then president. No one in the evangelical renaissance was more influential in shattering the legacy of fundamentalist withdrawal from modernity and insisting that evangelicals confront the toughest issues of modern times. The life and writings of Edward Carnell became a lens through which I could see and understand more clearly both my own heritage and certain important developments in American religious history.

However, although readers may be willing to grant me the appropriateness of my own interest in Carnell and recognize the legitimate interest of those whose personal backgrounds or professional responsibilities intersect fundamentalism or evangelicalism in various ways, not everyone shares these interests and concerns. Willy Loman's wife plaintively insisted that "attention must be paid" to the life and death of her very ordinary salesman husband. Should attention be paid to Edward Carnell? Does his importance transcend the parochialism of his own religious milieu?

A sizable number of twentieth-century historians have spent their professional lives elaborating the insight that American religious history holds the key to the American character: Perry Miller, Sydney Ahlstrom, William McLoughlin, Martin Marty to name just a few. Ahlstrom refers to "the Great Puritan Epoch" – a "unified four-hundred-year period" in the English and American experience.[4] McLoughlin discusses "the pietistic spirit of American culture itself," by which he means not narrow fundamentalist religiosity but "the sense of religious commitment and ideals that Americans inscribe to democracy and their way of life."[5] Both Ahlstrom and McLoughlin focus particularly on the decade of the sixties as a time of radical reorientation in America's religious faith and life and in its sense of its own identity. For Ahlstrom the sixties marked the end of the Puritan era:

The decade of the sixties was a time, in short, when the old foundations of national confidence, patriotic idealism, moral traditionalism, and even of historic Judaeo-Christian theism, were awash. Presuppositions that had held firm for centuries – even millenia – were being widely questioned.[6]

McLoughlin interprets the sixties in the context of a series of "great awakenings" – periods of "fundamental social and intellectual reorientation of the American belief-value system, behavior patterns, and institutional structure."[7] Basing his schema on a formulation of cultural change developed by anthropologist Anthony F. C. Wallace, he designates five of these periods, loosely dated as follows: the Puritan Awakening in both England and America (1610–40), leading to the beginning of constitutional monarchy in England; America's First Great Awakening (1730–60), leading to the founding of the American republic; the Second Great Awakening (1800–30), leading to the solidifying of the Union and the rise of Jacksonian democracy; the Third Great Awakening (1890–1920), leading to the rejection of unregulated capitalism and the beginning of the welfare state; and the Fourth Great Awakening, which began around

1960 and is still in progress.[8] Although evangelicals tend to equate awakenings with religious revivals, the McLoughlin concept clearly casts a much wider cultural and historical net.

The postwar "turn to religion" . . . went much deeper and wider than prayer breakfasts, mass evangelistic campaigns, and anti-Communist crusades. It constituted a general re-orientation of the whole social and intellectual climate of Western society, just as America's previous Great Awakenings had done. In the history books of the future, this revival will be associated with the rise of existential philosophy, neo-orthodox theology, the election of the first Roman Catholic President, the *aggiornamento* of Vatican II, the peace movement and the civil rights movement, the revival of pacifism, the war on poverty, and the quest for a new politics.[9]

Periods of reorientation, however, are profoundly unsettling. Normally we can process new information and experiences by relating them to familiar data. As Suzanne Langer says, "Our most important assets are always the symbols of our general *orientation* in nature, on the earth, in society, and in what we are doing." Under the mental stress that results when these symbols are threatened, "even perfectly familiar things may become suddenly disorganized and give us the horrors."[10]

According to Anthony Wallace, the first stage of a revitalization movement poses exactly that kind of threat; it is "the period of individual stress." In McLoughlin's words, it is a time

when one by one, people lose their bearings, become psychically or physically ill, show what appear to be signs of neurosis, psychosis, or madness, and may either break out in acts of violence against family, friends, and authorities or become apathetic, catatonic, incapable of functioning. Emile Durkheim described this as "anomie," or loss of identity. Often anomic individuals destroy themselves by drugs, alcohol, or suicide. By their friends, and by society in general, these early victims of social disjunction are seen as deviants, misfits, persons too weak or too psychologically infirm to cope with life. They are sent to ministerial or psychological counselors (medicine men) or to hospitals and asylums to be cured or to "readjust." But as the number of these individuals increases, the institutional bonds of society begin to snap.[11]

I shall not try to match up the details of Carnell's life with every trait on that list. It is a fact, however, that simultaneously with the first stage of the Fourth Great Awakening, Carnell was going through his own "period of individual stress" that clearly falls within the McLoughlin–Wallace guidelines. In April 1959, he resigned from the presidency of Fuller Seminary because of deteriorating health. Serious bouts with depression, exacerbated by insomnia and a growing dependency on barbiturates, led him to seek psychiatric help. In June 1961, he suffered a psychological breakdown, was hospitalized for several weeks, and was given electroconvulsive therapy. Through all of this he managed to cope with his teaching responsibilities, publish another book and several articles, and even gain some national attention as one of six young American theologians chosen to participate in a dialogue with Karl Barth on his visit to the University of Chicago in 1962. But the Carnell of these years was a seriously disabled man. In the spring of 1967, he somewhat reluctantly accepted an invitation to speak at a national ecumenical symposium, sponsored by the Roman Catholic Diocese of Oakland, to be held in the Claremont Hotel. He never delivered the speech. On the morning of his scheduled luncheon address, he was found dead in his room, apparently from an overdose of sleeping pills.

Were Carnell's troubles perhaps only personal? The fact that a man has difficulty sleeping does not necessarily mean he has internalized the world's existential anxieties, even if he does happen to be living during a time of collective cultural stress. If we look only at Carnell's *writings* and consider their general thrust, we might be led to infer that their author had retreated behind a battlement no more permeable to the spirit of modernity than the fortress of the fundamentalists. Admittedly, we can find little evidence of ideological uncertainty in his published writings (although now and again in his correspondence he let down his guard). However, as I interpret the total evidence, from the writings and the life, the confident assurance of the Carnellian apologetics, just short of arrogance at times, often masked a profoundly threatening insecurity that transcended exclusively personal dimensions and attached itself to the insistent and increasingly chaotic pressures of his particular religious milieu and of the world outside.

A single passage in a magazine article obviously cannot effectively demonstrate the propensity of a whole life, but it can open a window on a man's preoccupations at a certain time. Carnell wrote a short article for the July 1961 issue of *Eternity* magazine.[12] Its title promises nothing more than a routine devotional message – "The Secret of Loving Your Neighbor" – and indeed much of the discussion deals rather conventionally with the Golden Rule as an ethical standard. Throughout the article, however, runs a darker theme, "the pathetic effects of uprooted lives." What could have been a pious little homily rises to a climax in a paragraph that might almost have been written as a gloss on the first stressful stage of the McLoughlin–Wallace period of cultural reorientation. Said Carnell:

We are passing through a time of great social change, for a prophetic judgment is being leveled against tribal injustice, colonialism, cast privilege, racial discrimination, and denominational pretention in the church. The resulting disintegration of form can be ruinous for a person who is plagued by persisting childhood emotions, and who continues to imagine that he is a child in an adult world. He cannot cope with the feeling that he must stand mobilized against a hostile and changing social order. He desperately craves reassurance from those whose emotional maturity releases them to do as they would be done by. (CBC 139)

Then the paragraph's final sentence asks a question intended to be rhetorical: "And who is better able to give this reassurance than Christians who know the meaning of divine forgiveness?" But anxiety so thoroughly pervades the whole article that the confidently implied answer sounds more like whistling in the dark.

We should be making a serious mistake if we minimized the subjective risks involved in the confrontation between religious faith and secular modernity. Jewish philosopher Emil Fackenheim pictures that encounter as taking place on "the narrow ridge of total risk." Modern faith faces "the shattering possibility that all human witnessing to a divine presence ever made might have been based on a radical illusion: the possibility that man is, as secularism holds him to be, radically alone."[13]

Neither all believers nor all defenders of the faith, however, venture out on the narrow ridge. In a recent illuminating sociological study, James Davison Hunter has found ambivalence at the heart of evangelicalism's encounter with modernity. In the face of "the cognitive constraints of sociocultural pluralism" – that is, the various world views that compete for our allegiance – evangelicalism has chosen the basic strategy of "cognitive intransigence," by which Hunter means "ignoring the plurality by affirming the veracity of one tradition and the illegitimacy of the others."[14] But inevitably the strategy is imperfect in practice. A sociologically necessary interaction goes on constantly between religion and modernity. On the conscious level, says Hunter, "the dynamics of this interaction may be labeled *cognitive bargaining*" (15). Moreover, because of the "massive plausibility structures" that support the modern secular world view, the contest is slanted in favor of modernity (133).

Emil Fackenheim's "narrow ridge," in other words, is not the only risk in the self-exposure of faith to the modern secular world. In fact, on reflection his metaphor strikes one as misleading in its reduction of alternatives: The traveler either continues safely on the trail or plummets to destruction. Although for some religious believers the choice is that clear-cut (Carnell himself on occasion presented the alternatives in terms just as stark), Hunter's study suggests that we should include another risk metaphor, one less dramatic certainly but more subtle and more truly reflective of the complex life situation: the cognitive bargaining process. Along with their embrace of modern technology and their assumption of mod-

ern forms of cultural expression, evangelicals have adopted a more conciliatory stance toward modernity's intellectual pressures. So far, Hunter
says, the bargaining has led to a yielding only on more or less peripheral
issues – to, for example, "a softening of the dogmatic insistence on
conversion" (17). The long run may prove more problematic. Evangelicalism's essential traditional beliefs, "as long as they are firmly buttressed by a stable institutional matrix, can remain relatively protected
from the world-disaffirming realities of modernity" (134). That confident
claim describes very well the experience of Carnell the *writer*. The Christian orthodoxy of his books and articles held steady. Carnell the *man* was
not so firmly buttressed. My contention is that, even where bargains are
not consciously struck with the modern secular worldview, the inescapable ambiguities of modern existence probe insistently at the foundation of
Christian faith. Carnell exposed himself to both kinds of danger. At times
he walked "the narrow ridge of total risk," facing a mutually exclusive
choice between traditional Christian orthodoxy and secular modernity,
between faith and nihilism. At other times his choices seemed to be much
less definitive. As he internalized the intellectual tensions of his time, as
he won a point here, yielded a point there, he constantly faced the more
pervasive if less cataclysmic risk of the cognitive bargain.

We should not overlook the fact that the ambiguity inherent in faith
and doubt is a two-way street. Secularism often practices its own brand of
self-assured cognitive intransigence and also has its own erosion problems
to deal with. Again and again we have been told that in the modern era
the existence of God (the question to which all theological questions seem
ultimately to sift down) is a dead issue. Whereas in the premodern era it
was unthinkable not to believe in God ("The fool hath said in his heart
there is no God."), all thoughtful persons supposedly have not only left
behind that purportedly naive age but have also passed through the era of
radical doubt and intellectual struggle and come out on the other side
where they no longer even recall that there was once a problem. In the
new technological age, says J. Hillis Miller in *Poets of Reality*, we have
progressed so far beyond the mere assertion of God's death as to have
forgotten it. In fact, "many people have forgotten that they have forgotten the death of God."[15]

Serious theological inquiry, however, refuses to believe its own death
notices. Even if we make allowances for contemporary superstition,
evangelistic demagoguery, and civil religion – even if we label much of
today's God-talk a perfunctory response to the lingering anachronistic
influence of an earlier Age of Belief – we are still left with concerns that
refuse to give up the ghost. As Paul Johnson says in *Modern Times*,
"what is important in history is not only the events that occur but the
events that obstinately do not occur. The outstanding non-event of mod-

ern times was the failure of religious belief to disappear."[16] The point is not that we are in a new Age of Faith – not that the questions of faith and doubt, nihilism and ultimate concern have been satisfactorily resolved. It is true, however, that essentially the same theological questions that engaged the greatest minds and sensibilities of the past (Aquinas, Spinoza, Calvin, Pascal, Nietzsche, Melville, Dostoevsky, Emily Dickinson, Bertrand Russell, to name just a few from all over the theological spectrum) are still legitimate questions today, not merely as a residue from past arguments but as a perpetually relevant problem for some of the greatest minds and sensibilities of our own time, from a variety of backgrounds and disciplines. We may reject evangelicalism's cognitive intransigence, its strategy of ignoring the plurality of available options by affirming the final truth of its own tradition and the illegitimacy of all others, but Carnell's lifetime commitment to Christian apologetics at the very least reminds us that choosing instead the cognitive intransigence of modernity is no better an alternative. As an American evangelical at the beginning of the Fourth Great Awakening, Edward Carnell experienced the ambiguities of both resisting and yielding to the pressures of modernity. As he said in brief remarks to the audience at Fuller Seminary's Founders' Day Banquet less than three weeks before he died, "We face a future filled with exciting challenges and yet threatened by demonic uncertainties."[17] These are hard times for faith – any faith, not just Protestant evangelical Christian faith. These are hard times even for faith in the human spirit. What happened to Carnell is instructive for all of us – who continue to live within this turbulent period of reorientation and revitalization.

In the opening lines of a profoundly personal account of his own theological journey, Richard Rubenstein stresses the importance of the personal dimension in dealing with theological matters:

> When a theologian discusses his religious commitments, especially in scholarly writing, his readers seldom catch a glimpse of the anguish that moved him. What is affirmed often appears bloodless, as if arising out of intellectual reflection rather than experience. Nevertheless, every theologian has a story to tell. Good theology is always *embodied* theology. It arises out of and reflects life. And, in life, we are more often instructed by heartbreak and failure than success.[18]

Edward Carnell said much the same thing in his book *Christian Commitment:* "I am lifting the veil from *my* experiences in order that others might be guided into a more accurate understanding of their own."[19] Individual theologians may differ in how many of the connections between their lives and their theology they choose to bring to the surface. Or how clearly they themselves see the connections. But the connections are always there. "Every theologian has a story to tell." I have tried in this book to explore those connections – to engage occasionally with the writings as I discuss the life in Part One and to introduce the personal dimension where appropriate as I discuss the writings in Part Two.

Clifford Geertz says that interpretive anthropology "is a science whose progress is marked less by a perfection of consensus than by a refinement of debate. What gets better is the precision with which we vex each other."[20] I am not doing interpretive anthropology, but if this study of Edward Carnell makes a contribution to such "refinement" and "precision" in the continuing effort to understand the phenomenon called evangelicalism, I shall be more than satisfied. I suspect, however, that whatever success it may achieve along those lines, it will "vex" other readers in a different way. No one will mistake this book for a hagiography, but some readers may judge it to be unfairly critical of both Carnell and the evangelical movement. Perhaps, therefore, I should say a few words about my intent. I have no illusions that the Edward Carnell who has emerged in this book is an objective factual reproduction of the real thing, as if that were even possible. He is rather a Carnell that I have had a part in creating, out of several years of reading, questioning, interviewing, contemplating, and writing. As I reflect on the result, my presentation of the *life* seems to me reasonably sympathetic; of the ideas developed in the *writings* considerably less so. But Carnell's writings have already enjoyed extended expositions from a thoroughly sympathetic point of view.[21] I see this book as a friendly critique, which allows Carnell to develop his position in his own words but finally disagrees with it and with the evangelicalism it exemplifies.

At various points in parts two and three, I have offered some alternatives to the evangelical views my discussion of Carnell calls into question. It need hardly be said that Carnell would have been sorely "vexed" by what a supposedly friendly critique of his life and works could lead to, but perhaps this too can be thought of as consistent with Geertz's "refinement of debate" criterion. In any case, I would rather risk controversy on that account than be vexed myself by the recognition that I raised serious questions about Carnell's evangelical faith without pointing in what seem to me promising new directions. Indeed, although we discover in the making of Edward Carnell's mind the seeds of its eventual unmaking, the true measure of his importance may be that we can also detect, here and there throughout his life and writings, clues to what might have been – and to what might still be – the remaking of the evangelical mind.

CHAPTER II

The stigmata of fundamentalism

When Edward Carnell's father, the Reverend Herbert Carnell, retired in 1962 from a long career in the Baptist ministry, he and his wife moved from Michigan to southern California to live near three of their four children and their families. Herbert Carnell, however, was not the type to spend his retirement playing shuffleboard and working on his tan. In addition to fulfilling occasional preaching assignments, he began the ambitious project of writing an autobiographical memoir covering his entire life. The result: a 130-page typewritten unpublished manuscript that gives us an intimately personal view of Edward Carnell's paternal heritage.[1] It also conveys at least a few facts about Edward's own childhood and, more significantly, lights up the background against which that childhood was lived: the Protestant fundamentalist subculture of the American Midwest in the 1920s and 1930s. One additional fact underscores the importance of this manuscript in our study of Herbert Carnell's son; the closing paragraph reads as follows: "I wish to thank my son, Edward John Carnell, Professor of Ethics and Philosophy of Religion at Fuller Theological Seminary for his many helpful suggestions in the preparation of this volume. We are all debtors in one way or another."

In dealing with Herbert Carnell's memoir, we do well to remember that autobiography is never truth in any simple direct sense. Barrett John Mandel, in his illuminating article "The Autobiographer's Art," observes that "life itself is too big, too formless, too pointless, always too ugly in some of its details, and usually too tedious even in the hands of a great man to be rendered in all its complex reality."[2] As a consequence, every genuine autobiography is a "conscious verbal construct" that gives shape and artistic unity to that life according to the writer's larger organizing conception. And if that seems too sophisticated a self-imposed task for a retired Baptist minister whose only formal education after high school consisted of two years at Moody Bible Institute, Mandel insists that the

16

autobiographer (who we have to presume is consciously writing as well as he can) constantly makes decisions that involve not only selection but also such matters as emphasis, tone, syntax, and diction. "He may not consider himself literary, but built into his role as autobiographer will be options and decisions which are nothing if not literary."[3]

We do not have to look any farther than the title of Herbert Carnell's memoir to see exactly the kind of literary choice to which Mandel is referring: "From Wooden Leg to Pulpit." The elder Carnell reflects on what was unquestionably the most important experience of his childhood in the peat fen village of Hilgay, County of Norfolk, England, in the late nineteenth century. An innocuous accidental kick in the ankle when he was eight years old refused to heal. After the doctor prescribed several lancings, which gave only temporary relief, the inflammation spread up the entire leg and into the hip. Fortunately, the worried parents summoned a second doctor, who immediately took the boy to the hospital and began proper treatment. His life and his leg were saved, but the recuperative process was long and complicated. Before leaving the hospital he was fitted with a strange prosthetic device.

My natural leg was folded back and the wooden leg was attached to the stump formed by the knee. There certainly was nothing fancy about this accessory. It was made of plain wood, about six inches across at the top and gradually tapering down to about two inches at the bottom. The tip was reinforced with a ring of steel to help insure longer wear.

He was given orders to remove the wooden leg from time to time in order to maintain circulation in his natural leg and give it some necessary exercise. But all his walking for the next four years was done with the aid of this strange contraption.

When he returned from the hospital, he gave his mother the fright of her life. She was waiting for him at home, having just given birth there to her last child. What she saw, of course, was her son climbing down from the carriage with great difficulty on a wooden leg. As Herbert tells the story, she cried out, "Oh, my goodness! They did it! His leg is gone, and they didn't even tell me about it!" and then fainted on the floor by the bedroom window. He wore the device four long years until he was able to put it away at the age of twelve.

The word-picture of this young boy on his wooden leg presents a vivid and powerful image. But it is more than an image; it functions also as an effective symbol for Herbert Carnell's conflicting thoughts as he reflects on the events of his life. His autobiographical memoir is a deeply ambivalent account at the root of which lie the simultaneous feelings of resentment and gratitude. The resentment focuses on his deprivation, not only in the years from eight to twelve when he was a "public spectacle," but in a larger sense on the economic and educational deprivation that affected his entire life. A keen awareness of class distinctions and a painful sensitivity toward his meager formal education pervade the manuscript. On the other hand, the account sings a hymn of gratitude to God for a long, productive, and generally happy life. As the thirteenth child (there were fifteen altogether) of English laboring-class parents, he came a long way from his unpromising beginnings. The wooden leg, of course, was not solely responsible for either of these tendencies in Herbert Carnell's life, but it symbolizes both remarkably well. We have no difficulty empathizing with his hostility toward the artificial limb on which, as he says, he went "thumping along" through childhood. But, conversely, he never let himself be defeated by his physical predicament. He joined the neighborhood cricket and football games, won the hopping prize at the Sunday School picnic, and every day rode a borrowed bicycle to a house two miles outside the village, where he was given the kind of specially nourishing meal his own family was too poor to provide. His mixed feelings about the artificial leg show up clearly in his account of how he finally discarded it at the age of twelve:

So the wooden leg, which had been my faithful friend and companion for four years, was now laid aside with a prayer of thanksgiving. For quite some time I stored it under the bed, preserving it just in case I should have to use it again. But when I was positive that I would have no further need of it, I threw it on the old pile of wood in the back yard, eventually chopping it up for kindling. Since then I have regretted that I did not save it to show my posterity. But it was now gone, completely gone, and all I had was a memory.

Clearly the young Herbert Carnell had learned how to deal with a stigma – an "undesired differentness," which (as sociologist Erving Goffman describes it in his book *Stigma: Notes on the Management of Spoiled Identity*) can fall into one of three categories: physical deformity, blemish of character, or various tribal characteristics of race, nation, or religion. The remarkable thing about Herbert's experience with his physical stigma is how thoroughly and robustly he triumphed over it, in spite of the inevitable low periods. Riding out of the village on his bicycle, joining uninhibitedly in whatever games his friends were playing, he was much like those persons, mentioned by Goffman, who make a profession of their stigma – who, for example, take important jobs representing similarly stigmatized people. "Instead of leaning on their crutch, they get to play golf with it."[4]

In discussing Herbert Carnell's wooden leg, we are not so far from our main subject, his son Edward, as might at first seem to be the case. For

Edward Carnell grew up with a stigma of his own: the constant awareness of his second-class status as a member of a religious minority. From his earliest days, Protestant fundamentalism was by far the most significant and persistent force in the cultural matrix that shaped his life. He chafed under it as the son of a relatively uneducated Baptist minister who was usually at the bottom of the ecclesiastical pecking order in the various towns where they lived. As a college and seminary student, it was the fundamentalist faith he was grooming himself to defend. Later, as evangelicalism's intellectual spokesman, he explicitly disassociated himself from fundamentalism and redefined it as "orthodoxy gone cultic." In a 1959 magazine article, he said he was brought up in the "tyrannical legalism of fundamentalism." And finally, on the last evening of his life, as he reviewed the address he would not live to deliver the next day to the Diocese of Oakland National Workshop on Christian Unity, it was again fundamentalism on which his attention focused; for in the text from which he would have read he took special pains to explain the difference between an evangelical and a fundamentalist and the differing attitudes of each toward Roman Catholics. But an awareness of this lifelong preoccupation does not resolve the enigma of Edward Carnell's life. It only suggests certain boundaries within which the complexities of that life can most profitably be explored. To get to that territory we must first move farther along in the autobiographical memoir of his father.

In 1907, at the age of eighteen, with a series of unremunerative part-time jobs behind him, with only the dimmest prospects for success ahead of him in England, and with the offer of a loan covering the entire ship passage to America from his older brother Robert, who had emigrated there two years earlier, Herbert Carnell decided to make the break. He sailed from Southampton on February 7, disembarked at Ellis Island for the immigration entry process, then boarded a train for Illinois, where his brother had settled.

Even though the promises of better economic opportunity in America proved to be substantially true for Herbert, he increasingly felt drawn toward a different future – the Christian ministry. The thought was not a new one; he had previously rejected it, however, because of his inadequate educational background. Acceptance of his application for admission to Moody Bible Institute resolved that question. Within two years he had been graduated from the Moody Pastor's course, had married fellow student Fannie Carstens, and had assumed the pastorate of two small Baptist churches in Glassford, Illinois.

Thus began a career of serving a series of churches in Illinois, Wisconsin, Ohio, and Michigan – a career, however, not without the same kind of ambivalence we saw in Herbert's attitude toward his artificial leg. On the one hand he was fully cognizant of his limitations. As he listened at

Moody to outstanding preachers from all over the world, he refused to deceive himself into believing that he would ever rank with them. "People in the out-of-the-way places needed the Gospel just as much as those who worshipped in immense churches, and I decided that I would minister to those who dwelled in those hidden places." But he frankly acknowledges in his memoir that he envied those great preachers, and he resented the fact that year after year he and his growing family hovered around the poverty line. By the time Edward appeared on the scene (as the third of four children) the Carnells had moved to Wisconsin, first to Oakfield, where Herbert again pastored two small churches, and then to Antigo, county seat of Langlade County, some sixty miles northwest of Green Bay, where he was called to be pastor of the First Baptist Church. There, in the parsonage, on June 28, 1919, the same day that the Treaty of Versailles was signed officially ending World War I, Edward John Carnell was born, named for his paternal grandfather.

I have said that the autobiographical memoir written by Edward Carnell's father is useful for our purposes primarily because it gives us a perspective on the cultural milieu of Protestant fundamentalism within which Edward's early life was lived. But a second theme that has already been introduced – the ambivalent attitude toward money – demands further examination before we explore the fundamentalist subculture. The postwar decade was variously known as President Warren G. Harding's "Return to Normalcy," the "Roaring Twenties," the "Jazz Age," the decade in which President Calvin Coolidge declared that "the business of American government is business." The most surprising bestseller of the time was Bruce Barton's *The Man Nobody Knows*, which celebrated Jesus of Nazareth as the founder of modern business. Herbert Carnell was not one of those who amassed great wealth in the postwar boom. He did not expect to, of course. But he could not help resenting the continued economic deprivation he and his family had to endure while so many others were striking it rich. In retrospect he realizes he was infected with the same contagion that had spread like an epidemic through society: "When I looked into my heart and asked myself to state exactly how much money would make me content, I found to my surprise that I could not come up with a satisfying figure. It seemed, in other words, that I would be ready to take all the traffic would bear." He acknowledges that he trimmed his sails somewhat as a prophet of the Lord: "It was easy – all too easy – to damn the lives of the rich, as if they were guilty of a cardinal sin; when all the while we would be rich if we could." He bought a piece of land as a "speculative investment" and built a small cottage on it. His conscience did not rebuke him at the time, but writing forty years later he sees the move as yielding to "the temptation to make some money on the side."

Without a doubt, though, the most ill-considered decision Herbert Carnell made in his entire career – one that had far-reaching consequences for the whole family and to which he refers as a "tragedy" – was to leave the ministry, at least for a while, and earn some "real money." A number of things contributed to the decision. By this time he was pastor of a downtown church in Milwaukee, but still with a discouragingly small salary. He suggests also that his health had been deteriorating (though he gives no specific details) and that he felt that a temporary change in vocation might make him feel better. The situation was catalyzed by the arrival of another Carnell brother from England (Ted), who achieved immediate success as a salesman with the Phoenix Products Company of Milwaukee, a manufacturer of laundry supplies. Every time Ted returned from a successful foray through his sales territory, he dangled in front of Herbert the prospect of financial growth.

This was a frightful time for me, since I had to give serious thought to my ordination vows: how I had pledged to preach the Gospel as long as I lived, and that I should not become entangled with the affairs of this world. I began to rationalize by telling myself that I could leave the ministry for a while, and then, when I was back in shape financially, I could return. Despite an uneasy conscience, I proceeded.

Events took on their own momentum. More quickly than he had anticipated, Herbert resigned from the church, studied the line of products he would be selling, and hit the road. He did not repeat the instant success of his brother Ted. After assignments in New York and Florida, he was given the Cleveland area as his permanent territory. He put money down on an inexpensive seven-room house and moved the family to Cleveland. Finally he began to prosper.

But it was now October 1929.

I was in Detroit, making calls, when I received an unsuspected telegram informing me that I had been fired along with a number of other salesmen. My hand trembled as I read the telegram over and over. I did not want to believe what I read, but I was forced to. Now I had nothing.

It was the onset of the Great Depression, and the beginning of really hard times for the Carnells. Herbert cashed in his insurance policies, gave up the house, moved the family to cheaper quarters forty miles away in Oberlin, and tried with little success to sell disinfectant products door to door. Dorothy, the oldest child, recalls that when she was graduated from high school in Oberlin, it was made very clear that she was now on her own and could not remain at home. The next oldest, Paul, remembers that the whole family, not just his father, had to sell door to door to survive. It was a big treat for the Carnell children in those years to reach into their Christmas stocking and find such a simple gift as an orange. Edward was ten when his family and the entire nation plunged into the economic abyss. The experience to a degree shaped his life – not only the sudden catastrophic poverty of the turn of the decade, but the still modest family resources that during the late thirties made it necessary for him consistently to work some forty-five hours a week in the dining hall at Wheaton to put himself through college. And although by every criterion he was far more successful than his father, Edward (as a partial legacy, perhaps, of the traumas of the thirties) chafed his entire life under the burden of genteel poverty.

As for Herbert Carnell himself, however, it was not long until he was perceiving the "tragedy" as a "blessing in disguise." Even as his wooden leg took on the characteristics of a paradoxical symbol – that is to say, it was simultaneously a stigma and a mark of God's benevolent care – so this most devastating experience of his life proved to be a means of grace. It taught him exactly what he had to do. He set his sights on returning to the Baptist ministry with an unequivocal vocational and spiritual commitment. Once he had made that decision, he acted on it immediately. "With tears in my eyes I sat down and wrote a letter to one of the prominent pastors in Michigan, begging him to help me return to the ministry by placing my name before some church that needed a pastor. I suffered deep agony as I awaited a reply." He did not have long to wait. The answer came back with word that his name had been submitted to the First Baptist Church of Albion, Michigan. Within days a representative of the church came to Oberlin to interview him. The candidate went to Albion to preach. Both parties were pleased with the prospects. The pulpit committee voted to call him as pastor, and Herbert Carnell accepted. He was back in the ministry where he belonged. And the Carnell family moved into the ample parsonage at 116 Austin Avenue in the farming and industrial community of Albion, forty miles south of Lansing, halfway between Detroit and Chicago. It was here that Edward Carnell spent his teenage years until he left home to attend Wheaton College in 1937.

To say that Edward Carnell grew up in the context of Protestant fundamentalism is not to say that his father was a stereotypical fundamentalist. In his own eyes he certainly was not. He writes, for example, of attending the Northern Baptist Convention, which was held in Iowa during his first year at Antigo:

The Convention was one of the most disappointing I had ever attended, for the modernists and the fundamentalists were at each others' throats all the time. Frankly, I was ashamed to think that Christians would treat one another in such a way – even though they did disagree in many details of theology and biblical exegesis.

Clearly he places himself somewhere between the two contending groups. He disassociates himself also from some of the negative positions fundamentalists took on behavioral matters. He refuses to condemn, for example, the accepted practice of wine-drinking among the Christians in his English homeland:

They knew, although many Christians in America seem to have forgotten, that the Bible condemns immoderate drinking. It says nothing about moderation. Jesus, we know, created wine for the wedding feast, so in all probability He enjoyed a moderate use of wine Himself.

He is critical of what he calls the "hush-hush atmosphere" concerning sex at Moody Bible Institute during his student days there, an attitude inevitably resulting in hypocrisy:

I can't speak for the girls, but I know that the boys bore feelings of guilt because they could not talk out their true impulses. They masturbated and they were never quite sure whether the act was natural or wicked. Most of the time they concluded it was wicked. Constant self-condemnation hindered the boys from exercising the sweetness and nonchalance of Jesus Christ. Because they knew they were among those who watched pretty female legs – and not with mere ideas of anatomy in mind, either – they accused themselves of mental fornication.

While we must make some allowance for the fact that when he writes these words Herbert Carnell has retired from the battlefield and has had time to cultivate a measure of detachment, the facts do seem to verify at least some of his retrospective claims: it appears that he was never part of the militantly separatist wing of fundamentalism, whose adherents believed so strongly in the mandate to remove themselves from denominations corrupted by modernism that they condemned their theologically conservative fellow-Christians who chose to remain affiliated with those groups as a witness to the true Christian gospel. He considers it a worthwhile accomplishment to have brought the Milwaukee church back into active membership in the Wisconsin Baptist Convention. For three years in Michigan he was President of the Michigan Baptist Convention, in which capacity it was his officially designated task to visit churches that were contemplating withdrawal from the Convention and to try to dissuade them. In the 1940s, at a time when doctrinaire fundamentalists were still preaching the gospel of separation, he pursued a different ideal:

It was a joy to see the philosophy of separation give way to the philosophy of cooperation. The fight between fundamentalism and modernism was at its height. Pastors were accusing each other, and harsh words were flying between parishioners. For some reason the younger men seemed prey to what may be called ideological thinking. They tended to see all issues in absolute shades of black and white; there was no room for the sort of give and take which marks a man of God who has come to terms with the complexity of the biblical revelation.

Time and again in his memoir, he repeats his assertion that in the life of the church as well as the life of the believer the law of love should govern. If in later years Herbert Carnell's son, as president of Fuller Theological Seminary, had to endure what he referred to as five years of "unremitting attack" by fundamentalists, we can be reasonably confident that those letters to the seminary's founder Charles Fuller demanding Edward Carnell's scalp did not come from the likes of Herbert Carnell.

Then what, we may ask, was Edward Carnell referring to when he claimed, in a 1959 *Christian Century* article titled "Post-Fundamentalist Faith,"[5] that he was reared in "the tyrannical legalism of fundamentalism"? First, we must not forget that he helped his father edit the autobiographical memoir. I am not suggesting that he falsified or even distorted his father's attitudes and actions, but it is entirely possible (indeed it is highly probable) that the editorial hand of Edward Carnell is evident in such locutions (in the passage quoted above) as "ideological thinking" and "the complexity of the biblical revelation." One of the effects of Edward's editorial assistance may have been to round off some of the sharp edges in his father's fundamentalism.

For there were sharp edges. Herbert Carnell himself seems to have done some reshaping of his past attitudes. There is some evidence, for example, that the open-mindedness on sexual matters was to some extent a lesson learned late and then projected backward. Dorothy Carnell Campbell recalls that as a senior in high school she was given the opportunity to play a part in a dramatic production. Because the part demanded that she do a brief bit of ballroom dancing, she knew she might be in for trouble. What if her mother and father should come to the play? Her decision was to accept the role and hope that her parents would not come. But of course they did. Her father especially was shocked. He severely disciplined Dorothy and then preached a sermon the next Sunday morning on dancing as a form of adultery.

Whatever Herbert Carnell was really like, it was the entire fundamentalist subculture on which his son Edward in his maturity looked back in anger. He made a genuine effort to be fair. Don Weber, Carnell's brother-in-law (who, as Assistant to the President in the Carnell administration at Fuller, was as close to him as anyone in those years) has said that Carnell agonized over whether to include the "Perils" chapter (a negative critique of fundamentalism) in *The Case for Orthodox Theology* but finally decided that he could not in conscience leave it out.[6] Having made that decision, however, he obviously warmed to the task. He alluded to fundamentalism's celebrity converts being thrust into the limelight and delivering pronouncements on "science, the United Nations, and the cause of immorality in France." To attract a good crowd to a youth rally, "the fundamentalist thinks nothing of using 'an intelligent horse' for entertainment." And he chided the fundamentalist who ignores the weightier matters of mercy and justice because "he is busy painting 'Jesus Saves' on rocks in a public park." In the "Post-Fundamentalist Faith" article he counseled his readers that fundamentalists deserve our pity, not our scorn. But, not surprisingly, the remark earned him no gratitude from his friends in the fundamentalist camp; there is hardly an insult more scornful than being told one deserves pity. If these were isolated statements, we might be justified in concluding that they represented an occasional lapse, but similar comments appear throughout the last fifteen years of his life – in letters to friends, in interoffice memos to Don Weber, in class lectures. These are the responses of a man who was wounded – early and deeply – by what he later called "orthodoxy gone cultic."[7]

As I have claimed earlier, growing up in such an ambience was Edward Carnell's stigma. Whereas most of the illustrative material in Goffman's book *Stigma* concerns such overt characteristics as race, stuttering, hearing loss, blindness, facial scars, and crippled bodies, Goffman makes it clear that many stigmas are much more subtle. One authority he cites says that the number of stigma-suffering people is as high as we want to make it. When we consider those who have faced the problem at one time in the past, or will sometime in the future, even if only the problem of advancing age, "the issue becomes not whether a person has experience with a stigma of his own, because he has, but rather how many varieties he has had his own experience with."[8]

It should be seen, then, that stigma management is a general feature of society, a process occurring wherever there are identity norms. The same features are involved whether a major differentness is at question, of the kind traditionally defined as stigmatic, or a picayune differentness, of which the shamed person is ashamed to be ashamed. One can therefore suspect that the role of normal and the role of stigmatized are parts of the same complex, cuts from the same standard cloth.[9]

The really interesting question is how we manage the stigma problem. The most important goal for the stigmatized person, according to Goffman, is "acceptance" – that is, whether or not "those who have dealings with him fail to accord him the respect and regard which the uncontaminated aspects of his social identity have led them to anticipate extending, and have led him to anticipate receiving."[10] In the religious context, preachers can sermonize at length on the benefit of acceptance by God, but that is hardly a satisfactory substitute for human acceptance. And although the mutual support of his fellow fundamentalists (called the "sympathetic others" by Goffman) provided necessary and at times sufficient support, young Edward Carnell felt very deeply a sense of rejection by "normal" people outside the boundaries of his religion. He does not seem to have been the type who opted for a "method of disclosure" – such as carrying a Bible to school or wearing a "Born Again" button, thereby radically transforming the situation by voluntarily displaying a stigma symbol. On the contrary, all the evidence suggests that Ed Carnell solved the problem of personal acceptance by treating his religious differentness with disdain. He is remembered in Albion, Michigan, as the Baptist preacher's happy-go-lucky son, who did not do very well in school, who had an old wreck of a Model T Ford he called "Molly" that the young people rode around in, and who surprised everyone (not least his older brother, Paul) when he went off to Wheaton College and in time announced that he was preparing for Christian service.

In retrospect we can say that Edward Carnell's stigma as a youth was indeed lack of acceptance – but not personal acceptance. What festered in his mind was a more subtle but just as serious lack of acceptance – the inescapable and unendurable realization that everything his family stood for religiously was regarded by people outside the fold with indifference and often contempt. Carnell's experience in this regard was not at all unfamiliar to thousands of people in fundamentalist churches around the country in the 1930s. Fundamentalism had not always been obscurantist and not always an object of derision and contempt. Whether it is seen as a pietistic wing of late nineteenth-century evangelicalism, as a marriage of Millenarianism and Princeton Seminary biblicism, or as an early twentieth-century protest against the increasing liberal tendencies of the Protestant denominations, the movement was accepted at one time as a legitimate albeit somewhat anachronistic expression of historic Christianity. The pamphlets called *The Fundamentals,* appearing from 1910 to 1915, were by no means the scurrilous propaganda of militant ignorance. It was only after the debacle of the 1925 Scopes trial in Dayton, Tennessee, that fundamentalism retreated into its bunker mentality. As George Marsden says:

It would be oversimplification to attribute the decline and disarray of fundamentalism after 1925 to any one factor. It does appear, however, that the movement began in reality to conform to its popular image. The more ridiculous it was made to appear, the more genuinely ridiculous it was likely to become.[11]

Although as I have earlier pointed out, these were years in which fundamentalism expanded its own organizational network, it was virtually impossible to grow up in a fundamentalist church in the second quarter of the twentieth century (or to be a member of such a church whatever one's age) without seeing not only the church but all of life in Manichean terms. The forces of God were arrayed against the forces of the Devil. It was not difficult to sort people out in a light and dark world with no shades of gray. The controversial New York clergyman Harry Emerson Fosdick may have seen himself as a figure of moderation who was attempting to save Christianity as an intellectually viable option in modern times; yet there was hardly a fundamentalist in the country who could not unequivocally identify him as of the Devil's party.

The Manicheistic polarization in the subculture that nurtured Carnell is clearly reflected in his later criticism of fundamentalism. He maintained that in the absence of a clear connection with the historical creeds of the Church, fundamentalism's very existence was so dependent on a clearly defined enemy that when modernism collapsed, "the fundamentalist movement became an army without a cause." What persisted instead was a "mentality" with no essence except "status by negation."[12]

It took some time, however, for Carnell to gradually develop these views. One can turn up no evidence from his high school years that he gave much serious thought to the Christian faith that governed the Carnell household. Indeed, a study of his official high school record leads one to question whether this future holder of two doctoral degrees gave serious intellectual consideration to anything. The transcript, dated June 15, 1937, four days after his graduation, shows no A grades, 5 Bs, 16 Cs and 4 Ds, a record that hardly distinguished him as outstanding college material. As a matter of fact, Edward Carnell began the summer of 1937 with no definite plans to attend college in the fall. By mid-September, however, he was a resident freshman at Wheaton College in Wheaton, Illinois, embarked apprehensively and not very happily on the next stage of his journey.

CHAPTER III

Wheaton

> He was just in time to hear the chairman of the Evangelistic Committee say something about Miss Thurston's returning to Wharton in the fall for her last year. Of course, he had taken note of the remark, but had not seen anything of significance in it at the time, aside from the fact that it gave him a piece of information he was very glad to have. He wondered where this Wharton College could be. He had never heard of it.
>
> J. Wesley Ingles, *Silver Trumpet*[1]

If D. Randall MacRae, hero of J. Wesley Ingles's prizewinning Christian novel *Silver Trumpet* had never heard of Wharton (a not-even-thinly-veiled fictional equivalent of Wheaton College in Illinois), it was because he was a modern young pagan who had wandered into an evangelistic tent meeting out of nothing more than idle curiosity. If he had had any acquaintance at all with American fundamentalist Christianity, he would not have had to wonder about Wharton/Wheaton. He would have known. In the years between the two world wars – especially the late thirties and early forties, the period of time when Edward Carnell was an undergraduate – for a young person brought up in a devout Christian home, indoctrinated in a fundamentalist church, possessed of a desire for an academically respectable but religiously safe college education, there was no other place to go but Wheaton. That is not strictly true, of course, but in such matters it is the perception that counts. And in those years Wheaton had managed to build up, among a truly national constituency, a reputation not only for excellence but for superiority.

To some extent the reputation was deserved. At a time when the supply of thoroughly trained academicians sympathetic to Wheaton's brand of Protestant fundamentalism had all but disappeared, the college still managed to corral an impressive number of liberal arts scholars with doctorates from excellent graduate schools. This success stemmed in part from the efforts of a vigorous young president, J. Oliver Buswell, himself a

Ph.D. from New York University, who was wholly supportive of the cause of the fundamentalists in their struggle against theological modernism but did not let his ecclesiastical separatism undermine his commitment to a strong Christian liberal arts education. Even though the Great Depression began three years after Buswell became president, Wheaton continued to grow – in faculty additions, in buildings and grounds, and (amazingly) in the numbers of students it attracted. At a time of trouble for American higher education, Wheaton College became the fastest growing college in America, the largest liberal arts college in Illinois, and the eighth largest in the entire country.[2] Credit must be given also to considerable skill and hard work in public relations. The good word about Wheaton was spread around the country, by gospel teams, choirs, speakers, and by that greatest of all sales forces, hundreds of intelligent, enthusiastic young people working during summer vacation at camps and Bible conferences and in their home churches, adding the luster of youthful personality to whatever more objective criteria the public might have been aware of.

Silver Trumpet's hero, Randall MacRae, had no other criteria at all. All he knew about Wharton was that Fay Thurston was going back there for her final year of college. All he knew about Fay was her breathtaking beauty and musicianship. But that was all he needed. He decided definitely against returning to Princeton, where he had used up all his eligibility as the football team's star halfback and where his reputation as a student was less than outstanding. He gave up a well-paying position in his father's company, which was contributing every bit as much to his boredom and hostility as it was to his bank account. He packed his trunks, sent them off to Illinois, and got on a New York Central train for Chicago. His particular personal attraction may not have been typical of the students who chose Wheaton in those years, but the motivation of Ingles's hero does drive home the point that colleges attract students for all sorts of reasons.

Curiously enough, it seems that in the thirties and forties the novel *Silver Trumpet* actually played no small part in informing the Christian public about this unusual Midwestern college. The book was enormously popular, going through twenty-two printings over the years. More to the point, Dr. V. Raymond Edman, successor to Dr. Buswell as Wheaton's president, administered a questionnaire to freshmen one year during the forties. In response to a question concerning their reasons for having decided to attend Wheaton, more than half of the entering class included in their list a reading of *Silver Trumpet*.[3]

Ed Carnell was not persuaded to apply to Wheaton by anything so romantic as what lured D. Randall MacRae nor by anything so rational as solid academic reputation. In fact, well into the summer following his graduation from high school, it was not certain that he would attend college at all. Because of his mediocre academic record, those who knew Ed in church and town would not have been surprised to see him ignore college altogether. What did surprise them was Ed's choice of Wheaton, given his reputation as the wild one of the Carnell family. Ed had done at least *some* thinking about college. We know that his father drove him and two other young men from the Albion church, Lambert McLintic and Richard Weeks, to the Chicago area in May 1937, to visit first Moody Bible Institute, from which the elder Carnell had been graduated, and then Wheaton, where McLintic and Weeks had already been accepted as students. They did their best to persuade Ed to apply, but by July he still had not. According to his brother Paul, who had chosen to attend Albion College so that he could live inexpensively at home, Ed was not galvanized into action until he found out that as the son of a Baptist minister he would be eligible at Wheaton for a partial tuition scholarship. He applied hastily and was accepted only a month or so before the beginning of the fall semester.

On Saturday, September 11, the Albion boys were driven to Wheaton by a friend who loaded them and their luggage into his new 1937 Ford. They almost met disaster on the way. On U.S. 30, just west of Valparaiso, Indiana, while they were traveling up a long hill at seventy miles per hour, all four of the car's occupants in the front seat because the back was so loaded with suitcases and a trunk, a car swerved out from behind an approaching truck and in an almost fatal miscalculation attempted to pass. The driver of the boys' car instinctively wrenched the wheel to the right, avoiding a head-on collision. But a more narrow escape is difficult to imagine. The passing car grazed the Albion Ford as it careened past, spun it around on the highway, where it rocked back and forth, finally decided not to tip over, and rolled to a stop. That evening, as they joined with other freshmen in their first orientation session, a picnic supper on the athletic field, the boys felt fortunate to be alive.[4]

In the 1930s and 1940s Wheaton accepted a percentage of "non-Christian" students (today its policy is to admit only students who affirm faith in Jesus Christ as their savior), and in the fall of 1937 it wasted no time in getting down to the business of winning them to Christ. Registration was completed on Thursday, classes met in shortened periods on Friday, schedules were adjusted on Saturday, and on Sunday began a week of intensive evangelistic services led by Dr. Harry Ironside, pastor of Chicago's Moody Memorial Church, and Homer Hammontree, veteran song leader of countless revival campaigns. The college's efforts seem to have been successful. One of Carnell's classmates recalls how four years of evangelistic concern came to a climax: "It was an occasion of great joy – and relief – to all of us when it was announced at our Senior Retreat in Michigan that it was believed that all members of the class had come to know the Lord."[5]

In September 1937, however, graduation was four long years away. It is not unusual for the first year away at college to be a difficult one. For Ed Carnell the freshman year at Wheaton was especially trying. Even before his arrival on campus, a strong feeling of apprehension pervades a letter he wrote to the Office of the Dean of Students in late August. After asking whether it might be possible for him to room with the two other Albion freshmen, he elaborated briefly on the request: "If this cannot be done it is very necessary that I be put in a room with one or two boys because I have very peculiar habits when I am alone for any length of time. I said in my haste before that I desired a single room. May my stated wishes be carried out so that I may be a better student." The letter is remarkable not so much because it reveals that the young Carnell may have had certain "peculiar habits" but because of the attention he called to them. At the outset of his college career – a point at which we would normally expect young people to want to get off to a fresh start with no unnecessary baggage from the past – he virtually announced to the Dean of Students: "Watch me. I'm an odd duck."

The struggle was intense enough in his first year to make him think seriously of quitting. For one thing, a scholarship of $100 a year hardly solved his financial problems. In addition to the self-imposed pressure to do well in his studies, he had to work many hours a week just to stay in school. These conditions not only placed severe restrictions on the sort of life he lived but also contributed to unpredictable patterns of moodiness. He once wrote home to his parents that he was going to leave Wheaton and hitchhike to California. His roommate during the second semester, in the attic of a house on President Avenue, which had a small finished study room and beds in an unfinished area, recalls that Ed was seldom "civil" to him. "While there had not been any clashing of opinions or personal conflicts of any sort, Ed continued to be melancholy and hermitlike in his relationship to me. He had great difficulty in being social or communicative, to the extent that I much preferred to study in the library rather than in our cozy little study room at home." Carnell's roommate in his sophomore year tells much the same story.

If we stand back and look at his undergraduate career as a whole, we can see clearly that Edward Carnell was not the legendary "Big Man on Campus." He appears only once in the 1942 *Tower*, the yearbook for his 1941 graduating class; under his senior picture the caption reads simply: "Edward Carnell, Albion, Michigan, Philosophy." Campus leaders such as Hudson Armerding (who later became president of the college) have up to a dozen yearbook references and long lists of student activities, including election to "Who's Who in American Colleges and Universities." We would be far off the mark, however, if on the basis of first-year troubles and the silence of a yearbook we concluded that the undergraduate years at Wheaton were disappointing ones for Carnell. Years later in 1966, with his own daughter away at Westmont College in Santa Barbara, he wrote her a letter, reassuring her that she should not feel compelled to take a heavier load than she could manage and that she should feel relaxed about participation in extracurricular activities. Then the letter reflected on his own experience:

> When I went to Wheaton, I worked about 50 hours a week in the dining hall. I think I went to *one* football game during my entire four years at college. I did very little dating, for I had all I could handle with dining hall work and classes. But I don't look back with a single ounce of regret, for there were other things to do in life with the passage of time.[6]

Obviously college life was far different in the 1930s than it is today, even at colleges that did not call themselves Christian. What was life at Wheaton really like when Carnell was an undergraduate some fifty years ago? Marshall Frady has written a remarkably perceptive and generally fair biography of evangelist Billy Graham.[7] When he introduces Wheaton, however, where Graham arrived as a transfer student in the fall of 1940, the beginning of Carnell's senior year, Frady is guilty of some curious inaccuracies and perhaps a certain bias. He calls Wheaton "a doctrinaire evangelical conservatory set in the tawny plains south of Chicago."[8] A mere glance at a map shows that the town of Wheaton is arrow-straight west of Chicago's Loop (admittedly a minor point). And maybe we should not take serious issue with the adjective "doctrinaire" – although Wheaton was certainly far less so than, for example, Bob Jones College where Graham had once been a student. But then there is the curious term "conservatory." Wheaton had a Conservatory of Music, but it was only one part of the larger institution, and Graham had no connection with it. Is Frady obliquely alluding to Wheaton's acknowledged objective to *conserve* the faith of its students? Whatever the intent, the effect is to suggest that Wheaton College in 1940 was something different from (and, inevitably, inferior to) the regionally accredited liberal arts college it most assuredly was. The negative impression is modified somewhat by the additional comment that Wheaton was "a considerably more urbane and academically ambitious campus than Florida Bible Institute" (another of Graham's previous schools) – "the difference between them about comparable to that between a tub band and a chamber ensemble."

As a final touch to his account of Graham's debut on the Wheaton campus, Frady creates for us the image of a "rather gawky country youth" with "implausibly gorgeous pinstripe suits" – a youth who felt out of place on "that more staid campus of pince-nez sanctitude."[9] The fact that the usual campus dress was less flamboyant than "implausibly gorgeous pinstripe suits" might possibly mislead one into using the term "staid." However, none of the evidence available to us from that time period – yearbooks, student newspapers, archival bits and pieces, interviews with alumni – justifies the phrase "pince-nez sanctitude." It is not difficult, though, to risk a guess as to what gave it birth. For one thing, every campus has always had its share of stuffed shirts – humorless, self-impressed faculty, and students pathetically old beyond their years. Beyond that, Wheaton also carried its own distinctive legacy: the pietistic behavioral standards of Bible-belt fundamentalism. The Application for Admission filled out by every entering Wheaton student in those years summarized the rules governing conduct:

All are required to abstain from the use of alcoholic liquors and tobacco, card-playing, dancing, attendance at theaters (including moving picture theaters), and meetings of secret societies. Students who are not willing to cooperate in maintaining the Wheaton ideals of college work and life will be invited to withdraw whenever the general welfare demands it, even though there be no special breach of conduct calling for suspension.

Immediately following that paragraph was the question: "To what extent, if any, have you used tobacco within the past twelve months?" plus the notation, "This space must not be left blank." Finally, of course, there was the commitment: "If admitted to Wheaton College, I agree to abide by the above rules and any others which may be in force during my stay in Wheaton" and then a line for the applicant's signature. Inevitably some of the "non-Christian" students admitted in the 1930s and 1940s had serious misgivings about such standards. Nita Mae Carlsen, *Silver Trumpet*'s attractive rebel, called Wharton "a strange place. They've invented three hundred and seven new blue laws there in addition to the code of 1620." Even some of the students who came from churches and homes in total rapport with the Wheaton way of life felt uncomfortable with the pledge, not necessarily because they wanted to indulge in any or all of the forbidden practices but because they resisted the idea of signing away some of their freedom. By far, however, the largest segment of Wheaton applicants, when they signed the pledge, were simply affirming happily a standard of conduct in which they were already thoroughly comfortable. Even Nita Mae decided to return for a second year: "the place gets you somehow." To see the requirement as restrictive is to make the mistake outsiders have always made about what went on during those years at colleges like Wheaton. To be sure, rebels occasionally took the Aurora and Elgin into Chicago and sneaked into the movies. And there are alumni today who, in looking back on their college experience at Wheaton, make reference to "repressed sexuality," "authoritarian administration," "prohibitions on personal freedom," and "intellectual tunnel vision." But with alumni from the Carnell era, most of those comments represent the modified vision of maturity looking back on a world long past. These are the alumni who say, "I was happy there, but I don't think my kids would be." While they were students they enthusiastically enjoyed everything they expected college life ought to be. They had little or no money in the closing years of the Depression. Only a few of them had cars. So their lives centered on campus. And with a student population of around 1,200, everyone knew virtually everyone else, a situation which nourished a deep sense of personal camaraderie. There was plenty to do. If Carnell had to confine himself largely to work and study, others were more free to take advantage of a wide range of athletics and other extracurricular activities. In addition to the usual musical groups, debating teams, student newspaper, and various clubs, the Literary Societies (does the name mistakenly suggest pince-nez sanctitude?) dominated the campus's social life in those years, providing an acceptable substitute for fraternities and sororities. And when campus events were over, there was always the center of town, just a pleasant walk away, along suburban streets lined with giant elms, where ice cream parlors and sandwich shops remained open for such business as limited student budgets would allow.

Two powerful forces shaped Carnell's life at Wheaton and compensated for whatever deprivation he felt because he missed an active social life. The first was the very same dining hall in which he spent so many work hours week after week. Alumni of that era, when questioned about their memories of Ed Carnell, almost invariably say that though they did not have much contact with him they do remember seeing him at work in Upper Williston Dining Hall. One said: "My only recollection of him is as a busboy . . . superbly balancing a huge tray of filled dinner plates with one hand over his head." The important point is that with all of the seemingly endless hours of work, all of the understandable grumbling and boredom and weariness, the dining-hall crew, both staff and students, became a sort of second family for Ed Carnell. In January 1944, three years after graduation, when Ed and Shirley Rowe got married in Kenosha, Wisconsin, it was the presence of "Roggie" and "Ma" and "the old gang" from the dining hall that Ed specially mentioned in a letter to Dave Lovik, another member of the gang who apparently would have been best man but for his forced absence on duty in the Merchant Marine. The dining hall and kitchen themselves became not only a place to work but to fraternize, have Christian fellowship, eat leftover food, and significantly further one's education. Larry Kulp, who went on to a distinguished career in science (as J. Laurence Kulp), which included a number of years as director of the Lamont Geochemical Observatory at

Columbia University, learned his organic chemistry on the job in the Upper Williston kitchen, placing three-by-five cards where he could now and then glance at them while he scrubbed stoves. Lars Granberg, who went on to become Dean of the Social Sciences at Hope College in Michigan and for a time was Carnell's colleague as De n of Students and Associate Professor of Psychology and Counseling at Fuller Seminary, now gives him fifty percent of the credit for his undergraduate education because of Carnell's insistence on pursuing for hours, while at work in the dining hall, the further implications of issues that had been raised in class. Sometimes these questions and comments had to be shouted back and forth over the clatter of dishes and pans, the hiss of steam tables. An alumna recalls that during one semester when she was at the cash register and Ed was carrying trays of dirty dishes back to the kitchen, he would pose a philosophical question to her as he headed for the kitchen and insist that she have an answer for him when he returned for another load.

Not surprisingly, the place of such hard work became at times a place to let off steam. Jim Tompkins, later a student with Carnell at both Westminster Seminary and Harvard and one of his closest friends at Wheaton, recalls such an occasion, which for the full effect must be described in his own words:

In the summer of 1940 I stayed on campus to take a course in physics. Ed stayed for some other purpose, but as usual we met in the dining hall kitchen or dish room. Normally we worked from 6 A.M. to 8, were in class or lab from 8 to 11:30, worked from 11:30 to 1, were in class from 1 to 4:30, and then worked from 5 to 8:30. Weekend work in the dining hall was slightly lighter, but most of us put in 35 to 45 hours per week. By the end of summer school we were exhausted and living on raw nerve.

On one night toward the end, something snapped. I was scraping, Ed was stacking dishes and pushing them into the washer. The temperature was nearly 100 degrees; no air-conditioning; soaking wet with sweat; bone-tired. There were five or six of us working as fast as we could to finish. I don't recall how it started, but someone said something to someone else, probably as a joke, and the latter reached into the garbage pail for a handful of discarded mashed potatoes and gravy. Somebody got that handful squarely in the face, also probably as a joke.

For the next fifteen minutes the place was a riot. The fifty-five gallon drums (into which we put waste food for pigs) were emptied panfuls on end into each other's hair or down the neck or shot across the room to splat against a wall. Two guys would gang up against a third and baptize him in sour milk or squash yesterday's peas and beans inside his shirt. Others would wrestle on the floor swimming in grease and pour catsup in each other's ears. One guy was stuffed into the dumbwaiter and half drowned with hoses directing water at him full force and he with no means of escape. When we finally ran out of ammunition, we stopped and surveyed the mess. The ceiling dripped with garbage; cupboards and shelves were in complete shambles; windows, doors, equipment, everything –

splashed with refuse. It was hilarious. We laughed until we were almost sick, and then pitched in together and thoroughly cleaned the entire area. In the end, it had never been so spotless.[10]

The Dionysian abandon of this scene counterpoints not only the hours of sweaty work in a 100 degree kitchen but also the Apollonian rigor of serious academic study, the second powerful shaping force that increasingly dominated Carnell's life at Wheaton. It is no exaggeration to say that he found himself intellectually at college, discovering a love and capacity for learning that set the direction for the rest of his life. The evidence from his Wheaton transcript clearly indicates it was philosophy that captured his mind. Whereas he was a good enough student to graduate with honors in 1941, he ranked no higher than 48 in a class of 205. But his grades in philosophy were outstanding and his performance on the philosophy comprehensive exam was ranked as Superior.

The faculty member most responsible for igniting Carnell's intellectual fires was the late Gordon Haddon Clark, who had come from the University of Pennsylvania in 1936 as visiting professor of philosophy and joined the permanent faculty the next year. It is important, in our effort to understand Carnell, not to pigeonhole Clark as merely another faculty member among many. In an appreciative introductory essay to a Clark Festschrift, Carl F. H. Henry states that at Wheaton Gordon Clark "made a lasting contribution to a score of young scholars who were to articulate Christian theism aggressively in the contemporary milieu. Among these were Edward John Carnell, Edmund P. Clowney, Clair Davis, Billy Graham, Paul K. Jewett, Robert K. Rudolph, and the present writer."[11] In Carnell's case the influence was lifelong and doubly significant in that during the last years he and Clark were profoundly alienated from each other.

Who was this man who, in Henry's words, cut such a "wide and deep swath" on the Wheaton campus? In a school that often seemed to place more importance on chapel sessions and semiannual evangelistic campaigns than on academic concerns, Clark held out for the primacy of the classroom. Many Wheaton alumni, even some who in subsequent years have strayed far from Clark's philosophical rationalism and dogmatic theology, still think of him as the one person most responsible for rousing them from intellectual slumber. One alumnus who abhorred chapels remembers only one of any consequence: "Dr. Gordon Clark spoke once for five minutes! and *said* something." Another recalls that during the revival meetings that began each semester, when the chapels would unpredictably go into overtime at the sacrifice of classes, Clark and a couple of students who had cut chapel that day could have been found stewing impatiently in a classroom, waiting for chapel to end, wanting to get on with Kant or Aristotle. Clark thoroughly enjoyed teaching and communicated his enthusiasm to his students. "He was funny in a poker-faced way," says an alumnus from that time. "He would be expounding away at some idea or other, making it sound good, arguing for it, but we just knew he didn't believe it. Students would say, 'But, Dr. Clark, is this true?' He'd ignore them and go on with his exposition." When teaching Plato he would be Plato, answer questions as Plato. And so on with Aristotle, Descartes, Spinoza. He would make sure, however, to round off his presentations with a critique of each philosopher.

Other traits of Clark were not looked on as so admirable. As an unabashed rationalist who pursued truth with the mind, he was deaf to other dimensions of the philosophical enterprise and totally incapable of dealing sympathetically with, for example, a theologian like Karl Barth. On one occasion, a student who had read just about everything by Barth that had been translated into English was goaded by other students into attending one of Clark's classes on Barth. He was appalled to realize that Clark's negative pontifications were based exclusively on a reading of only one of Barth's earliest works. When the student pointed out in class discussion that Barth, in a more recent book, had changed his mind on a certain issue, Clark was nonplussed. That was simply not how one should operate in such matters. Having once made up his mind on an issue, after a full exercise of the intellect, he did not change it.

Inevitably this dapper, self-assured, combative man aroused controversy. As a strong Calvinist in a school with a deeply ingrained Arminian history, Clark was obviously tweaking the tiger's tail when he took on the leadership of a small group of pro-Calvinist students who became his protégés and were subsequently perceived by the rest of the college community with considerable ambivalence. Although excellent students, they were a breed apart, sometimes arrogant in their orthodoxy. Both Carnell and Tompkins were included among Gordon Clark's boys, as was Paul Jewett, who also went on to Westminster and Harvard and later joined the faculty of Fuller Seminary as Carnell's colleague. Once again, from James Tompkins's sharp sensory memory we get a vivid picture:

I recall on one occasion, following a particularly lively session with Clark, that we trooped out together across the campus. Clark (who, I suppose, was about five feet seven inches in height) was in the lead. Ed, who may have been five-ten or eleven, fell in behind Clark, walking in his footsteps with Paul Jewett next in step, etc. The order may not have been just so, but at least there were four or five of us imitating Clark's gait and manner like goslings following their mother goose. Of course it was all in fun; but Clark did have that kind of hold over us.[12]

John Graybill, who went on to earn a Ph.D. in Assyriology and become an Old Testament professor, credits Clark with teaching him the crucial historical fact that the fundamentalism of the 1940s must not be equated with historic Christianity.

When I began to see that most of the distinctive features of the thought-system in which I had been raised were really first stated (in the form I knew them – and that *form* was always considered to be of the essence) late in the last century or early in this, and often by men not too well educated and out of touch with the sources (the Hebrew and Greek Bible and the church fathers), that really set me to thinking and studying, and from this exercise I have never recovered. It saved my faith for me (to the extent it has been saved). I have come greatly to admire the church fathers and Protestant reformers, and I have Clark to thank for this. He moved among these ancients as among friends; so have I.[13]

Ironically, though, Clark was something of a fundamentalist himself. One thinks of the Princeton and Westminster New Testament scholar J. Gresham Machen as a comparable figure. Ned Stonehouse, in his biographical memoir of Machen, points out that he did not like to be classed as a fundamentalist. The term carried implications of some strange new sect, whereas he considered himself to be defending the central tradition of the historic Christian faith. But he accepted the label for the sake of the cause. Stonehouse quotes Machen directly:

"Do you suppose, gentlemen, that I do not detect faults in many popular defenders of supernatural Christianity? Do you suppose that I do not regret my being called by a term that I greatly dislike, a 'Fundamentalist'? Most certainly I do. But in the presence of a great common foe, I have little time to be attacking my brethren who stand with me in defense of the Word of God. I must continue to support an unpopular cause."[14]

Clark too had mixed feelings. On matters such as biblical inerrancy his fundamentalism was rock-ribbed. But his strict Calvinism was alien to Wheaton's brand of Arminian fundamentalism (which stressed free will and responsibility) and was perceived by some of his critics to be fatalistic and thus inimical to evangelism and the missionary enterprise. Clark of course did not see it that way at all. The conflict intensified in the early 1940s under a new administration and culminated in a private heterodoxy hearing before the college board of trustees. In the Buswell regime the confrontation probably never would have taken place. But the firing of President Buswell in January 1940 made Clark's eventual departure almost a certainty. The new president, V. Raymond Edman, was a popular choice. His promotion to the presidency from the college's history faculty held out the hope of a more democratic administration, although if Edman proved to be more democratic than the sometimes imperious

Buswell, it was more a matter of style than substance. More significantly, the new president represented a basic shift at Wheaton from head religion to heart religion. Edman was an intellectually shallow nan – some have called him anti-intellectual – and although he was enormously successful at raising money for Wheaton through wealthy business interests, he alienated certain members of the faculty. Clark never got the chance to resign. At the end of the 1943 spring semester he was ousted; shaking from his feet the dust of the Christian college, he moved on eventually to the secular campus of Butler University in Indiana. By the time this happened, Carnell had graduated and was doing his seminary work at Westminster in Philadelphia, but he knew what was going on at Wheaton and deeply resented the shabby treatment of his beloved professor. Even ten years later, when Carnell would write to Clark from Fuller Seminary, the memory obviously still rankled: "I have a feeling that if I had been treated by Wheaton as you have, on sheer disgruntlement I would never want to see the place again."[15]

But Wheaton, of course, did not treat Carnell the way it treated Clark. Wheaton represented the beginning of a redemptive process, healing the wounds left by "the tyrannical legalism" of his fundamentalist boyhood. Wheaton was no less representative of fundamentalism than Herbert Carnell or the First Baptist Church of Albion, but it was fundamentalism with a touch of class. Under Clark's tutelage especially, Carnell began to see Christianity as intellectually respectable. Painfully aware of the gulf between his new understanding of the Christian faith and the severely limited version of it represented by his father, he felt himself drawn more and more toward a career of committed Christian scholarship. But he also became convinced that he would never get a fair hearing for the faith unless he had not only the best academic credentials but satisfactory answers to whatever questions unbelief might pose.

David Roberts, later to become Wheaton College's Director of Development, was another of Carnell's classmates, one who knew him well because he worked beside him in the dining hall for four years. After more than four decades, one incident dominates Roberts's mind when he thinks of Carnell. It epitomizes what was happening to this young man and pulls aside just a little bit the curtain that shields our view of the future. Roberts and Carnell used to indulge in friendly argument while they worked. On this particular day Carnell was especially troubled. He had been a member of a gospel team conducting a street meeting the night before. While witnessing to one of the onlookers, he had been asked a question he could not answer. He was more than troubled; he was shaken. Here at work in the kitchen the next morning he was declaring that he would never again let himself be put in a spot like that until he had all the answers. Roberts argued that we could never have all the answers, that it was our responsibility to witness, to share Christ, not to give answers to all questions. But Carnell adamantly stood his ground.[16]

With that kind of an outlook, the choice of a seminary weighed heavily on his mind in his senior year. Most of the more theologically conservative seminaries sent recruiters to the Wheaton campus every year. But Carnell wanted to sample the possibilities firsthand. During spring vacation he went on a 1,700-mile hitchhiking tour that took him to four seminaries on the eastern seaboard: Eastern Baptist, Princeton, Westminster, and Faith. The first two were affiliated with major denominations; Westminster (in suburban Philadelphia) had split off from Princeton in the late 1920s as a result of internal modernist–fundamentalist dissension among the Presbyterians; and Faith Seminary (in Wilmington, Delaware) came into being as a result of still further dissension in that extended separation process. In late April, Carnell made his decision. Along with his application for admission to Westminster he sent a personal letter clearly defining his primary goal and pinpointing the reason for his choice:

I feel, after sitting in on the classes of the various schools, that you offer the most scholarly defence of the Gospel of Jesus Christ, and so I am prepared, if I am accepted, to join with the student body and faculty at Westminster to fight against all forms of anti-Christian systems, and to preach to the world as consistent as possible the Whole Council [*sic*] of God.[17]

Fourteen years after his graduation from Wheaton, returning to speak in chapel as an Illustrious Alumnus, president of a sister institution, Carnell expressed gratitude to Wheaton for its permanent impact on his life in three areas: scholarship, discipline, and personal relationships. In the first category, he noted that whereas he learned *more* in graduate school than he did at Wheaton, he did not have to *unlearn* anything. In the second category, he hailed Wheaton for inculcating in him the meaning of time and the dignity of labor. The college, he said, taught him to be the steward of the minute. Finally, on the third point, he expressed his appreciation for Wheaton as "a family where love prevails."[18]

Not much there to make us sit up and take notice. Carnell succeeded in finding things to say that were both true and affirmative. What transposes these positive remarks into a new key, and significantly increases their value to us in our effort to understand Carnell, is the implicit presence in each of them of darker tones that we can detect mainly by hindsight. When our biographical study has moved farther along, his note of gratitude to Wheaton for teaching him to be "a steward of the minute" will make us think not only of productive self-discipline but of an almost compulsive drivenness that led him to say once to a friend soon after his breakdown, "Learning to loaf is one difficult piece of pedagogy for me. Where I am racing all the time, well, that's the mystery."[19] When we hear him describe Wheaton as "a family where love prevails," we will think not only of the close-knit kitchen gang but of Carnell's growing alienation, his tendency to isolate himself from colleagues and friends. When he commends his Wheaton education because he did not have to unlearn any of it when he got to graduate school, we will think not only of the superb quality of Gordon Clark's undergraduate philosophy courses but of the inner conflicts later generated in Carnell by the clash of Clark's rigid rationalism with his own more existential impulses.

But those experiences will come later. Now it is 1941, and the young man who had vowed never again to witness for Christ until he had all the answers was ready for the next step of the journey: matriculation at a theologically conservative seminary where presumably he would learn more of those answers.

CHAPTER IV

Westminster

In order to understand Westminster Seminary, where Carnell enrolled in the fall of 1941, one must first know something about Princeton Seminary, for Westminster would never have come into being except for certain developments that split Princeton into factions in the 1920s. Since its founding in 1812 under the leadership of the Reverend Archibald Alexander, who was appointed its first president by the Presbyterian General Assembly, Princeton had stood unbendingly for strict Calvinistic Reformation theology as articulated in the writings of the seventeenth-century Swiss scholastic François Turretin. The boast of Alexander's protégé and successor, Charles Hodge, that "a new idea never originated in this seminary," should not be dismissed as stubborn anti-intellectualism but should be seen rather as the serene confidence of one who is convinced that God has vouchsafed eternal truth to human care in the inspired words of the Bible, that the Reformation rediscovered the truth buried under centuries of ecclesiastical debris, and that the mandate of modern Christians is simply to deepen their understanding of and commitment to the truth, which never changes. As *his* successor Francis Patton once said:

Now Princeton Seminary, it should be said, never contributed anything to these modifications of the Calvinistic system. She went on defending the traditions of the Reformed Theology. You may say that she was not original: perhaps so, but then, neither was she provincial. She had no oddities of manner, no shibboleths, no pet phrases, no theological labels, no trademark. She simply taught the old Calvinistic Theology without modification: and she made obstinate resistance to the modifications proposed elsewhere, as being in their logical results subversive of the Reformed Faith. There has been a New Haven theology and an Andover theology; but there never was a distinctively Princeton theology. Princeton's boast, if she have reason to boast at all, is her unswerving fidelity to the theology of the Reformation.[1]

But in the 1920s, everything nailed down at Princeton started coming loose. Controversy was nothing new to the Princeton conservatives. Indeed, in doctrinal struggles within the Presbyterian denomination in the 1890s, they had demonstrated not only their ability to tackle potentially explosive issues but their ability to prevail. They engineered the General Assembly's formal action against three influential progressive seminary professors: Henry Preserved Smith, Arthur Cushman McGiffert, and Charles Briggs (the first from Lane Seminary, the latter two from Union). In the early 1920s the Princeton conservatives were still riding high. They won a significant victory in persuading the 1923 General Assembly to set in motion the complex parliamentary machinery designed to whip the New York Presbytery into line in its treatment of the controversial Harry Emerson Fosdick. By the 1924 Assembly, however, it had become apparent that even though by their maneuvering they could force Fosdick to resign his position at New York's First Presbyterian Church, they were unable to get action on substantial doctrinal issues. The extreme conservatives now faced serious opposition not only in the denomination but within the seminary itself. During the following year positions polarized around two leaders, both Princeton Seminary professors: Charles Erdman led the moderates and J. Gresham Machen, highly respected New Testament scholar, championed the cause of the extreme conservatives. At this point in history, the basic fundamentalist argument that theological liberalism represented a new religion antithetical to historic Christianity (a position given its most articulate argument in Machen's 1923 book *Christianity and Liberalism*[2]) had gained considerable respect in both the religious and secular worlds.[3] But at the 1925 General Assembly, the balance of power began to shift. Erdman was elected Moderator. A power play by the exclusivists – designed to force doctrinal conformity – failed when the question was referred to a special committee for study. In *Fundamentalism and American Culture* George Marsden underscores the irony:

It was not immediately obvious that the exclusivist fundamentalist movement in the Presbyterian Church would be killed by referral to a committee. In fact it was. The working strength of fundamentalism everywhere depended greatly upon the national mood. In the early summer of 1925 fundamentalism was at its peak; by the next year its strength was rapidly sinking.[4]

Having lost a battle, Machen returned to Princeton to continue the war. But his position grew more and more untenable. The 1926 General Assembly, in connection with its delaying tactics on Machen's appointment to the prestigious chair of Apologetics and Ethics, set up yet another committee to review the controversies at Princeton. Not unexpectedly, when in 1929 that committee mandated a new plan of seminary governance that would guarantee a more inclusivist orientation, Machen led a faction (including Professors Oswald T. Allis, Cornelius Van Til, and Robert Dick Wilson) out of Princeton to Philadelphia, where they founded Westminster Seminary. Their resolution to form a new seminary, which was passed in the summer of 1929, made clear their pedagogical and theological conservatism: "We believe that immediate steps should be taken for the establishment of a new theological seminary which shall continue the policy of unswerving loyalty to the Word of God and to the Westminster Standards for which Princeton Seminary has been so long and so honorably known."[5] As the heir to the long tradition of Princeton conservatism, Westminster Seminary carried into the mid-twentieth century what they perceived to be the orthodox Reformation dogmatism of Alexander, the Hodges, Patton, and Benjamin Breckinridge Warfield.

Between 1929 and the fall of 1941, when Carnell and several other Wheaton friends arrived at Westminster, the separatist nature of the institution intensified. Machen was suspended from the Presbyterian ministry in 1935 and a year later, with a small group of his followers, founded a new Presbyterian denomination, later called the Orthodox Presbyterian Church.

One is tempted to look on Carnell's three years at Westminster as an interlude between his intellectual awakening at Wheaton and the enormously influential period of graduate study at Harvard and Boston University. From one point of view, that idea has much credibility: The Westminster theology did not win Carnell's full allegiance. To be sure, he studied diligently and worked hard. He earned two degrees (Bachelor of Theology and Master of Theology) at the end of his stay, and won the William Brenton Greene, Jr., prize in Apologetics for his thesis "The Influence of the Philosophy of Immanuel Kant on the Theology of Frederick Schleiermacher." He appreciated the solid grounding he received in the history of systematic theology under Professor John Murray.[6] Professor Cornelius Van Til, the theologian who most completely represented the seminary's version of Calvinism at the time, later wrote that Carnell was not only a student of his but a friend, that he wrote a brilliant master's exam, and that there was every indication "we were in agreement regarding apologetic methodology." But sharp differences arose between the two men. The actual breach came later, according to Van Til, during Carnell's matriculation at Harvard.

He was sure, as he told me during a whole day we spent together discussing these matters, that since I did not do justice to Aristotle's fourth book of the *Metaphysics*, my faith must be a blind faith. He was sure I could make no intelligible contact with the unbeliever. Everything he wrote in his first book on apologetics, and in all those to follow, he wrote with full consciousness of the differences which arose between us during his days at Boston.[7]

There is reason to believe Carnell experienced the alienation earlier. Looking back in a 1953 letter to James Tompkins, his Wheaton and Westminster classmate who had by that time drifted away from orthodoxy, he compared and contrasted his college and seminary years and explicitly declared his preference for Gordon Clark over Van Til: "Like yourself, I rejected Van Til; but unlike yourself, graduate studies presented no option superior to that which Clark taught me."[8] Without minimizing the importance of the differing apologetical stances, one suspects that the gap between the mentor and his student was in part a matter of pedagogical style. Lloyd Dean, another of Carnell's companions at Harvard, recalls Carnell's explanation of the differences between Clark and Van Til:

"You'd ask Clark a question, he'd think for a minute, then give you a one-sentence answer. And you'd say to yourself, 'That's no answer.' But you'd go home and think about it – and after a while you'd come around to the view that it was a pretty good answer after all. Which is exactly the process Clark intended you should get involved in. You'd ask Van Til a question, he'd talk for half an hour, and you'd be sorry you asked the question."[9]

Clark and Van Til became antagonists of a sort in 1944. Clark, having been let go by Wheaton, was interested in a Westminster teaching position and applied for ordination in the new Orthodox Presbyterian Church. At a series of hearings, which a number of Westminster students regularly attended, the discussion of certain rather abstruse theological issues had the effect of pitting Clark's ideas against those of Van Til.[10] By this time, Carnell had already graduated and gone on to Boston, but he was kept informed by fellow Clark sympathizers still enrolled at Westminster. Their perceptions were that, whatever the official outcome, Clark argued his case far more skillfully than those arrayed against him. In any case, it was after these confrontational hearings that Clark decided his academic future lay not in a Christian college or seminary but in a secular university. Carnell, already smarting over Wheaton's treatment of Clark, could hardly have avoided focusing some of his resentment on Van Til. Ultimately, however, the reason for the Carnell–Van Til split (and for Carnell's lack of enthusiasm for Westminster Seminary as years went on) was not Van Til's pedagogy or apologetical assumptions but the very characteristic of which Hodge had boasted and which Westminster came into being to perpetuate: unyielding resistance to theological change of any kind. To be sure, Carnell had his own privileged sanctuaries that enclosed beliefs not open to change. Rare is the theologian who does not. But we are talking here about a fundamental distinction between theological openness and inflexibility, and on that criterion Carnell differed radically from Westminster.

Nevertheless, while a student there he absorbed much of value. He deepened his knowledge of all the things orthodox seminarians study – most especially a particular Calvinist perspective on theology. In later years many of the things he learned at Westminster remained intact in his own theology; other things were treated more as a base from which to explore in new directions. But taken as a whole, the study at Westminster unquestionably provided a solid foundation that enabled Carnell later to benefit much more readily from the educational opportunities at Harvard than would otherwise have been the case. His younger friend from college, Glenn Barker, traveled a different route and was painfully aware of the consequences; moving directly from Wheaton to graduate study at Harvard Divinity School, he discovered that he was ill-prepared and had to work doubly hard to fill in the knowledge gaps.[11]

But even seminary life has to be more than classrooms, library, and examinations. The Wheaton transplants were accumulating a supply of dissatisfaction with what seemed to some of them a lifeless orthodoxy. James Tompkins recalls that he and Carnell visited and considered transferring to Eastern Baptist Seminary:

The warmth and enthusiasm of Wheaton was so noticeably absent at Westminster that we really felt isolated. What we seemed to be searching for was the theological rigor of Calvinism joined to the spiritual exaltation of Fundamentalism. Eastern was theologically superficial; Westminster was spiritually dead. With such a choice, we settled for the corpse.[12]

Carnell's problems at Westminster went beyond theological differences and spiritual incompatibility. For the first two years there, he was frankly unhappy a good deal of the time. The problem was not with his living conditions. Student accommodations were considerably more elegant than they had been at Wheaton, the seminary having purchased a former estate in Chestnut Hill, a well-to-do suburb northwest of Philadelphia. The presence of a number of college friends provided the potential for good camaraderie. Carnell roomed for the first year and a half with fellow Wheaton graduate Delbert Schowalter, but they were not especially close. As Schowalter remembers those years, Carnell was "a very serious fellow. It was typical of him to be wrestling with philosophical problems, almost to the point that he was overwhelmed by them."[13] Schowalter is undoubtedly right to a degree. However, although we should not minimize the intellectual dimensions of Carnell's behavior, it is important to remember that he had been perceived as moody right from the start as a Wheaton freshman. Except for the kitchen crew, he had been a loner, but a loner who did not revel in his solitariness. The isolationist pattern intensified at Westminster. In discussing experiences of Carnell's later years, at which time we will have accumulated more evidence, we will need to make some interpretive judgments concerning his complicated personality. David Roberts's anecdote in the previous chapter has already revealed a theologically oriented compulsiveness in his academic quest – an effort to find sufficient answers to all the objections one might confront in persuading another person to become a Christian. At seminary, additional pressures – both external and internal – deepened the negative moods related to his pattern of loneliness.

The heating-up of World War II exerted some of this pressure. Although the United States did not enter the war officially until the Japanese attack on Pearl Harbor on December 7, 1941, Carnell's first year at Westminster, war had for some time been in the foreground of the American consciousness. The distant thunder of the Japanese–Chinese hostilities in the Far East, the Nazi blitzkrieg through Europe, the fall of France, the Battle of Britain, President Roosevelt's call for America to be the "Arsenal of Democracy" for the Allies: These events all had taken place during Carnell's Wheaton years. And whereas James Tompkins later referred to Wheaton as "an oasis in a world on fire,"[14] that description was only relatively true. When the Selective Training and Service Act became law on September 16, 1940, the reality of the war was brought home in a new way to the young men of the country, not excluding those at Wheaton College. Then, during the summer after Carnell's college graduation, German armies invaded Russia. In October a German submarine torpedoed and sank the *Reuben James,* the first American naval vessel to go down in the rapidly escalating hostilities. After Pearl Harbor, of course, life changed dramatically for everyone. By 1945 over twelve million men and women were serving in the various American armed services. Casualty statistics from distant places with unfamiliar names – Corregidor, Guadalcanal, Salerno, Anzio – summed up only the most obvious of war's tragic consequences. Men and women in round-the-clock shifts in the nation's factories waged war in a different way. And young men in theological seminaries, holding tightly or loosely to their 4-D draft deferment cards, faced every day their own brand of consequences, less overtly dangerous than those faced by a soldier in combat but rather more insidious because of their subtlety. Conscientious seminarians could not help but face some survivor guilt as the casualty lists mounted from the battlefields around the world.

We know that over the course of his career Carnell gave much thought to the Christian's proper stance toward war. He dealt with the issue in the seminary classes he taught in later years. During the Korean War he wrote a carefully thought-out-article entitled "Should a Christian Go to War?" for the Inter-Varsity magazine *His*.[15] Although he never served in the armed forces himself, his position as a philosopher, a theologian, and a man was unequivocally to insist on the Christian's obligation to support the government in "defensive warfare," which he defined as "simply the use of a national police force to destroy gangsterism on an international scale." If in these post-Vietnam years such confidence in the ability of a nation (and its individual citizens) to decide when a war is "defensive" and not "preventive" or "aggressive" seems naive, we should note that in the *His* article Carnell did acknowledge the ambiguities that complicate the effort to determine whether a government is defender or aggressor, "for motives are infinitely compounded with the subtleties of propaganda and emotion." Furthermore, the issues seemed so clear-cut in World War II and in the "police action" in Korea that there were virtually no conscientious objectors among American fundamentalists and very few from the major denominations. For the most part the C.O.s of that era came from "peace churches" such as the Quakers or the Mennonites. In any case, for Carnell the issue had profoundly personal implications. For a time he seriously considered satisfying the competing calls to duty simultaneously by enlisting in the chaplaincy. In fact, when the Wheaton student newspaper announced in the summer of 1943 that Ed Carnell had returned to the campus to study German and to resume his old job as cook in Upper Williston, it added this comment: "He intends to go back to Westminster next fall to continue his work and after completing his training there, he will go into the Navy as a chaplain."

The problem for Carnell and other young men in seminary was not whether the war itself could be justified but whether they themselves could justify their existence if they did not directly participate in it. Guilt feelings goaded many of them into herculean academic efforts to prove themselves worthy of their special status. Inevitably the strings were often wound too tight.

The exhaustion resulting from overwork was, in Carnell's case, exacerbated by his insomnia. In his 1956 book *Christian Commitment*, he allowed his readers a rare glimpse into one of the horror chambers of his life:

Although I have always been reasonably healthy, insomnia has plagued me from adolescence until now. Only those who are unable to sleep at night can appreciate the distressing toll this ailment takes on one's life: the omnipresent sense of fatigue, the susceptibility to irritation, and the grossness of an unrefreshed mind. All through the university I struggled against a never ending torpor, mental and animal. Each night the disquiets of mind prevailed over weariness. And the more the tensions of graduate work mounted, the more I fought off the effects of insufficient sleep.[16]

He mentions one specific incident in which the emotional lid blew off. The exact time and place of this experience is unimportant. (It probably happened in 1946 when he was studying at Harvard and living in Marblehead, Massachusetts.) Clearly, as he tells it, the incident is intended to represent many others like it. He had been cramming long into the spring nights for language examinations and had also been losing sleep from insomnia with depressing regularity. "My mind was like a mass of live rubber: continually expanding, it threatened to divide down the center." Impulsively he picked up a stack of German idiom cards, threw them against the wall, and within minutes was walking the railroad tracks leading away from town. Then his perspective changed.

Never before had the difference between my own roily soul and the serenity of nature stood out in sharper contrast. Although I longed to be identified with the natural harmony of the grass and the trees, I knew that this could only be enjoyed by denuding the self of all that comprises the essence of freedom. This left me with an overpowering sense of my own finitude. I could *consider* an ant, but I could not be one; and the more I tried to be one, the more I used moral freedom as an escape from the perils and responsibilities of moral freedom. Everything I conceived became a burden; every anticipated obligation threatened to impale me. Even so ordinary a responsibility as conversing with others overwhelmed me with consternation. Nor dare I conceal the fact that even suicide took on a certain attractiveness.[17]

Philosophically he grasps a truth from this experience: "*One's ability to see reality is somewhat conditioned to the tone of one's affections.*" What is more significant is that in Carnell's retelling of this incident we find evidence of certain tendencies, attitudes, and responses that were present in his life as early as the Westminster years and continued to play an increasingly important role as the years went on. His own account places the most stress on the insomnia. But we must not fail to note that, on this one occasion at least, he claims he went so far as to contemplate suicide. An especially revealing clue to his later troubles quietly rises to the surface in the same paragraph as the italicized philosophical insight: acknowledging that an extended loss of sleep eats away at his will to live, he writes, "But after a powerful sedative, I see things in a different light. The harmony of nature is restored; I am patient with others; the zest for creative living revives." By the time these words appeared in *Christian Commitment*, he had made a further discovery: Sleeping pills are addictive. And ten years after that, an overdose of barbiturates killed him.

The passage, however, also sounds a hopeful note. Carnell had discovered the restorative values of walking. He was a walker all his adult life. He walked the streets of Boston and Cambridge, the coastline along the picturesque town of Marblehead; he walked to work at Fuller Seminary from his home in Pasadena; several times he had his wife drive him to the top of Mount Wilson so he could walk back down the mountain; and one particularly troubling day he walked all the way from Pasadena to downtown Los Angeles. We know that at Westminster he was already dealing with his depressing moods by going on long solitary walks.[18] And as we picture this tall figure walking away from the campus toward the town of Glenside, we cannot help but recall another detail of the autobiographical incident just quoted: "Even so ordinary a responsibility as conversing with others overwhelmed me with consternation." This man who in a few years would be so thoroughly at home behind a teaching lectern or a pulpit always felt most threatened, with rare exceptions, by the prospect of confronting one other human being face to face. Consequently, while he reaped the physical benefits of vigorous extended walks, he slipped ever more deeply into his pattern of aloneness.

That pattern was interrupted in his final year at Westminster. During the summer of 1943 he met the young woman who was to be his partner for life. The previous summer, following his first year at seminary, he had lived with his parents at their parsonage in Lansing, Michigan (where his father had been called late in 1940 to be pastor of the Olivet Baptist Church). He continued his foreign language study at Michigan State and served as interim pastor of the First Baptist Church of Perry, Michigan, a few miles northeast of Lansing. It was a busy summer. In addition to the intractable demands of language study (at which Carnell was never especially adept), he preached twice on Sunday, prepared a brief sermon for the children, taught a Sunday School class, and led a midweek Bible study and prayer meeting.[19]

But his psyche was still tuned in to the Wheaton frequency. He had hoped to do his language study there instead of at Michigan State in the summer of 1942, but plans did not work out. In 1943, however, his experience and faithful labor as a college cook and general kitchen worker paid off. He was hired back at his old job in Upper Williston dining hall. Also on the Wheaton campus that summer was a young woman from Kenosha, Wisconsin, named Shirley Rowe, a public school teacher who had attended a two-year normal school in her home state and was taking further college courses in summer school. Carnell asked her to attend a concert with him in Chicago's Grant Park. It became clear early in the relationship that neither wanted this to be just another summertime romance. After they went their separate directions in August, they conducted a courtship by correspondence until Wheaton's Homecoming

Weekend in October, at which time, after the football game with De-Kalb, they announced their engagement in the time-honored Wheaton way – ringing the tower bell with the help of close friends from the kitchen alumni.

In recounting the events of the weekend in a letter to his college friend David Lovik, on duty in the Merchant Marine, Carnell obviously was still savoring both the sweetness of reunion with his fiancée and of reliving undergraduate memories with old classmates ("Then we went into Roggie's kitchen and sang to her all of the old hymns of the dining hall such as 'Alfalfa Hay.'") However, he sensed also, with a tinge of regret, that they all knew they had to leave the past behind. "It was not like the days when we cooked together and Elliot was there to burn the rice and Ma hollered at you all of the time. Those days are gone forever.")[20]

The only thing that tempered Carnell's joy over his engagement to Shirley was that they had to separate again. He went back to Westminster, of course, and she to her job in Wisconsin, for which she had signed a teaching contract. At this time their plans were to marry in the summer of 1944 after Ed's graduation from seminary. That decision was influenced by the Westminster position on student marriages: they were considered an impediment to the primary task of serious scholarship. So for a while Ed and Shirley continued to subsist on a diet of letters. Ed wrote a long letter every day of the week, even arranging mailings so that Shirley would receive one on Sunday via special delivery.

But plans changed quickly. As Shirley explains the situation, Ed was so lonely that they decided not to wait. She took the radical step of breaking her teaching contract in order to get married during the semester break and return to Philadelphia with Ed for his final term at Westminster. Rapidly planned weddings were the norm in those wartime years of short service leaves and unexpected travel orders. Just as several of the kitchen alumni had helped Ed ring the tower bell to announce his engagement, so these most important people in his life were present less than three months later to give him a proper matrimonial send-off. The wedding took place on New Year's Day in Shirley's family home in Kenosha. The ceremony, performed by Ed's father, was followed by a church reception. It was a source of considerable satisfaction to Carnell that the list of guests included not just the usual family and friends, and many of the Wheaton kitchen crew, but also Professor and Mrs. Gordon Clark.

The honeymoon consisted of a single night at Chicago's Blackstone Hotel and a journey by train back to Philadelphia. However brief, they enjoyed it fully. "The trip back to Philly was a lot of fun; we ate turkey in the diner and lived like kings till we got here to our apartment. Then the reality of life commenced."[21] The Carnells lived that semester in what was formerly the chauffeur's quarters, a small apartment over a garage at the foot of the estate next to the railroad tracks. Shirley studied Latin and took a course at the seminary. Ed continued to shovel coal and, when spring came, to trim trees on the campus at sixty cents an hour. The academic work was no less hard, the schedule no less rigorous. But the presence of Shirley kept the loneliness at bay.

Although Carnell considered graduate study at the University of Pennsylvania (where Gordon Clark had received his Ph.D.) and even mentioned in a letter the possibility of a teaching fellowship at Northern Baptist Seminary in Chicago, there was never much doubt that Harvard was really where he wanted to go. Shirley says that he told her right away of his plans to attend Harvard. "I am gunning for my Ph.D.," he frankly admitted to Dave Lovik. He made his formal application to the Divinity School on January 31, 1944. The most fascinating item in the packet of materials he sent was a letter to the Office of the Dean. For the purpose of setting up an illuminating contrast, before quoting from this letter I shall repeat the crucial paragraph of a previously quoted letter – the one written to Professor Paul Woolley three years earlier when he was applying to Westminster:

I feel, after sitting in on the classes of the various schools, that you offer the most scholarly defence of the Gospel of Jesus Christ, and so I am prepared, if I am accepted, to join with the student body and faculty at Westminster to fight against all forms of anti-Christian systems, and to preach to the world as consistent as possible, the Whole Council [sic] of God.[22]

Now in January of 1944 he proposes to the Harvard Dean an entire doctoral program in the history and philosophy of religion:

I wish to relate very specifically the question of epistemology to each of the six fields in which I shall engage myself in study. The first three fields, which are required, will provide me with an opportunity to apply methods of epistemology to Christianity and to some other chosen religion through a study of the contents and literary history of each. Also, I shall be able to do research work in the abstract question of the methods of knowledge and truth when related to religion and religious convictions. This probably will constitute my critical study of a phase of Philosophic Thought. The fourth field will be in the field of mysticism, conversion, and religious experience, a branch of epistemology viewed subjectively, a field which has always intrigued me because of the discrepancies in convictions, yet all appealing to objective reality. The fifth field will be in the study of ethics, its demands and relation to religion; yet always I shall tease out the theory of knowledge which each theory appeals to for its basis and verity. The last field will cover the problem of metaphysics involved in a religious view of the world. This, finally, will bring the theory of knowledge into relation with science and other phenomena of reality, and religious convictions to the structure of the objective universe. Thus, through this tentative schedule, I expect to apply my time and talents to this one critical problem as it manifests itself in these six fields of study.[23]

One cannot help but be impressed by the contrast between the two letters. The difference in tone and substance cannot be fully explained by the normal intellectual growth of a graduate student or by an appropriate switch in rhetorical strategy. The writer is like an aircraft about to take off from a carrier deck, its engine at high pitch, waiting for the restraining wires to be released. But if Carnell had any illusions that he was going to take Harvard by storm, he was mistaken. The admissions committee was not overwhelmed. A letter in Carnell's permanent Harvard file states the committee's agreement that he should be admitted but eased out at the end of the first semester if he did not measure up. Carnell knew only that he was accepted and bound for the mecca of American graduate education.

As noted earlier, he finished his work at Westminster with academic distinction. In late May he was ordained to the Baptist ministry under the Northern Baptist Convention in his father's church in Lansing. In June he and Shirley once again headed for Wheaton, where they worked to accumulate as much money as possible against the uncertainties of a new life in Cambridge. By September they had settled into a small apartment at 27 Irving Terrace, three short blocks from the Divinity School.

CHAPTER V

Fundamentalism-on-the-Charles

"My parish, with Wesley, is the world."

Edward Carnell[1]

In March 1940 Willard L. Sperry, Dean of Harvard Divinity School since 1922, referred in a "Dean's Letter" in the Divinity School *Bulletin* to the recent appearance at Harvard of a type of student quite new to that institution: "a man who has already had one theological course in a conservative-to-fundamentalist seminary, and who is now anxious to begin all over again another three years of theological re-education."[2] It is not clear exactly how many such students there were. Dean Sperry does number "a half-dozen in the three regular classes," but is vague about those on upper levels ("to say nothing of the Graduate group"). More important, he seems to have some anxiety as to how the Divinity School constituency is going to react to this new development. Acknowledging that these men present an academic problem "in that they have seldom had the four years of regular college work, which we technically require for admission here," he points out that some of them have come with an A.B. in Theology. And whatever the value of that degree, they do have certain qualities that highly commend them: "They already know their way around the major biblical and historical fields and their store of relevant facts-in-advance, awaiting reinterpretation, is much in excess of that of the ordinary college graduate." The experience with these men, he says, has on the whole been encouraging.

It was only the beginning. For whatever reasons, fundamentalists kept on applying to Harvard Divinity School, and through the 1940s and 1950s the school kept accepting them, giving them what Dean Sperry called a "theological re-education," and sending them out with baccalaureate and graduate degrees. While classification by theological label is always suspect, and especially hard to decipher in a rear-view mirror,

54

the number of self-acknowledged fundamentalists (or evangelicals, as they later began to call themselves) who were granted Th.D.s or Ph.D.s from Harvard in the remaining thirteen years of Sperry's deanship was at least twelve. Two others who received their degrees in the 1960s took most of their classwork within that earlier time span. In addition, perhaps another ten or twelve men of similar background and conviction were matriculating at the Divinity School during this time, working at the master's or bachelor's level or subsequently transferring to other institutions. And while these figures may not at first seem significant, it should be noted that the average number of annual graduates from all programs at the Divinity School during the 1940s was less than twenty.

These were not barbarian hordes overrunning the citadel of learning. The roster of Harvard fundamentalists now reads like an honor roll of mid- to late-twentieth-century American evangelicalism. In addition to Carnell, who received his Th.D. in 1948, the list includes such names as Kenneth Kantzer, theology professor at several evangelical colleges and seminaries and for a time editor of the movement's unofficial house organ *Christianity Today* (Ph.D. 1950); the late Merrill Tenney, longtime dean of Wheaton College Graduate School (Ph.D. 1944); John Gerstner, church historian at Pittsburgh Theological Seminary (Ph.D. 1945); Harold Kuhn, professor of philosophy of religion at Asbury Theological Seminary since 1944 (Ph.D. 1944). No less than three Fuller Seminary faculty appear on the list in addition to Carnell: theologian Paul King Jewett, interpreter of the works of Emil Brunner and author of the controversial *Man as Male and Female* (Ph.D. 1951); the late George Eldon Ladd, author of several books on the Kingdom of God and moderate evangelical voice in the sensitive area of New Testament criticism (Ph.D. 1949); and the late Glenn Barker, a New Testament scholar who was granted his Ph.D. in 1962 but did most of his class work within the period of time on which we are focusing. The remainder of the list: Burton Goddard, dean emeritus, Gordon-Conwell Theological Seminary (Th.D. 1943); Roger Nicole, professor of theology at Gordon-Conwell, now retired (Ph.D. 1967); Samuel Schultz, professor of Bible at Wheaton College, now also retired (Th.D. 1949); George Turner, emeritus professor of biblical literature, Asbury Theological Seminary (Ph.D. 1946); J. Harold Greenlee, formerly professor of Greek at Asbury, more recently a consultant with Wycliffe Bible Translators (Ph.D. 1947); Jack P. Lewis, professor of Bible at the Graduate School of Religion, Harding College (Ph.D. 1953); Lemoine Lewis, professor of Bible at Abilene-Christian College (Ph.D. granted in 1959 but all classwork done in the 1940s). Two other men who did not actually receive Harvard doctorates warrant mention because they play significant roles in the discussion: Lloyd Dean, professor of philosophy at Rhode Island Junior College, went on to complete his Ph.D. work at Boston University; the late Terrelle B. Crum, dean of Barrington College and an indispensable figure in the founding and ongoing work of the Accrediting Association of Bible Institutes and Bible Colleges, studied at Harvard Divinity School from 1937 to 1941 but did not finish his degree.

Carnell was far too much of an individual to be designated as typical of all these Harvard fundamentalists, but his experience does shed light on the experience of others. He was an unlikely Harvard applicant, as the son of a Baptist minister whose only post–high school education was two years at Moody Bible Institute and as a graduate himself of Wheaton College, which, despite its reputation for academic respectability, was a fortress of fundamentalist theology and moralistic pietism. So too with Kantzer, Jewett, Ladd – all of them – hardly typical Harvard men. What lay behind this curious symbiotic relationship between students and an institution theologically so far apart?

Let us look at the institution first.[3] Whereas in the minds of most American church people Harvard Divinity School in the 1940s was generally thought to be affiliated with the Unitarians, its denominational status was by that time a thing of the past. In 1879 Dean Francis Greenwood Peabody had argued before the Board of Overseers for an unsectarian school whose system would be determined by belief in "sound methods, broad knowledge, and quickened interest." Noting that this kind of school or faculty had long been known in Germany, he felt that Harvard should be such a school in the United States. In its undenominational classification, Harvard was virtually unique in this country for some time; as Levering Reynolds points out in a historical survey of Harvard Divinity School in the twentieth century, the *New Schaff-Herzog Encyclopedia of Religious Knowledge* in 1911 listed only Harvard as undenominational, "although Union Theological Seminary in New York could have fairly laid claim to the distinction."[4] More significant, however, is the educational philosophy and methodology that underlay Dean Peabody's proposal to the Board of Overseers. His stress on "scientific" study essentially meant the historical method, an approach that remained in effect at the Divinity School through the era we are discussing. Of six new faculty appointed between 1880 and 1883, five had studied in Germany. Their influence was decisive in making Harvard Divinity School "the most advanced expression of the liberal religio-historical Protestant scholarship of which Germany was the homeland, but in which most of the leading scholars in all major American Protestant seminaries participated."[5]

Although for a while the institution forged ahead, the second quarter of the twentieth century proved to be a time of trouble. For one thing, the president of the University from 1932 to 1953, Dr. James B. Conant, a scientist whose broader interests were in general education both within the university and in the society at large, had little interest in and gave little support to the Divinity School, believing theology a divisive force in education. Another problem was the depressed state of American religion in general. Historian Robert Handy has referred to the years 1926 to 1935 as "the American religious depression," a period when, in all but the rural areas of the nation, the Protestant churches had lost most of their influence.[6] Under the Conant administration, needing students to justify its very existence, Harvard Divinity School showed no substantial increase in student enrollments. Like so many of America's factories operating at less than full capacity through the years of economic depression, the Divinity School, with its impressive array of learned scholar-teachers, was falling far short of its potential contribution to the University, the church, and society. When interest in theology did begin to awaken, it was a Barthian or Niebuhrian neo-orthodoxy that carried the day, at a considerable remove from Harvard historicism, and the seminaries more favorably oriented ideologically to this position tended to attract the growing numbers of theology students. In short, Harvard Divinity School needed students. In the lean years of the late thirties and early forties, applications from a new potential reservoir of students, even from within the ranks of fundamentalism, were not to be dismissed out of hand.

What about those fundamentalists? What were *their* motives?[7] In one sense we hardly need ask. Young men who had progressed far enough on the academic ladder to seriously contemplate graduate education could hardly have avoided at least thinking of Harvard. Why not the best? Or at least what they perceived to be the best. No less a personage than historian Theodore White acknowledged that during the same era he and many others selected Harvard for their undergraduate education because of "the Harvard badge, which says 'Veritas,' but really means a job somewhere in the future."[8] Some had additional personal reasons, such as, in Merrill Tenney's case, the proximity of Harvard to his teaching responsibilities at Gordon College and Divinity School. Several found Harvard's offer of scholarship money decisive. (Carnell was given a $200 scholarship his first year.) J. Harold Greenlee says: "I chose Harvard because it was the only university I knew of with a Ph.D. in Biblical Greek." At a deeper level there had to be mythic undertones – encountering the Beast of Scholarly Unbelief in his own labyrinth and emerging with new confidence and new powers. As Roger Shinn remarked, reviewing a subsequent book by Carnell, "In some circles he is described, somewhat glibly, as one of the new generation of brainy fundamentalists who have studied at Harvard in order to learn the arguments they will spend the rest of their lives attacking."[9] Shinn is correct in his insistence that the description is less than fair, for the mythic truth that underlies the observation has been too easily parodied. But it was a factor. John Gerstner of Pittsburgh Theological Seminary says: "I went there because it was ultraliberal and academically competent, desiring my conservatism to be put to its tests." And Samuel Schultz of Wheaton: "Although I was quite fully informed about the perspective in the Harvard Divinity School prior to enrollment, I valued this opportunity of firsthand exposure to a naturalistic viewpoint on the Bible which confronted me with a sincere examination of my approach to biblical scholarship."

Young fundamentalist scholars had another, more significant, perfectly sensible reason for choosing Harvard in the 1940s. The decisive factor was the Divinity School's thorough dedication to historicism as its educational philosophy and methodology. The institution's position at the far left of the theological continuum did not discourage them at all from coming; in fact, ironically, it was the very characteristic that made Harvard more attractive than many other graduate schools of religion. These young men suspected that if they went to the nation's prestigious liberal and neo-orthodox schools of religion, they would be pressured to conform to a certain theological mold. At Harvard they knew that they could continue to keep the orthodox faith at the same time that they devoted themselves to a historically oriented, theologically neutral program of study. All that Harvard would ask of them was academic excellence. It was a fair bargain all around.

Academically Harvard was every bit as rigorous as Carnell and his fellow fundamentalists expected, but atmospherically it was more benign than they could have hoped. "I think the conservative went to Harvard," says Jack P. Lewis, "expecting to meet the Devil and instead encountered gentlemen of the highest character who were far kinder to *us* than *we* would have been to them had the case been reversed." More than any other faculty member, it is Henry J. Cadbury, New Testament scholar and Hollis Professor of Divinity, who stands out in their minds as the exemplar of rigor and fairness. Merrill Tenney had Cadbury as advisor for his Ph.D. program in Biblical and Patristic Greek: "While he knew that my theological convictions were the opposite of his, he was never abrasive or contemptuous in his treatment of me, whatever he may have thought. His attitude seemed to be that if I did the work that he expected, he would support me irrespective of my beliefs." Glenn Barker determined early in his own teaching career that he would always want to treat those who differed from his own theological position with the same complete respect showed toward him by Professor Cadbury. Referring to Cadbury as "a man of complete intellectual honesty," Carnell recalled how he would chide those nonfundamentalists in his class who were handling the Greek text irresponsibly. "We may not agree with Paul,"

Cadbury would insist, "but let us at least be honest with what he says."[10] Cadbury was memorable also for his Socratic teaching method, for which the fundamentalists were a perfect pedagogical foil. He seemed better able to provoke confrontation with the issues he wanted to pursue if some fundamentalists were present in the class, and if they were slow to join the interchange he was not the least bit reluctant to ask one of them for his view on a given question. And he was not above a playful jab now and then. "If you have praying mothers," he would say at the beginning of a class in which he would be taking a radical position on a sensitive issue, "they'd better be on their knees this morning."

Professor Nock was another matter entirely. Get together any group of Harvard Divinity alumni from that era and they will soon be swapping Arthur Darby Nock stories. A classicist and historian of early Christianity, Nock possessed a store of learning second to none but is remembered as the poorest lecturer on the faculty, lacking in the usual social graces, pacing back and forth while he muttered under his breath in a British accent difficult to catch. Tenney recalls one seminar with him in which he used to rub cologne on his forehead and swear at the students. Terrelle Crum never forgot his first meeting with Nock. Already teaching at Providence Bible Institute, Crum was going to be in Cambridge only on Fridays, so before the first class of the semester he asked Nock for a conference appointment on Fridays. According to Crum, "Professor Nock hit the ceiling. 'Young man, as a Harvard graduate student you come when your professor says to come, even if you have to travel from the other side of the world!' I crawled back into my shell until after class, when he came up to me, apologized gruffly, and said, 'See me on Friday.' "

One concludes that Nock's students learned rather quickly about graduate school standards. He was brutal in cutting through sham and careless scholarship, and it is said that each of his students can recall the episode in which he felt Nock's scathing criticism most severely as if it happened yesterday. However, Jack P. Lewis says: "Despite it all, good students learned fast under him, all lamented his early demise, and all speak of him with loving respect."

But our interest goes deeper than the nostalgic memories of revered teachers and the usual triumphs and tragedies of graduate school days – sacred detritus lodged permanently in the lore and legends of all alumni of all graduate schools. Something more important was happening to the Harvard fundamentalists. We must not overlook the fact that this group of students inherited all the emotional wounds of the fundamentalist–modernist wars of the 1920s, one result of which was a tendency in fundamentalist ranks to discredit the value of the free pursuit of truth in the educational process. These young men were aware that they were the advance guard of a new interest in education within a tradition that for a generation or more had been distrustful of it. This realization did not mean, however, that all of them responded identically to their graduate study at Harvard. In the eyes of certain of their nonfundamentalist fellow students, some of them appeared to be interested less in learning than in gaining the prestige that went along with a Harvard degree. It is also true that some of the fundamentalists began their Harvard programs relatively late, having already settled into an understanding of the Christian faith that satisfied their intellectual demands. And whereas, as previously mentioned, some came to Harvard precisely because they eagerly anticipated the prospect of putting their faith to the test, others majored in areas highly technical rather than philosophical (such as ancient languages) and thus, whatever their personal interests, had less time for the struggle with conceptual problems. Consequently, while the fires of the academic crucible burned hot for some of them, others survived like Shadrach, Meshach, and Abednego, with not a hair of their heads singed. Except for Carnell, the angst level seems to have been surprisingly low.

The first year in Cambridge was not easy for the Carnells. For one thing they faced the familiar gnawing problem of having barely enough money to get along. In late summer they had settled into an apartment on Irving Terrace, a pleasant elm-lined street only a block long, just a few minutes walk from the Divinity School. But neither the $200 scholarship nor Shirley's job in a law library met their financial needs. Ed tried to find a student pastorate in the Boston area, with duties flexible enough so that he could give his primary attention to studies. But he was unsuccessful. Instead he prepared food at the Harvard Faculty Club and on occasional weekends worked for the New Haven Railroad.

Carnell's problems that year were academic and intellectual too. Generally speaking he did very well. There is no evidence that the administration ever found it necessary to consider implementing the terms of the memo in Carnell's admission folder (that he should be admitted but eased out at the end of the semester if he did not measure up). Carnell's permanent Harvard file does, however, yield some revealing evidence from one of his courses. Professor D. Elton Trueblood, the Quaker theologian who was teaching at the Divinity School in the fall of 1944, noted that Carnell had written some poor papers, concluded that he was "greatly inhibited by narrow dogmatism," and sensed "some emotional disturbance," which he attributed to the theological problems he was facing. One bit of further evidence suggests that Trueblood analyzed the problem correctly, for Carnell told fellow students that he had come to Harvard with a sack full of arguments in defense of the faith, only to find to his dismay when he reached into it one day that the sack was empty. The young man who had declared to David Roberts at Wheaton that he would never again witness for Christ until he had all the answers to all the objections an unbeliever might raise was finding the quest tough going at Harvard. Small wonder that Trueblood detected "some emotional disturbance" and shrewdly diagnosed the problem as theological.

Inevitably, of course, Carnell had to modify the compulsive and self-defeating kitchen manifesto he had made to Roberts. We recall that in 1942 he preached for the entire summer in the First Baptist Church of Perry, Michigan. And, although presumably still not privy to all the answers, toward the end of his first year at Harvard he once again took on the responsibility of proclaiming the evangel and shepherding a flock. He was invited by the First Baptist Church of Marblehead, Massachusetts, to become their interim minister, replacing temporarily the regular minister who had just left for active duty in the chaplaincy of the United States Army.

The pastorate carried an annual salary of $1,560 plus $390 a year for rental of a parsonage. Marblehead is a delightful place to live any time of the year, but especially in the summer, and the Carnells wasted no time in moving to their new quarters. Located on the shore north of Boston, the town was settled in 1629 and first called Marble Harbor because to approaching boats the cliffs along the water's edge looked like marble. For two centuries the town's life was dominated by the fishing industry. One of the more tragic but less glorious incidents in that long maritime era was immortalized by John Greenleaf Whittier, with something less than complete historical accuracy, in the ballad poem "Skipper Ireson's Ride" ("Old Floyd Ireson, for his hard heart, / Tarred and feathered and carried in a cart / By the women of Marblehead!"). Both the Baptist Church and the parsonage were nestled right in the center of town, among the densely packed old buildings in the thicket of streets that wind around in conformity to the rock ledges on which the town was built.

Carnell did not have an abundance of free time for relaxation in his new home and surroundings. For in addition to his graduate studies (which do not come to a halt when formal classes stop in May) and the new obligations connected with the church, a call from Gordon College offered him a position on the summer school teaching roster made vacant by a last minute cancellation. Carnell must have had some misgivings about taking on yet more duties. But whatever the increased demands on his time and energy, this was an offer he could hardly refuse. Indeed, as we shall subsequently see, once he got his foot in the door of academia, Carnell never looked back.

This is not to say he was in any way derelict in fulfilling his responsibilities at the church. In the seventeen months he ministered there he conducted three services a week. In response to a parishioner who bemoaned the sparse Sunday evening attendance, Carnell said: "If there were only myself and my wife, we would still hold a Sunday evening service." A woman who is now a teacher and married to a Presbyterian minister recalls that during her junior high school days in Marblehead Carnell took time Saturday mornings to teach the Westminster Catechism to her and a friend. She thinks of those sessions as the most important spiritual influence of her life.[11] Two of the church's members, a married couple well along in years when I talked with them in 1977, were especially close to the Carnells during their stay in Marblehead. Noting that his preaching was "often over our heads," and that he found it difficult to relate to people personally (a failing he frankly acknowledged to them), these parishioners were nonetheless extremely fond of Carnell. They also worried about him. He seemed to them to be tired most of the time. So they were not surprised when he submitted his resignation in September 1946.[12] The official church record gives the reason for leaving: "He found that a pastorate in addition to his other duties was becoming too much of a strain on his health."

Without questioning the genuineness of Carnell's physical exhaustion, we should keep certain things in mind. First, it was not at all uncommon at this time for young scholar-minister-teachers to fill demanding multiple roles – studying at a seminary or graduate school, teaching usually at a Christian college, and serving as the minister of a church. Sometimes these fragmented lives were spread rather widely on the map, demanding many hours of travel by car or train each week. Life was not easy for any of these men and their wives, but they more or less accepted their lot as necessary to the achievement of their objectives. In Carnell's situation, the almost compulsive intensity he brought to all of life's activities made his round of duties especially tiring. And we must not forget the always present problem of insomnia.

Carnell's most compelling reason for resigning the pastorate at Marblehead was that with the teaching experience at Gordon he knew without a doubt that he had found his true vocation. As a matter of fact, in July, two months before he wrote his letter of resignation, he and Shirley had moved out of their quaint and comfortable Marblehead parsonage to a fourth-floor apartment (no elevator) at 42 Buswell Street in Boston, not far from the Gordon campus. In the next chapter, we shall have occasion to study Edward Carnell in some depth as a teacher. Let it suffice at this point to say that almost four decades later, Gordon alumni of that era still talk about the excitement generated in his classes. One of his Gordon students says: "I have never known a more exciting and even dramatic lecturer. His classes were an experience. He never seemed to do anything off the cuff, but rather was a meticulous craftsman in all that he did."[13]

Meanwhile, Carnell was gaining confidence as a student also. In addition to his Th.D. studies at Harvard, he enrolled at Boston University in graduate philosophy courses taught by Professors Edgar Sheffield Brightman and Peter Bertocci. He was not a shrinking violet in any of his classes. Lloyd Dean, whose friendship with Carnell went back to the first class the latter taught at Gordon College, recalls one especially touchy moment. One year they both took a course with Professor Nels Ferré at Andover-Newton School of Theology. Once a week they dashed from Gordon to Dean's house in Winchester, downed a quick supper, then sped to Ferré's home in Newton where about a dozen students met for the seminar. "It was typical of Ed," says Dean, "that he was a little disturbed when we were frequently a few minutes late. He used to say that we did have an obligation to be there on time." But late or not, Carnell was not about to retire shyly into the shadows. Dean recounts what happened on this particular evening:

Ferré was quite authoritarian in the classroom – and Ed was a rather blunt questioner. This night Ferré was carrying on about the problem of evil and expressing a troubled concern for the worms being eaten by the robin, when Ed raised his hand: "Dr. Ferré, has it ever occurred to you that you might be wrong?" There was a moment of stunned silence while Ferré pulled himself together. I had received a good grade from Ferré in the previous semester, but at this point I was a little apprehensive at being identified as Carnell's friend.[14]

But what about the "emotional disturbance" Elton Trueblood perceived in Carnell during his first semester at Harvard that he attributed to the theological problems he was facing? How did Carnell deal with that problem in the final years of graduate school? To answer these questions, let us return to the empty sack – that is, to Carnell's admission to fellow evangelical students that he had come to Harvard with a sack full of arguments in defense of the faith only to find to his dismay when he reached into it one day that the sack was empty. We must balance that remark with another piece of evidence. In 1958, during his tenure as president of Fuller Seminary, speaking at a fund-raising dinner in Chicago, Carnell reflected on some of his reactions at Harvard: "The more I exposed myself to the competing ideologies, the more convinced I became that the Christian world view can be accepted with the consent of all our faculties. A conviction grew in my mind as I cast myself on the perils of graduate study that any fair-minded individual who is open before the facts, if he pursued a course carefully and with patience, would arrive at the biblical, theistic position."[15]

If we allow for some fraternal exaggeration in the empty sack remark and some presidential rhetoric in the Chicago speech, these two statements are not so far apart as initially they seem, certainly not irreconcilable. I suggest that what was missing in Carnell's sack at this time was not a confident Christian faith but an apologetical stance. He had been thoroughly immersed for three years in the Calvinism of Cornelius Van Til at Westminster but grew to believe that Van Til, in his unwillingness to acknowledge that the unbeliever is capable of arriving at *any* valid truth, was eliminating every point of contact between the believer and the unbeliever, thus undercutting the task of apologetics and leaving the faith without defense. For his own part, Van Til charged that by insisting that faith must have a rational foundation, Carnell was making man autonomous, the creature in effect setting up a standard that the Creator was being forced to meet. The mutually acknowledged rift between the two men was permanent.

We noted in the previous chapter that Carnell explicitly declared his allegiance to Gordon Clark over Van Til. Was there nothing left in the sack of arguments from the formidable Clark? There was indeed; but Carnell came to believe that the legacy of Clark did not completely meet his needs at this stage of his quest. While Carnell did not turn his back on the law of contradiction, the formal basis of Clark's system of deductive rationalism, he became convinced that Clark, like Van Til, was severely limited in his apologetical usefulness. The law of contradiction was the means by which one could ferret out the inconsistencies and illogicalities of opposing systems, and that, according to Clark, is the main task of apologetics; but Carnell was looking for something more positive. In Clark's view there is no evidence that can certify the God of Calvinistic orthodoxy, for if such evidence existed it would be more foundational than God himself and therefore undermine his status as a first principle. However logical, this point of view struck Carnell (as he took philosophical inventory at Harvard) as unnecessarily constricted, doing justice to neither the full dimensions of human life nor the breadth of Holy Scripture.

So he wrote a book. To be sure, Carnell is not the first graduate student to have published a scholarly volume while still a degree candidate, but not many such books are greeted with quite the acclaim received by *An Introduction to Christian Apologetics* in the spring of 1948.[16] One of fifty manuscripts submitted to the William B. Eerdmans Publishing Company in an Evangelical Book Award contest, it won the $5,000 first prize and is generally cited – along with two of its contemporaries, the symposium *Modern Science and Christian Faith* and Carl F. H. Henry's *The Uneasy Conscience of Modern Fundamentalism* – as heralding the dawn of an evangelical awakening.[17]

Appearing in the spring just prior to his reception of Harvard's Th.D., *Apologetics* gave a big boost to Carnell's career. However, events related to the publication of the book also caused him some unexpected trouble at Harvard. January 1948 was a traumatic month for Carnell. In December he had submitted copies of his doctoral thesis to both his adviser,

Professor Auer, and the second reader, Professor Ferré of Andover-Newton. Johannes Abraham Cristoffel Fagginger Auer (one alumnus recalls that a telephone man arrived at Auer's office one day expecting to install five phones) had come to the Divinity School in 1929 and been designated Parkman Professor in 1930. In 1942 he had taken over the responsibility of directing the programs of graduate students particularly interested in theology. In fact, during his last dozen years on the faculty, he was the *only* professor of theology, a fact that takes on added significance when one knows that his own theological position was Humanism. But he was a warm, genial, fair-minded man, and Levering Reynolds's claim that "he never failed in his respect for other men's opinions, however much he might disagree with them,"[18] is substantiated by the group of evangelicals. When Paul Jewett was ready to begin his thesis on Emil Brunner, it was Auer who suggested and then arranged for Jewett to spend a year studying in Switzerland.

Carnell's thesis was on Niebuhr: "The Concept of Dialectic in the Theology of Reinhold Niebuhr." Auer approved it but Nels Ferré did not. On December 30 Ferré wrote Nock to the effect that he found the thesis inadequate in historical background, deficient in relating Niebuhr's dialectic to contemporary thought, and therefore unacceptable. He further accused the writer of superficial generalities and of unfairly caricaturing Niebuhr's ideas in order to get the better of an argument. We can get just an inkling of how much of a blow this rejection was to Carnell in a letter he wrote to Dean Sperry on January 10. Emphasizing that he had already talked with Ferré by telephone, he said, in part: "I want you to know that I am so anxious to do things right at Harvard that I will rewrite the entire dissertation with the criticisms of my readers in mind." He asked Sperry, if possible, to keep the matter confidential, "since there is a certain academic disgrace connected with the experience that is difficult to bear."

Carnell kept this close call a secret, not even telling his wife. He may have confided in some of his close friends among the graduate students, but I have not found any who knew. Carnell was overreacting a bit perhaps. It is not a disgrace to have to revise a doctoral thesis. As a matter of fact, the revisions required by Ferré cannot have been very extensive, for he signed the completed dissertation later in the spring semester. But Carnell's reaction in January has to be seen in the context of his emerging career as an evangelical scholar. The agony caused by Ferré's negative response to his thesis was balanced by the ecstasy of hearing that he had won the Eerdmans prize for *Apologetics*. After the initial high feelings had worn off, Carnell must have come down hard when he realized what a cruel irony it would be if word got around that the author of this acclaimed book could not even get his doctoral thesis approved. Moreover,

he sensed a threat to his academic career, for at this very time he was being considered for a faculty post at Fuller Theological Seminary. Such apprehensions may have motivated in part his appeal for confidentiality.

In any event, sometime between January 10 and 31 Carnell sent Dean Sperry a copy of the Eerdmans notice concerning his award. Unknowingly, he was setting himself up for another potentially devastating response. Sperry's reply, though warmly congratulating Carnell on the book prize, went on to question him soberly on two pieces of information in the Eerdmans publicity release. First offender was the statement that Harvard Divinity School "is also awarding him the Th.D. degree in June 1948." To Sperry this was presumptuous and entirely improper, on the grounds that no one can be assured of a degree until the faculty so votes. Then the very next sentence of the news release caused an even more serious objection: "He is now a candidate for the Ph.D. degree at Boston

University, studying under the outstanding contemporary personalist, Prof. E. S. Brightman." Sperry clearly indicated that this was news to the Divinity School faculty, and that it violated a university rule that forbids candidacy for two degrees at the same time. Sperry's opinion that these developments would not necessarily affect adversely the approval of Carnell's thesis must have been small comfort. Other correspondence reveals that Dean Sperry was not being picayune but genuinely felt that Carnell was indulging in sharp practices that bordered on dishonesty.

Fortunately for Carnell, he had the right answers. After apologizing and acknowledging at least partial responsibility, he addressed the two complaints. In answer to a query from the publisher, he had said that he "expected" the Th.D. from Harvard in 1948, but had not intended to presume the institution owed him a degree, and was given no copy proof to review before the statement was released. As for the second charge, "I feel even less responsible." He pointed out that he had come to Harvard ignorant of the rule and fully intending to take two doctorates. But the Harvard Graduate School itself, when they informed him that this would be impossible at Harvard, advised him to try another institution. Far from indicating anything wrong with the procedure, they even sent his transcripts to Boston University. The entire affair blew over when Nock got in touch with Brightman, who told him that he thought very highly of Carnell, was fully aware of his work at Harvard, and could see no danger of an overlap on dissertation material. A conciliatory letter from Dean Sperry informed Carnell that he was exonerated, and he continued his way toward June commencement with no further pitfalls.

It would be a mistake, however, for us to drop without further comment the mild controversy between Auer and Ferré over Carnell's dissertation. In subsequent chapters we will explore in some detail Carnell's treatment of Niebuhr (especially in connection with the book *The Theology of Reinhold Niebuhr*, which is an elaboration of that dissertation). It is enough now to note one significant aspect of Auer's and Ferré's contrasting responses. If we conceive of the variety of theological positions as arranged on a continuum from extreme liberal to extreme conservative, we can agree, without getting down to fine points, that Auer the humanist must be placed at the liberal end and that Carnell, still calling himself a fundamentalist, belongs close to the conservative end. Whereas Reinhold Niebuhr's exact place on the continuum would be open to considerable disagreement, there would be an overwhelming consensus that he should be placed somewhere in the middle, certainly between the positions represented by Auer and Carnell. As a humanist, then, Auer had no ideological quarrel with Carnell's rejection of Niebuhr's neo-orthodoxy, though he surveyed the issue from the opposite end of the theological continuum. Ferré, though, would have had an investment in the kind of theological exploration represented by Niebuhr, for he too devoted his career to exploring the middle ground between historic orthodoxy and humanistic liberalism. Carnell makes abundantly clear his rejection of the middle-ground strategy in the closing lines of his thesis:

Niebuhr must either turn to revelation in Scripture seriously, in which case he must go all the way with the problems which attend special revelation; or he must break with the appeal to special revelation and take up empiricism seriously, in which case he must go all the way with the scientific method. There does not seem to the author any stopping point between these two termini.[19]

The same bifurcation of thought systems into Christian and non-Christian permeates the argument of *An Introduction to Christian Apologetics*. Because "the reach of metaphysics is absolute," starting with the wrong assumptions can lead one astray at every point along the road. This kind of either–or thinking permits Carnell to claim, for example, that only a Christian has the right to make statements and expect to be understood (because only a God whose very nature is the guarantee of meaning can provide the basis for intelligible communication).

With no sovereign God to set the course of reality and to give promises of hope to man, there is a 50/50 chance of anything happening. In five minutes, not only may elephants fly and roots grow up, but doors may have only one side, spinach may grow in patches of square circles, the sun may turn to silk, the moon to mink, up may be down, right may be left, and good may be bad.[20]

The choice is clear: either the fundamentalist interpretation of historic orthodox Christianity or absurdity and nihilism. So although Carnell perceived himself to be filling an apologetical vacuum, it is clear that he had no inclination to explore the middle ground between these alternatives. At this stage of his career, Carnell was still very much a Clarkean. After three years of study at Harvard and Boston University, he acknowledged only two live competing choices: either the fundamentalism with which he came or the scientific method whose end was nihilism. And whereas the Divinity School cannot be blamed for the tendency of Carnell's logic to rule out any middle ground between alternatives, it is a fact that theology was not Harvard's strong suit in these years. The July 1947 "Report of the Commission to Study and Make Recommendations with Respect to the Harvard Divinity School" expressed grave concern that Harvard offered a total of only three courses in theology and philosophy of religion and none in Christian ethics, adding that "the tendency to stress the historical rather than the constructive aspects of theology is in itself a symptom of theological decline."[21]

In the course of an interview with one of the Harvard fundamentalists,

I asked him how his graduate study at Harvard Divinity School influenced him as a Christian scholar. The answer: "Harvard didn't change what I believed, but it certainly did change the way I held my belief." At first my inclination was to accept that statement at face value – in the way he sincerely intended it should be taken – as an affirmation that while he remained an orthodox Christian believer, he came to hold his faith less dogmatically, open his mind to a variety of new ideas, and act charitably toward those who differed with him. As I reflected on his statement over a period of months, however, I began to see that it could be interpreted otherwise. Whereas it is true that some of the Harvard fundamentalists were profoundly influenced by their graduate school experience and have throughout their careers shown a willingness to think new thoughts theologically, a number of these men adopted a theologically neutral historicist methodology that enabled them to become thoroughly learned scholars who could debate more effectively those with whom they disagreed while at the same time shielding their own religious beliefs in a privileged sanctuary.[22] Carnell had a foot in both camps. Although he later explicitly disowned fundamentalism and delivered a harsh critique of the movement in *The Case for Orthodox Theology*, his published books and articles reveal that as a thinker he never broke completely free from much of fundamentalism's ideological baggage. What we must not forget, however, is that even though Edward Carnell had almost overnight become a name to be reckoned with in an already resurgent evangelicalism, he was still only in his twenties. He had not stopped growing intellectually. The positions staked out in his first book were to shift significantly in later works.

In the fall of 1947, before the troubles with his dissertation and before the Eerdmans book prize, Carnell realized he was coming to a fork in the road. He felt confident that he could complete all his residence requirements for the two doctoral degrees by the following spring. He knew also that his position at Gordon College and Divinity School was secure, if he wanted to stay there. However, it was almost inevitable that a mutual attraction should develop between Carnell and the newly founded Fuller Theological Seminary. Fuller opened that September in Pasadena, California, on short notice with four faculty members and only thirty-nine students. But the evangelical world knew enough not to misjudge this modest beginning. For one thing, Charles Fuller's international radio broadcast, "The Old-Fashioned Revival Hour," gave the seminary instant name recognition. And although the evangelist had not previously been linked with higher education, he had managed to demonstrate the seriousness of the institution's intent by its first appointments. First to come into the fold was Harold John Ockenga as president. Long a powerful force in the New England area as pastor of Boston's Park Street

Congregational Church, Ockenga had legitimate academic credentials, with a seminary degree from Westminster and a Ph.D. from the University of Pittsburgh. The four members of the founding faculty came to Fuller from teaching positions at other institutions: Everett Harrison from Dallas Theological Seminary, Carl F. H. Henry and Harold Lindsell from Northern Baptist Seminary, and Wilbur Smith from Moody Bible Institute, along with the fourteen thousand books in his personal library.[23]

Recognizing immediately the importance of the new seminary and knowing that once the limited number of faculty slots were filled there would probably be no more openings for years, Carnell went into action.[24] Ockenga, of course, had kept an eye on the cadre of young evangelical scholars doing graduate work just across the Charles River in Cambridge. He knew Carnell especially well. Like some others in the group, the Carnells had become members of his church and worshipped there regularly. Moreover, Ockenga had read and commented on sections of Carnell's book manuscript.[25] In early September 1947, just prior to the arrival in Pasadena of Fuller's first class of students, Carnell sent a letter to Ockenga formally applying for a faculty appointment the following September. He first staked out a position on the common ground he shared with Ockenga: "From my years of fellowship with you I have discovered that our world-views coincide almost jot for jot and tittle for tittle. You combine a happy appreciation of Reformation Christianity with a love for the Fundamentalists of our present day." Then he briefly related the substance of several conversations he had had during the spring and summer months with Carl Henry, already on board as one of Fuller's founding faculty, with regard to their possible collaboration on scholarly projects:

It would be impossible, however, to do this without our being near each other for consultation. If I could take over the division that Dr. Henry is to lop off in time, that would solve the problem perfectly. Henry is now teaching both systematic theology and philosophy of religion. When he decides which field he would prefer, I would love to work over the other. I have had equal training in systematic theology and philosophy of religion. Collaboration with Dr. Henry could mean the publication of a series of contemporary volumes of great worth.[26]

Finally he added a page of the usual data on formal training, experience, and works in progress.

Ockenga relayed the application to the appropriate faculty committee at the seminary. Although Carnell was not the only candidate under consideration, news of his Eerdmans prize put him on the inside track. In a reply to Ockenga's congratulatory note, Carnell brought up once again the possibility of a Fuller appointment. Claiming that his motives were "as altruistic as a sinful human being can formulate them," he made clear his conviction that "there is such a coincidence between the total aims and goals of Fuller and my own life visions, that a tremendous mutual edification could result."

> Whether the other faculty members need me I am not sure, but I know unequivo-cally I need them. I need the fortification of an able faculty to serve as a backdrop for future research and publication. At present there is not a single man on Gordon's faculty competent to criticize my work. For this reason I had to send all five copies of the second draft of the prize book to men outside. I have no interest in being a lone-pebble-on-the-beach scholar. I want to submerge my efforts within collective agencies of a committee of scholars.[27]

With his new notoriety, he obviously found it difficult to keep his enthu-siasm and self-confidence within bounds:

> Finally – and I add these items to give you a full-rounded picture of myself for your future discussion over the problem – through my four years under Professor Murray at Westminster I feel I have a grasp of the history of systematics. Then with a doctoral dissertation for Harvard on Niebuhr and one on Brunner for B.U., I will have the contemporary scene down cold. In addition to this I have studied Catholic systematics for about eight years now and I think I can lay my finger on their trouble in a nice solid volume in a few years.[28]

He assured Ockenga that if other doors did not open he would "labor with deepest love here at Gordon and attempt to bring the school from its present state of obscurity to the broader light of academic recognition." His sights were trained, however, on bigger things: "My parish, with Wesley, is the world."

By late February, Fuller made an offer and Carnell accepted. His one misgiving was that Gordon College would not get a fair return on its investment in him. Gordon's president, Dr. T. Leonard Lewis, had been an enthusiastic supporter of Carnell, and all along the way the college and seminary had arranged convenient teaching schedules and relieved him of committee duties so he could concentrate on his research. Moreover, just before the Fuller appointment was sealed, the dean of the college an-nounced that Carnell had been promoted to full professor.[29] Although many at Gordon resented his departure, most amicably recognized its inevitability.

With their number increased by the addition of a baby girl, Jean, born while they were living in their fourth-floor walk-up on Buswell Street, and with their possessions augmented by new clothes, a washing machine, a living room suite, a radio-phonograph, a small library of new and secondhand theological books, and a new Buick, all purchased with the Eerdmans prize money, the Carnells in the summer of 1948 headed west to southern California and to Fuller Seminary, the institution he would serve for the remaining years of his life.

CHAPTER VI

Fuller Seminary

It does not take a powerful imagination to appreciate the sense of satisfaction and accomplishment with which Carnell undertook his teaching duties at Fuller Seminary in September 1948. Still a year short of his thirtieth birthday, he had not veered one degree off course since that time ten years earlier when he had caught the vision of how the life of the mind could serve the cause of Christ. With a doctorate from Harvard, the prospect of a second doctorate from Boston University, a prizewinning book on apologetics, a prestigious teaching position, a wife and a baby daughter, and (no small acquisition for the man whose primary interest in high school was a cherished Model T Ford) a brand new Buick Roadmaster, he was moving ahead with a sense of inner authority. For the first time, the future did not present a formidable array of higher and tougher obstacles. Rather it seemed to level out on a high plain of anticipated accomplishment where he could continue to fulfill even more successfully what he had already demonstrated was his sacred calling.

And for a while, that is exactly how it was.

A. The pre-presidential years: 1948–1954

"I would like to see this exchange of letters symbolize the titanic struggle between supernaturalism and naturalism."

Carnell to Tompkins, April 29, 1953

"As you see, I have no very clear cut pattern of investigation in mind; but if we play with these ideas long enough, the friction of handling may turn them into fireballs."

Tompkins to Carnell
May 31, 1953

73

The westward move and the new job were exhilarating but not without problems. Finding a place to live topped the list. In 1948 the American economy had not yet completed the transition to postwar recovery, and many parts of the country desperately needed more housing. A Boston University friend whose family lived in Pasadena told Carnell that to his knowledge there had not been a rental unit in the Pasadena area since 1943 and advised him to buy. Inability to raise a down payment made that impossible, but the Carnells did succeed in finding a house to rent (at $1,500 a year) in Alhambra, a few miles south of downtown Pasadena.

For the entire preceding academic year, the seminary itself had been dealing with a serious housing problem. Because the postwar shortage of materials had prevented Charles Fuller from beginning construction of new seminary buildings, in the spring of 1947 he had purchased the Cravens estate on South Orange Grove Boulevard in Pasadena: five acres of property and a thirty-two room mansion that would meet all the immediate needs of the school, scheduled to open in September, just a few months away. However, an unfavorable decision by the Pasadena zoning board on the seminary's request for a use variance (a request Dr. Fuller had every reason to believe would be granted in a changing neighborhood that already had one school directly across the street) necessitated a drastic shift in plans. The Lake Avenue Congregational Church, whose pastor was a longtime friend of the Fullers, offered to let the new school use the assembly rooms of its education building as classroom space. Faculty offices, library, and single student housing remained at the Cravens estate, two miles from where the classes met. In the long run, this last-minute rescue had much to commend it, for the church was only a few blocks from the downtown property, which later became the permanent location of Fuller Seminary. In the short run, everyone endured much inconvenience. Dan Fuller, Charles Fuller's son, recalls the first few days of the 1947 fall semester: "We members of that first class will never quite forget the incongruity of hearing Carl Henry's insights into the theory of religious knowledge while sitting on kindergarten chairs taking notes."[1]

No one really minded. It was an exciting time. When Carnell arrived on the scene for the beginning of the second year, morale was even higher. On September 8, 1948, he wrote to Ockenga, still president-in-absentia but about to make one of his many flights from Boston to Los Angeles for the fall convocation: "The seminary is everything I pictured in my mind. My office is magnificent – I am quite unworthy of it – and I am moved in and ready for the serious business of philosophical apologetics and systematic theology."

As a scholar, Carnell's first order of business was to complete requirements for his Ph.D. in philosophy at Boston University. Having passed his French exam the previous February, his German and two of his qualifying exams in April, he had hoped to take the two remaining qualifying exams in the summer before heading west. However, with summer school responsibilities at Gordon and a share in getting ready for a 3,000-mile move, he had to put the exams on hold. So on arriving in Pasadena, in addition to his new teaching responsibilities and his scholarly writing, he had to devote large segments of his time to studying for exams and beginning research in depth on Kierkegaard for the dissertation. Coincidentally, this schedule put him on almost exactly the same track as his new colleague Carl Henry, in the final phase of their graduate education. Both had the same adviser at B.U. (Edgar Sheffield Brightman); both mailed in their dissertation outlines on the same day in October 1948; both were assigned the same second reader (L. Harold DeWolf); and both came east on the same spring day (May 2, 1949) for their oral examinations – Carnell's at 2 P.M., Henry's at 3:30. It was a happy conclusion to a long arduous journey. Back in Pasadena the next day, Carnell shared his enthusiasm in a letter to Ockenga:

Dr. Brightman congratulated me enthusiastically upon my completion of all of the Ph.D. work. Dr. DeWolf told me that the dissertation was more than worthy of publication. All of these indicia of success in the last of the academic ventures into formal degrees are heartwarming.[2]

When Carnell and Henry came east again for the university commencement in early June, they were given the added pleasure of sharing Ockenga's pulpit at Boston's Park Street Church.

With the celebrating over, the Carnells headed immediately for some welcome vacation time in Kenosha, Wisconsin, at Shirley's family home. For Carnell, of course, vacation meant free time to write. During the first year at Fuller, he had not had time to do much on his next scheduled scholarly project, revising for publication his Harvard thesis on Reinhold Niebuhr. He had, however, managed to write the first draft of a book on television and now set out to complete it. The subject was timely and popular, with a potentially large readership among his publisher's usual clientele in the churches. Carnell was candid about his purpose for writing the book: He was convinced that evangelicals needed guidance on the television question, but he also wanted to make some money ("I want very much to crack this housing problem in California"[3]). In December 1948, just over three months after arriving in Pasadena, he sold the new Buick in order to buy a stove and a refrigerator – convincing evidence that the financial problems were neither imagined nor overstated.

Carnell had raised the salary issue with the seminary administration early in January, after he had been elevated in rank but given no financial increase. His letter of protest to President Ockenga, trying hard to communicate extreme disappointment without offending his main benefactor, disclosed his feelings in a style so formal and constricted one can almost feel its forehead throbbing. In between the opening ("Dear Harold: Your good letter was received.") and the closing ("We wait your impending visit with eagerness – as usual. I remain, Your servant in Christ, Ed") were these two paragraphs:

> While I appreciate exceedingly the thoughtful offer of the trustees to elevate my professorial standing, without attending salary balance, I should far prefer to retain my present rating with its simultaneous academic and financial limitations; for not only would I deem it prudential and encouraging of self-confidence to wait for the honor of a full professorship until such time as my maturities of teaching, publishing, and gaining of degrees places me in a category equal to those already on the staff enjoying that standing, but also, though less remote in importance, it would prove to be no small source of embarrassment to me among friends who would conclude from my title that I was receiving a commensurate income and who would as a consequence expect more from me socially. I do not covet the title "full professor" as an end in itself.
>
> I sense a shift in policy, do I not? A shift seems to be on hand, for last year I gathered that tenure and elevation were to be coterminous in my case. If that does not prove to be so, at least I shall have the right to conclude that it was rather foolish of me to pick up a Ph.D. when I could have devoted myself to the publication of lucrative books.[4]

If by "lucrative books" he had such projects as *Television: Servant or Master?* in mind, he was primed for disillusionment. When the book came out in 1950 it netted him virtually nothing.[5] In any case, by May 1949 Ockenga had arranged an increase for Carnell, who thanked him for "assuring my economic security in this new and unexpected way."[6]

Two other books, appearing in successive years, made up in prestige – at least within the evangelical constituency – what *Television* failed to supply financially. *The Theology of Reinhold Niebuhr*, a revision of his Harvard Th.D. thesis, assumed a critical stance in its systematic exposition of Niebuhr's theological views. A few months before the book's actual publication, Carnell wrote to Lloyd Dean, his close friend and fellow student from Harvard days: "Without any attempt to brag, I think I have put Niebuhr in a rather embarrassing position at certain points. I have what I feel are some crucial arguments which apply not only to Niebuhr but also to the whole neo-orthodox tradition."[7] Then a year later, in 1952, came *A Philosophy of the Christian Religion*, his second major work of apologetics, building its argument on the question of values and concluding that only conservative Christianity could stand up to close scrutiny on the crucial axiological issues. Together these books

solidified the reputation Carnell had tentatively established in the evangelical community with the meteoric appearance of *Apologetics*, which by 1952 had gone through four editions.

In his letters to Ockenga exploring the possibility of an appointment to the Fuller faculty, Carnell had stressed the importance of collegiality, especially the value of collaborating with Carl Henry. He had mentioned the desirability of faculty members complementing each other in their work, reading each other's manuscripts. In those early years at Fuller, collegiality was in fact a strong force. The men had lunch together often and set up a schedule of monthly meetings at which they tried out papers on each other. Furthermore, they had been attracted to Fuller partly by the prospect of increased time and opportunity for scholarly productivity: eight-hour teaching loads, three months off in the summer, and all the clerical help they needed. Their professional lives, however, were not quite so unencumbered with academic duties as these facts may suggest. The lack of a president-in-residence inevitably meant that faculty had to assume many duties that would have ordinarily been handled by the administration. Nevertheless, George Ladd, another of the "Harvard evangelicals," is a good example of how well the arrangement worked in some cases. Ladd had been teaching four courses at Gordon Divinity School in Boston. He wanted to write a book on "The Kingdom of God" but needed a large block of time for additional research. When Fuller offered him a two-course load, he eagerly accepted – and wrote nine books on the subject before he died.[8]

Carnell shared fully in this collegial ferment. When in December 1948 the seminary invited Bela Vasady, a Hungarian evangelical, to the campus for extensive conversations prior to a possible faculty appointment, Carnell was quite willing to table his misgivings about Vasady's refusal to indict Barthianism in view of the candidate's "plenary agreement to hold bi-monthly discussion groups together within the department until settlement is reached." He looked forward eagerly to Vasady's joining the faculty ("Around the table next fall the two continents can talk about theology and ecumenics.") and did his best to harmonize pride and humility in his comments to President Ockenga:

I believe that with the Henry-Vasady-Carnell block here in apologetics-systematics-philosophy of religion, Fuller Seminary will have one of the strongest departments in the world for both undergraduate and graduate studies. I append myself to the triad with humility, for no one is more keenly aware of the fact that if Vasady had appeared earlier, I would doubtless be still in Gordon College.[9]

Even with Carnell's rapidly rising reputation as one of the young men to watch in evangelical scholarship, it was as a classroom teacher that he shone most brightly. In the pre-presidential years, enrollment in his classes nearly always reached classroom capacity. His colleagues Carl Henry and Wilbur Smith both referred to him as a "master teacher," Henry specifically remarking on his ability to make the material experientially real. Along the same lines, an alumnus mentions the "existential ambience which convinced the student that Carnell knew where you were in your own problems." David Hubbard, who has been Fuller's president since 1963, names Carnell as the most significant influence in his own life and says that for many students he meant the difference between believing and not believing.[10] Another alumnus commends him for his honesty: "He did not put on airs. You did not feel he was putting on a show. He taught theology, but didn't claim that the truths studied were all fully in his experience." Several former students recall that he lectured on highly technical material without ever consulting a note. In fact, some refer to his having "memorized" his lectures, and one alumnus remembers walking down a seminary hallway, stopping to look into a classroom, and seeing Carnell practicing his lecture. Another remembers occasions when he excused himself from class early because he had not thoroughly mastered his material. If that sounds ordered and compulsive and not very much like a "master teacher," file the thought away for future reference, but reflect also on the fact that Carnell was apparently at his best fielding unexpected questions from the class. Says one former student: "His capacity to hear a question, to reflect on it for a moment, and to speak to it in detail and with precise organization never ceased to be a wonder to me and many other students." As a teacher, Carnell placed great value on the maieutic method, thinking of himself not as the bringer of truth but as a Socratic midwife helping students give birth to their own ideas.

In the years before his breakdown, Carnell eventually attained that enviable positi n where even his shortcomings were considered more or less endearing eccentricities. At one point during his first few years, however, a fairly sizable number of students were troubled enough over his unapproachability (as contrasted, let us say, with Clarence Roddy and other professors who were gifted with more open, more convivial personalities) to draw up a petition requesting that Dr. Carnell be less aloof toward students. A likeness to Mount Rushmore was even suggested, though most likely not in the actual petition. Carnell got wind of this and was rather hurt by it. He began a class period one day with a few words of personal defense (which, according to an alumnus, went something like this): "I am E. J. Carnell. I am not Clarence Roddy or anyone else. Don't try to make me over into somebody I'm not. They tell jokes and play golf on their day off. I don't. I go for long walks." Nothing more was heard of the petition.[11]

The students, of course, had found a sore spot. Throughout his adult life, Carnell was least comfortable in one-on-one situations, except for a narrow circle of family and close friends, mostly of long standing. He avoided such encounters when he could do so without serious negative consequences. Sensitive, painfully vulnerable, he lived behind protective stone walls, cool to the touch. Even when he tried to unbend, he could not quite pull it off. At one faculty–student retreat he consciously dressed down to an informal green leisure outfit and was promptly dubbed "The Green Hornet." His everyday southern California garb – a black suit with a stiff-collared white shirt and even at times a homburg hat – is central to "the Peggy Lovik incident," far and away the most often retold story in the collection of Carnell reminiscences. Lovik, an undergraduate classmate from Wheaton days, went on to teach Physical Education at Westmont College in Santa Barbara. One drab, cool day in spring, body-surfing into an almost deserted beach, she was unceremoniously dumped at the feet of a lone man walking along the shore. Here is how Lovik remembers the incident:

As I stood up dripping like a mermaid, there in front of me was Ed Carnell, complete with homburg, cane, and black suit. The greeting was as though we were in the middle of a semi-formal dining room. While Ed was reserved he was always warm towards me and the family. With a bit of a smile he said, "Hello, Peg," mentioned something about each of my brothers that he knew. It had been years since I had actually talked with him so I was enjoying the visit. We said goodbye and he continued walking along the beach as I swam back to the waves. The incident must have tickled his funny bone because he attended a banquet that weekend and I began to get reports back about our meeting from his friends.[12]

Although his formal attire quite clearly helped to armor him against unwanted intrusions into his private world, it surely did not hide him anonymously in the crowd. Willing to be a bit of a spectacle, he came to class one day with a terrible cold, stood at the lectern, plugged in a heating pad, held it against his chest, and carried on with business as usual the entire period. When he walked down the seminary corridor – a tall figure (six feet, approximately 185 pounds) with a military stiffness, face steadfastly set in the direction he was headed – he would almost always have under one arm a large book. Many students assumed at first it was a Bible. It was not. It was a dictionary. Carnell, in fact, was a dictionary addict, following the dubious practice of trying to improve his vocabulary by systematically studying it literally page by page. After the family moved to a house on South Oakland Avenue, a pleasant mile-and-a-half walk from the seminary, Carnell would tear a sheet out of his dictionary and study it on the way to work. Lars Granberg recalls standing with him one afternoon on a family outing, looking out over the Angeles National Forest. "When Ed said to me, 'Aren't you impressed by nature's fecundity?' I knew he was in the f section of his dictionary."[13]

The annals of higher education bulge with anecdotes, some admittedly apocryphal, chronicling the antics of pedagogy's certifiable crazies, and these modest quirks are hardly state-of-the-art calibre. They do, however, reflect a mildly surprising dimension of Carnell's character and personality and must be included in any effort to understand him. His droll (sometimes sour) self-deprecating sense of humor, for example, while not a particularly unusual trait, deserves notice because of the almost total absence of humor in his books.

In the winter of 1953, Carnell revived through correspondence an old friendship. James Tompkins, whom we have met earlier in these pages, had traveled a parallel course to Carnell's, from Gordon Clark's philosophy classes and the dining hall crew at Wheaton, through exposure to Cornelius Van Til's brand of Calvinism at Westminster Seminary, to extensive informal dialogues at Harvard, where Tompkins did graduate work in philosophy while Carnell studied at the Divinity School. During the years at Harvard, however, their theological journeys began to take radically different directions. Then they separated geographically. At about the same time Carnell moved to Pasadena, Tompkins dropped out of Harvard and settled in Portland, Oregon, working in the management controls division of Remington Rand. Early in February 1953, after speaking in Portland at the National Sunday School Convention, Carnell was told, just before leaving for the airport, that Tompkins was living in the area. When he got back to Pasadena, he wrote him a letter, filling him in on personal and professional data and offering to send him a complimentary copy of *A Philosophy of the Christian Religion,* which had been published a few months earlier.

Thus began an unusual correspondence – a seven-month island of nine letters surrounded by silence – a correspondence noteworthy not merely because it gives clear proof of Carnell's almost hubristic self-satisfaction at this stage of his career but, more significantly, because it drops clues that his edifice of faith had been erected over a fault line of doubt that could be ignored but not completely obliterated.[14]

Carnell tips his hand in the first letter. After telling Tompkins that as he wrote the book he had in mind many of the problems they used to talk over at Harvard, he adds: "It is still my deepest conviction that you are merely passing through a phase change in your thinking and that the Lord will bring a complete adjustment between the head and the heart before long" (2/9/53). Tompkins's response is missing from the correspondence, but it is clear from Carnell's next letter that he had replied warmly and looked forward to receiving a copy of the new book. Carnell then asks him to note any flaws he finds in the book's reasoning. "I have never been personally satisfied," he says, "that I have grasped the problem which you have wrestled with over these years and which has caused your dissatisfaction with the Wheaton position" (2/24/53).

The next two letters are from Tompkins, one mostly to thank Carnell for the book, which had just arrived. In the second, however, he moves quickly beyond innocuous pleasantries and touches on sensitive material. Referring to Carnell's earlier declaration that he is "only one who is interested in being led into the truth," Tompkins comments bluntly:

Let me say at the outset that I honestly believe that you honestly believe that you have no other motive than this. But let me add that I also believe that there are two Ed Carnells involved in this three-way correspondence. There is the ideal Ed Carnell who looks with dispassionate, disinterested objectivity at philosophic problems and who cares not one whit which way the chips fall so long as he hews to the line of truth. There is also involved the Ed Carnell who advised me 10 years ago in seminary: Doubt all you please, but while doubting, don't neglect to pray for guidance out of this morass.

The former is the pursuer of truth; the latter the defender; the former, the investigator of truth; the latter, the invested with truth; the former, the philosopher; the latter, the apologist. Paul had clear insight into human psychology when he wrote in Romans of the warring selves. (4/20/53)

He asks Carnell what will happen if the philosopher in him gets the better of the apologist in this dialogue: "What are you prepared to lay upon the altar of truth? All that you hold dear? Even your own soul?" Tompkins acknowledges that Carnell could ask the same questions of him.

But whereas it would cost me nothing to be convinced of error and I, presumably, would have everything to gain, what of you? A meteor falling from heaven, casting its evanescent light across the Christian horizon? In such a crisis would the apologist rise up in holy indignation and quash the philosopher? (4/20/53)

In his reply, Carnell leaps on this point:

Do not minimize the price which *you* must pay if investigation shows that you are wrong and I am right. You may even find renunciation more difficult than I. It will take more humility for you to *come back* than for me to *give up*. Furthermore, as a result of having empirically shifted from the very view which I am defending, you may be tempted to assume the hauteur of one who, having been through the war, now looks on little brother's sandlot scuffles with comfortable aloofness. Such complacency may only add blindness. (4/29/53)

He reiterates that he is prepared to accept all the consequences of truth. He brushes aside Tompkins's implied charge that he is playing with a stacked deck. "A man," he says, "is entitled to believe in the finality of his position until he can be persuaded of its error. Apparently you have been sufficiently sure of your own view to withdraw from orthodoxy. You are at least *that* certain that you are right."

Then Carnell reveals just how much importance he attaches to what they are doing:

I would like to see this exchange of letters symbolize the titanic struggle between supernaturalism and naturalism. Let us agree in advance that there shall be no rush. What if it takes us a full year just to clarify the problem?

I also trust that this exchange of letters will keep you from mental stagnation. I hope to press you back to the place where you are forced to give a precise account of yourself. Please do the same of me. (4/29/53)

With Tompkins's reply, the correspondence escalates to a new level of intensity. Referring to the two objectives Carnell proposed (i.e., symbolizing "the titanic struggle between supernaturalism and naturalism" and pressing each other to "give a precise account" of himself), Tompkins says he might be pleased to do one or the other or both, but not simultaneously.

> Each activity has its own particular plane. If you want me to pounce on specific passages of your *PCR,* quote in opposition (in the same fashion as the Fathers quoted Thomas and with probably the same results) the learned views of naturalists to embellish the standard of liberalism – well, it might be fun, and I suppose it would keep me from a certain species of "mental stagnation." But that procedure, I venture to suggest, will never become more than a superficial bickering over trivia. You will only know when we complete our exchange how badly your argument outstripped mine, and I, how mine, yours.
> If, on the other hand, we really want to get down to the root issues, the exchange must be on another plane. It must be completely personal. No third parties shall be allowed to deprive us of freedom to bare the heart. That, of course, eliminates dictation, for no man can be his naked self who must always be asking subconsciously: If I say X about myself, what will my secretary think? (5/10/53)

Carnell agrees – no secretaries. And he seems to opt for the second of the two alternatives: "Naturally I expected that we would bare our hearts. If you and I cannot unbosom, who may?" (5/18/53).

Nevertheless, much of what they write to each other at this stage is primarily philosophical rather than personal. They argue points of view amicably and acknowledge painful ambivalence in the process of arriving at their respective present positions. In a letter dated May 31, Tompkins muses on what they have accomplished so far:

> As I look at our mutual problem, it seems to me that investigation may well show that we share many common views: but strangely enough the optimism which rides in plain sight throughout your writing seems to me to betray a fundamental pessimism: the fear of exposing oneself to the choice of a wrong option. And the pessimism which seems to ride in the arms of agnosticism reveals itself to be the optimistic notion that in spite of errors honestly entertained, all will be well with the soul anyhow. Funny, isn't it?

Then, as if to recognize that his previously stated dichotomy between impersonal ideas and personal reflection is far from absolute (a view we are inclined to support on reading even these brief excerpts from the correspondence), Tompkins concludes his letter with these words: "As you see, I have no very clear cut pattern of investigation in mind, but if we play with these ideas long enough, the friction of handling may turn them into fireballs" (5/31/53).

The whole summer goes by without an answer from Carnell. Finally, in early September, he replies. It is the last letter in the correspondence. The universal problem of death is on his mind. One of Fuller Seminary's most gifted and promising graduates, president of the previous year's student government, has within the week become ill with polio and died. In the letter Carnell quotes the soliloquy from *Macbeth* that begins with "Tomorrow and tomorrow and tomorrow" and ends with the observation that life is "a tale / Told by an idiot, full of sound and fury, / Signifying nothing." His mood changes as he reminisces on what it was like to teach Kierkegaard in a summer school course at Wheaton. He remarks on the irony of his having walked again "the trails which we walked on in fellowship, speaking in concord of the things which now form the subject of our debate." He chides Tompkins for "the familiar attitude of complacency which I have tried to challenge before," and he repeats a charge he had made in an earlier letter, namely, that it would be psychologically more difficult for Tompkins to admit that his faith reversal was wrong than for Carnell to declare himself an unbeliever. "In a way you would have to apologize and repent, and such postures are among the most difficult in the world to maintain. If my fears of losing my faith in God are strong – and they are – how much greater must your fear be of having to bow in repentance before the God whom you now doubt?"

He concludes the letter, which began on a somber note of premature tragic death, by focusing on the issue of eternal destiny. Here is the final paragraph of the seven-month correspondence:

> Your task is to prove to me that this is a type of universe in which ultimate differences in individual destiny do not depend upon attitudes which we take toward reality here and now in time. I think you have unconsciously assumed a philosophy of reality to be congenial with your expectations, and now you ask me to start my inquiry with you at that point. I am perfectly willing to believe that we may be complacent about destiny, but as yet you have not given me any clinching reasons to make me believe that complacency is preferable to faith. (9/2/53)

James Tompkins has no recollection of why the correspondence stopped. Rereading it after a gap of some twenty-five years, he can see several points he would like to have explored further, but he can locate no other letters. Obviously, since the final letter was from Carnell, who clearly at that point assumed the exchange would continue, we cannot assign to him the responsibility for bringing it to a close. What we *can* say with some assurance is that, for whatever reasons, both participants were content to let it subside into silence. There was no further contact of any kind between Edward Carnell and James Tompkins.

I should like to suggest two reasons why Carnell did not try to keep the correspondence alive – even after initiating it himself, investing it with cosmic significance, and committing himself to the long haul. ("Let us agree in advance that there shall be no rush.") The first reason is guesswork, but is supported by evidence from the letters and from the nature of the Carnell–Tompkins relationship. The correspondence, I think, posed an enormous threat to Carnell. In saying this, I do not mean to imply that Tompkins won the intellectual struggle. I do mean that Carnell entered the dialogue fully expecting that he could convincingly demonstrate the superiority of his philosophical position, could win Jim Tompkins back to the faith they shared at Wheaton College. After all, Carnell was riding a wave of popularity and influence within the national evangelical constituency. From his perspective, he had put to rout the enemies of orthodoxy in his two apologetics books. When it became apparent to him that his intellectual arguments were not putting Jim Tompkins to rout, Carnell, I suggest, was deeply troubled. Tompkins's opposing views could not be handled in the same way as John Dewey's or Bertrand Russell's. The evangelical apologist could rationally tear their ideas to shreds in his books without facing effective rebuttal. Tompkins was different. Ed and Jim had been brothers in Christ. Their friendship had been forged in the sweatbox of the Wheaton kitchen as well as in the classes of Gordon Clark and Cornelius Van Til. Furthermore, they already had a history of sharing, at least to a certain limited depth, their questions about religious faith and doubt. When in this exchange of letters (completely honest, by mutual agreement, and kept free of curious secretarial eyes) Carnell said, "If my fears of losing faith in God are strong – and they are –," he gave us a rare glimpse into his inner life. He was showing the kind of candor which his students seemed to sense in the classroom but which is absent for the most part from his books. James Tompkins, therefore, should be seen not merely as an intellectual combatant whom Carnell could not overcome in an argument. He was a sort of alter ego, giving voice to serious doubts and questions that troubled Carnell's own intellectual life at the deepest level. To have continued the correspondence with Tompkins on this level of personal honesty – even if not another soul were ever to see it – would have threatened the very foundation of all that Carnell, at this point in his life, had every reason to believe he was doing uncommonly well. If they were to play with these ideas long enough, as Tompkins had said, the friction of handling might indeed "turn them into fireballs."

There is a possible second reason why Carnell might have let the exchange of letters lapse. In the fall of 1953, a set of circumstances was developing at Fuller Seminary that at some point began to make heavy demands on Carnell's time and attention. We know that in just a few months he would be deeply involved. The situation, however, did not develop overnight, and it is entirely possible – indeed, I should say, quite probable – that as early as the previous fall the correspondence with James Tompkins was shunted aside by the unsettled problem of Fuller Seminary's presidency.

B. Appointment to the presidency: 1954

"The situation was such that I simply could not sit back and watch the school go into the wrong hands by default."

Carnell to Gordon Clark
October 25, 1954

When Charles Fuller and Harold John Ockenga brought Fuller Seminary into being in the spring and summer of 1947, the logical choice for president of the new institution was Ockenga himself. He had earned a Ph.D. in history at the University of Pittsburgh and was recognized as one of the half-dozen top evangelical leaders in the country. But Ockenga was fully occupied as minister of the large and influential Park Street Congregational Church across the street from Boston Common. As a temporary solution to the immediate leadership problem, Ockenga agreed to be president-in-absentia for three years and then come to Pasadena as resident president. According to Carl Henry, "We all took our jobs under that assumption."[15] But after three years had passed, Ockenga was still not ready to make the move.

Matters were brought to a head in the fall of 1953, when the three-story classroom and administration building was completed and all the facilities were finally united at the seminary's permanent location. All concerned recognized the need for a full-time president on the scene in California and agreed that Ockenga was by far the best man for the job. The one serious exception was Ockenga himself, torn between east and west, Park Street Church and Fuller Seminary.

In the midst of this indecision, Carl Henry recalls, Ockenga came to the Henry home for Thanksgiving dinner. After lengthy discussion, he finally agreed to make the move. As a testament of his good-faith decision and his commitment to come to Pasadena the next fall as president, Henry had him turn one of the dining room chairs upside down and sign his name to the bottom. But the commitment came unstuck. On his return to Boston, Ockenga regretted the decision and backed down.

No one at Fuller was untouched by the uncertain situation. As one of Ockenga's most loyal supporters, Carnell was especially troubled. On February 12, high above the Pacific coast in a United Airlines Mainliner on the way to a week of lectures in Seattle, with a portable typewriter on his lap, he wrote a three-page letter to Ockenga – "a few thoughts regarding the presidency."[16] In it he stressed the need for an on-the-scene president, repeated that Ockenga was his first choice, but recognized that he could not leave Park Street Church without a full sense of rightness about the decision. What he *could* do was influence the choice of a successor – someone who would "continue the standards and policies that you would have pursued if you were to blueprint the goals of the institution in person." The problem was that as a legacy of the school's more or less democratic ambience in its early years (operating with its president three thousand miles away) "many self-appointed guardians of the school's administrative policies are at work." The line between academics and administration had been blurred. Then he waxed philosophical:

Wise administration always meshes best when its actions are taken in hearty conjunction with faculty interests, for the entire responsible body ought to speak pro and con in important matters. But when this preliminary venting is finished and the trustees conscientiously decide what is best for the institution regarding the ruling head of the school, *this verdict should be handed down as an administrative decision to be accepted and obeyed, not as a fruitless suggestion about which free debate may continue.*

We should not be misled by the authoritarian ring at the end of that statement. What troubled Carnell will become increasingly clear: He was afraid that a theologically and educationally small-minded faculty would gain ascendancy over a progressive administration. If he had perceived himself to be part of a progressive faculty chafing under a backward-looking president, his argument would have taken a different course. What the seminary needed, he said, was a "first rank scholar and teacher, as is the policy of Harvard," though it might take time to find and groom such a man.

But I urge you that when a man is found who will most likely perpetuate your own ideals of Christian scholarship, spiritual deportment, and world-wide cultural and academic integration, stay with that choice and impose it for the good of all in the school. Convince the trustees; sell it to the Fullers and the Smiths; persuade the faculty. Apart from this forceful preparation the new man will be so denuded of prestige that he will command neither the authority to pioneer new educational techniques nor the confidence of the very faculty whom he seeks to inspire. A real president of this great school I should sincerely envy; but a footman or a lackey I deeply should pity.

If one reads the letter as a hint that Carnell himself possessed certain qualifications for the job, that suspicion is strengthened by another three-page letter less than a month later. In the interim there had been talk of offering an additional incentive to attract Ockenga to Pasadena – something like the pastorate of the Lake Avenue Church. Carnell strongly dissented, convinced that *"the presidency of Fuller is an office sufficiently demanding in obligations and sufficiently replete with prestige to be an end in itself."* He returned to the subject of Ockenga's grooming a successor:

> As I see it, you have worked yourself into two situations of relative indispensability; and that to emerge from either without destroying the work which you have already put in, you will have to extend your care by communicating your manner and methods to an understudy. I am completely convinced that when, and if, the Lord puts it in your heart not to take up administration in education as a full-time assignment, you will cast about for one here at the Seminary who can be your understudy in learning the techniques of running this institution.[17]

This time, although again he did not say so directly, he left little doubt that he had himself in mind. One revealing clue is his use of pronouns. He referred to the Fuller faculty as "they," not "we." In his mind he was already set apart from the others: "Again and again the faculty has asked whom they would follow as they now follow you, and inevitably they have ended up with the admission that they had no one in mind." And in another paragraph: "Not only are there problems of temperament when you assemble a group such as these men are, but more important there is the temperament of the school." He also appended an embarrassingly transparent postscript. Referring to one of his colleagues, he said: "I have given considerable time counselling ———, and I know you will be happy to learn that he is squaring away nicely. For some reason he confides in me and I do my best to clear his perspective." Ockenga, presumably, would see the "reason" immediately; although one of the younger faculty, Carnell was looked up to by his colleagues as a wise and mature adviser.

It would appear that Carnell's campaign had its desired effect, though not without complications. Sometime in May, Ockenga took Carnell aside and discussed privately with him the possibility of his assuming the presidency. To my knowledge, no record of that conversation exists; we have only Carnell's comments in a subsequent letter to Ockenga, thanking him for considering him for the presidency ("a warm memory to be shared by us alone") and releasing him "from any unspoken commitments of last May."[18]

Later events prove that at the time the conversations were only exploratory. For during the summer, Ockenga ostensibly stopped vacillating and decided definitely to become full-time president on the scene in

Pasadena – definitely enough, at least, to warrant informing the media. The seminary, however, did not reckon with the persistence of Ockenga's Boston congregation. Officially refusing to accept his resignation, they extracted a promise to reconsider. Then many of them joined in a cavalcade of cars that drove to Ockenga's vacation retreat in New Hampshire as a demonstration of their love and support and determination. Their importunity succeeded. After another agonizing period of indecision, early in September Ockenga reversed what had already been publicly announced, wiring the seminary to cancel forthcoming publications containing his name as president.[19]

On retreat when the telegram came, the faculty reacted calmly, probably because they were not especially surprised, knowing a reconsideration was in process. Carnell immediately wrote a long letter to Ockenga (the letter referred to earlier in which he released Ockenga from any tentative commitments made to him concerning the presidency in their May conversation). He commended Ockenga for his courage and reassured him that he was still held in high esteem at the school. As for the presidential vacuum that clearly had to be filled soon, Carnell elaborated on why he did not want to be considered. His sense of separateness from the rest of the faculty had intensified. The previous evening, Dr. Fuller had held a sort of "testimonial dinner" during which each faculty member gave his views about the current situation and the future of the institution. Carnell was not pleased at what he heard: "It was a revelation to me of what kind of a new myth they wanted to start. They meant to imply that the next president would be the mirror of some undefined, ill-developed ideal . . . sort of an evangelical Dale Carnegie to be a front and public relations man; one who would be 'promotionally' good for the school; and one who could soak the rich." Such thoughts, of course, ran completely counter to Carnell's conviction that the president should be first of all an educator. Furthermore, he said that he could not condone his colleagues' "fantastic dreams of being 'America's leading evangelicals.'"

Stress was made of the fact that the new president ought to lead the faculty out in the publication of world-shaking literature. Has it not occurred to them that in the seven years they have had to show deeds rather than words, that not one man on this faculty has published as much as one article in a scholarly journal; let alone publishing a book with a major house. This faculty has an amazing sense of its own virtues. If I were president, I would only irritate them; for I refuse to be party to their fantastic schemes.[20]

"So, do not bother trying to put my name across," he said, "It is a lost cause."

Within eight days, the new president of Fuller Theological Seminary was announced: Edward John Carnell.

Carl Henry, who spoke against Carnell's appointment, provides a glimpse of what went on behind the scenes that week. Ockenga, who had come to the campus following his telegraphed change of mind, called Henry and invited him to join himself and Dr. Fuller in the president's office. Acknowledging their recognition that the school needed a president, they asked Henry whom he would suggest. He named Dr. Frank Gaebelein, headmaster of Stony Brook School on Long Island and a well-known evangelical leader. Dr. Fuller asked, "What if we stay inside the faculty for our choice?" This time Henry suggested Charles Woodbridge, Professor of Church History.[21] Ockenga then asked, "What about Eddie Carnell?" Henry expressed disapproval and gave four reasons: (1) Making him president would remove a master teacher from the classroom; (2) it would undercut the scholarly productivity of a man whose books are extremely important; (3) he did not have the necessary administrative experience; (4) he had very little pastoral experience. At this point Henry realized that the situation had turned awkward. Ockenga then informed him that they had already selected Carnell. "I was shocked," says Henry, "because of course I would not have said all those things if I had known."[22]

Before the appointment was officially announced, Carnell did some vacillating of his own. On Tuesday evening, September 21, after Carnell had accepted the invitation of the trustees to become president, he felt the need to consult with Harold Lindsell, at that time the school's registrar. So the Carnells paid a visit to the Lindsell home. According to Mrs. Carnell, their response was cordial but reserved.[23] Carnell saw the evening rather differently. He was so disturbed that in the morning he fired off a note to Ockenga in which he complained that Lindsell clearly indicated that "he is going to dump everything on me" except those duties that strictly belong to the registrar. "Candid conversation with him left me with such a feeling of apprehension about the wisdom of this move to make me president that I spent most of the night tossing and meditating." He had made too big an investment in his education, he said, to "throw this away for an office in which I have to decide how many dozen towels the school should order." He asked that the matter be thrashed out immediately with Lindsell, Dr. Fuller, and the trustees. In a subsequent letter to Ockenga, he pinpointed the reason for Lindsell's attitude that evening: "Dr. Lindsell, as we both know, was deeply crushed to see one of his juniors elevated over him to the presidency."[24] In any case, the problem was solved to Carnell's satisfaction (at least for the moment) and formal announcement of his appointment was made the next day as planned, Thursday, September 23, at the seminary's eighth annual convocation.

As subsequent events will demonstrate, Edward Carnell had just made the most fateful decision of his life. Why did he say yes? He would have been the first to agree that Carl Henry's four reasons gave an essentially correct appraisal of his academic and administrative strengths and weaknesses. One need only to look back on the correspondence with Ockenga during the previous winter and spring to find the answer. In his view, his own personal destiny took second place to the future of Fuller Seminary as an institution. A young school, barely seven years old, faced a crucial decision. If the wrong person were to become president, its future as a progressive leader in evangelical theological education almost certainly would be jeopardized. Carnell was convinced of this because he knew the ideas, goals, and standards "they" held – meaning many of the colleagues about whom he had written to Ockenga. As he said to Gordon Clark when he wrote informing him of the presidential appointment, "The situation was such that I simply could not sit back and watch the school go into the wrong hands by default . . . To see this school fall into the hands of those who would let it develop into a mediocre, fundamentalist institution, would be more than I could stand."[25] Whatever compromises he had to make with his personal aspirations paled before the higher priorities of Fuller Seminary. In somewhat different terms, he laid out his reasons to the faculty (and reported them later to Ockenga): "I consider myself a sacrifice, in a sense, for the school. Preferring to remain in the cloistered walls of scholarship, I am glad to bring whatever gifts and wisdom I have to bear on the office of president. For the first time in my life I have done something really sacrificial. Up until now I have been guarding my own interests. Convinced that *someone* must head the school who knows education, theology, and the art of diplomacy, I could not in honesty let another do a task that I had been called to perform." If we conclude, as many have, that Carnell made a mistake in agreeing to become president, we must recognize that he did so with his eyes wide open to the risks involved.

Moreover, Carnell had some reason to think he could wear two hats successfully. He had, to begin with, a definite concept of the president's role as shaper of educational philosophy and architect of long-range institutional strategy. His repeated references to Harvard reflect not only the pride of an alumnus but the presence in his mind of a working model. He saw Presidents Conant and Pusey as educators first; they were not saddled with the onerous tasks of day-to-day operations. As for the Divinity School, with which Carnell had his closest acquaintance, the late Glenn Barker, one of the Harvard evangelicals and subsequently Fuller's

Provost, remarked that "everyone knew that Miss Prescott ran the school."[26] When longtime Divinity School faculty member Ralph Lazzaro heard about this comment, he laughed and acknowledged its essential truth.[27] As in many educational institutions there is one chief staff person in the main office who has a knowing finger on all administrative details, so at Harvard Divinity School Miss Prescott was that person. No one could guarantee Carnell a Miss Prescott, but he was given assurances that he would not be burdened with either operational details or fund-raising responsibilities. Finally, his commitment was not long-term. He agreed to serve for three years, specifying that at the end of that time he would take inventory and decide whether to continue. At the same time, of course, the board of trustees, under Ockenga's leadership, would go through a similar evaluative procedure.

C. The presidency: the first eight months: 1954–1955

"I promise, God helping me, to preserve and propagate the glory of this Seminary with a spirit of humility and joy."
Edward Carnell, Inaugural Address, May 17, 1955

In academia as in politics, new administrations tend to enjoy a honeymoon period during which differences are swallowed and tensions eased in a genuine effort to work together. Carnell's honeymoon lasted until his formal inauguration the following May, but the intervening months were not problem-free. For one thing, the presidential change had been made so rapidly that there was no time to find a replacement for Carnell in the classroom. In addition, therefore, to his new administrative duties, he was teaching a full load of classes. Enthusiasm, however, overcame exhaustion. Faculty attitudes modified – or perhaps Carnell's perception of them changed from his new vantage point. Whatever the cause, the same faculty whose commitment to solid academic values he had seriously questioned in September now "are especially happy over the fact that the Trustees made a decision to make education the first task of the administrative head of the school here at Fuller."[28] To those same trustees, who he knew were more concerned with personal piety than academic prowess, he wrote reassuringly about the vibrant spiritual life at the seminary – the full weekly chapel period set aside for prayer, the regular Monday morning faculty prayer meeting in his own office.

Within days of taking office he set the faculty about the task of finding a new man to take his place teaching Systematic Theology, giving them as a high-priority possibility the name of Paul King Jewett, also a Wheaton–Westminster–Harvard alumnus at that time on the faculty of Gordon Divinity School. A search began for a Professor of Evangelism, in conjunction with a promised grant from the Pew Foundation. A faculty committee was formed to begin plans for a new library building.

On November 19 an event took place on campus that, while certainly not considered unimportant at the time, looms rather more large in retrospect, partly because it was emblematic of the Carnell presidency. A distinguished visitor, Dr. Daniel Day Williams of Union Theological Seminary in New York, spent the entire day at Fuller interviewing faculty and administration as part of an American Association of Theological Schools study project funded by a grant from the Carnegie Foundation. Realizing how good and bad impressions could spread throughout the academic community, Carnell held a preliminary briefing session with the faculty and, when Williams's visit was over, commended them for acquitting themselves superbly.[29] One can imagine what the briefing session was like from Carnell's later comment that Williams "was impressed with the fact that we as a faculty refuse to believe that we have arrived at all truth. We are always anxious to learn and to grow."[30]

Although Carnell had to shelve temporarily his own current scholarly project – a new book on apologetics – he continued to hold monthly faculty colloquia, taking his own turn in November by reading a paper on Reinhold Niebuhr. But if his own aspirations were held down, his hopes for the seminary at times seemed boundless: "One of my dreams is to create a research center here, on the order of the Institute for Advanced Studies at Princeton, New Jersey."[31] Even the daily grind was made more tolerable by a shift in the attitude of Harold Lindsell, of whom Carnell said that he had "made the adjustment to the presidency here a lot easier by his cooperation."[32] Although he never personally enjoyed traveling, Carnell realized he must not shirk that necessary dimension of public relations. So he spent the first two weeks of March on the road, making visits to Wheaton College, Northern Baptist Seminary in Chicago, Taylor University in Indiana, and three seminaries in Kentucky (Asbury, Louisville Presbyterian, and Louisville Baptist). On a quiet Sunday in New York City, he talked with Mrs. Reinhold Niebuhr (Niebuhr himself was ill) and roamed through the unlocked sections of Union Theological Seminary, "trying to capture the reason why the very atmosphere of the Union quadrangle excites a tingling sensation of being centrally about the work of theology." On the way back west, he stopped at Houghton College in upstate New York, visited with family in Michigan, and checked out the new four million dollar library at Wayne State University in Detroit.[33]

The trip was far more than a public relations junket. The impressions he garnered, the information he collected, the counsel he received – all filtered through his consciousness and became part of his preparation for the greatest challenge of his life up to this point: the address he would be called on to deliver at his official inauguration, scheduled for the evening of May 17. Knowing his motivation for agreeing to assume the presidency, we can be sure he wanted to sound a note that would transcend fundamentalist parochialism. Knowing his concerns as a conscientious and practical administrator, we can be equally sure of his desire to retain and deepen the support of the evangelical community. Most of all, for those inside and outside the church, inside and outside academia, his purpose was to glorify the noble calling of theological education.

The inauguration ceremony was held at the Lake Avenue Congregational Church. In addition to students, faculty, staff, and friends, representatives were present from some forty-five educational institutions around the country. The presidential address, "The Glory of a Theological Seminary," may have been Edward Carnell's finest hour. At his best an extremely effective public speaker, he apparently was in top form on this occasion. Dan Fuller says that he rehearsed the speech while walking eight times the nine-mile trek down the road from Mount Wilson.[34] William LaSor, who was sitting next to Dean Earl Cranston of the University of Southern California School of Theology, recalls that after the address Cranston turned to him and said, "My, that was a masterful statement."[35] No one in the audience could possibly have been surprised by or resentful of Carnell's first characteristic of a seminary's glory: "That with spiritual conviction and firmness of moral purpose the seminary strives to preserve and propagate the theological distinctives that inhere in the institution itself." One would expect the same firmly grounded emphasis of their uniqueness on the part of neo-orthodox and liberal institutions. But Carnell's second and third points did raise some eyebrows. The second had to do with educational breadth and freedom of conscience: "that in preserving and propagating its theological distinctives, the seminary make a conscientious effort to acquaint its students with all the relevant evidences – damaging as well as supporting – in order that the students may be given a reasonable opportunity to exercise their God-given right freely to decide for or against claims to truth." The third characteristic concerned the primacy of love and the attitude of tolerance toward those with differing theological views: "that the seminary inculcate on its students an attitude of tolerance and forgiveness toward individuals whose doctrinal convictions are at variance with those that inhere in the institution itself."[36]

However, like the famous dog (in the Sherlock Holmes story) that did not bark in the night, the inaugural is every bit as important for what it did *not* say as for what it did. Not once in the entire address did Carnell use the word *evangelical*. Acknowledging that the Eternal Gospel (the expression he used some nineteen times to refer to the priceless treasure entrusted to the seminary) is an abstraction that must be translated into concrete terms, he nevertheless mentioned creed only once – a reference to the traditional Apostles' Creed, whose first two articles he quoted: "I believe in God the Father Almighty, Maker of heaven and earth, and in Jesus Christ His only Son our Lord." Nowhere did he bring up explicitly any of the items in the unofficial evangelical creed: not the faintest hint of an allusion to biblical inerrancy, no declaration of faith in the historicity of the resurrection (let alone the historicity of Adam and Eve), no outline of the plan of salvation based on the forensic necessities involved in the substitutionary atonement, nothing about the promise of heaven or the threat of hell, no repetition of the arguments for philosophical theism. To be sure, one might point out that he did not have to say these things; they were all taken for granted. Nevertheless, Carnell was consciously setting the tone of his administration. Consequently, whereas his first affirmation promised the perpetuation of the seminary's heritage (which everyone knew was evangelical), his decision not to identify that heritage by name moved the seminary another step toward a genuinely ecumenical future.

The dean of the School of Theology at USC may have been pleased with the address, but several Fuller faculty were not. As LaSor tells it, "When I went up to my office (which is across the hall from the president's office), four faculty members were waiting for Carnell to arrive, and they went in with him and told him in strong terms what they thought of his address. As I remember them, they were Henry, Lindsell, Woodbridge, and Smith – but my memory could be faulty."[37] Carl Henry does not recall that there was a delegation but does acknowledge dissatisfaction with the address. Some of the faculty, he says, were dismayed "over a failure to emphasize what specifically justified Fuller in distinction from already existing schools – that is, the elaboration of its distinctive mission."[38] All reports agree that Wilbur Smith harbored the deepest resentment. Smith, who had Charles Fuller's ear though not his full sympathy, called Dr. Fuller to protest. Then Fuller called Carnell, who later told his friend Bernard Ramm, "I knew exactly who would be calling, and I got a lump in my stomach that didn't leave the entire time I was president."[39] Since Dr. Fuller unequivocally supported Carnell throughout his years at the seminary, we may safely infer that the lump was caused by the recognition that within the faculty ran a serious undercurrent of distrust. One immediate result of the faculty protest was that Carnell impounded the transcript of the address and never let any copies of it be distributed during his lifetime.[40]

What was it about Carnell's inaugural address that Wilbur Smith and the others found so threatening? David Hubbard, Fuller's current president, sees it this way: "Carnell had been hired to come to Fuller to teach apologetics, and to these men that meant the rationalistic stress on propositional revelation. When he made love an apologetic touchstone, it was as if the seminary was being basically changed in their eyes."[41] As Carnell himself put it in a letter to Charles Fuller shortly before he left the presidency in 1959:

Since the night I tried to express a few fresh ideas about the law of love in my inaugural address as president, I have had to stand alone in the defense of the classical tradition, and in the persuasion that we ought to express the more gracious and gentle attributes of Christ as well as thunder in the defense of doctrine.[42]

Whatever the reasons, one thing was clear: For President Carnell, the honeymoon was over.

D. The presidential years: 1955–1959

"The accomplishments of the Seminary are sound measurements, I believe, of the distinguished leadership which Dr. Carnell gave to it during those formative years of his Presidency."

> Robert Rankin
> Member, Accreditation Team
> American Association of Theological Schools

In our attempt to reach some kind of an understanding of the tangled events of Carnell's presidency, let me first suggest another image that lingers in the mind. Carnell is walking around a city block – once, twice, three times. He has an appointment with a corporate executive, a potential channel for large donations to the seminary. He is trying to screw up his courage to walk through the revolving doors. Finally, of course, he does, but not happily. He said it again and again, in many different ways: I am not a fundraiser, I cannot go around begging with a tin cup. In accepting the presidency in the first place, he had hammered out an agreement with the trustees: They and Dr. Fuller would find the money; he would take care of the academic side. But if he really thought that such an agreement would work, he was setting himself up for disillusionment. The complicated reality of Fuller Seminary's financial condition affected virtually everything Carnell did for the remaining four years of his administration. Even in the eight-month honeymoon period, we can see an occasional straw in the wind. Four months after taking office, he referred to "the mystery of the finances of the school" and complained that he could get no information out of Dr. Fuller.[43] In the spring of 1958, he was still singing the same tune: "I know no more about our true financial picture than I did four years ago when I took the office."[44] To be sure, he was exaggerating – by that time he not only knew more but had effected some important changes – but his statement accurately measured the depth of his frustration.

The roots of the problem extend back to the 1920s. Charles Fuller had made a great deal of money buying and selling orange groves in the Los Angeles area in the decade before the Depression. As a clergyman, however, his deepest interest was in Christian evangelism, especially through the relatively new medium of radio. After conducting various radio programs in connection with his pastoral ministry, he ventured out on his own in Christian broadcasting in the unpromising year of 1933. In 1934, he began a program called "The Old-Fashioned Revival Hour," which by 1937 was being heard coast to coast. Because of the need to oversee the handling of the financial contributions that came in from the growing national audience, he formed a nonprofit corporation called The Gospel Broadcasting Association. In 1942, a second board was set up, the Fuller Evangelistic Foundation, in order to distribute funds more widely to various religious, charitable, and educational activities not subsumed under the category of broadcasting. Included in the monies made available to the new foundation was a substantial trust fund set up in 1918 by Charles Fuller's father to serve the cause of missions and evangelism. It was this new organization, the Fuller Evangelistic Foundation, that supplied the startup money for Fuller Theological Seminary in 1947.[45]

At first the arrangement worked satisfactorily. The seminary did its best to become self-sustaining, but with no denominational backing and no history of cultivated friendships with wealthy donors, it was at a severe disadvantage. According to Harold Ockenga, in the seminary's early period Charles Fuller simply arranged for the Foundation to make up any deficit at the year's end.[46]

The system might have lasted indefinitely but for two reasons. The first was the unpredictable manner in which Dr. Fuller controlled the funds. Comparing his moods to a fever chart, Carnell said, "One week he will come to us announcing the glad tidings of all the new possibilities of funds from the Foundation, and then the next week he will come and tell us not to spend money even for library books, because of the pinch in the economy."[47] Under such circumstances, drawing up annual budgets was difficult and long-range planning next to impossible.

What finally forced some change was Fuller Seminary's decision to seek accreditation from the American Association of Theological Schools. In September 1955, Dr. Fuller revealed to Carnell that the Foundation had borrowed some $900,000 for the seminary and that interest on the loans amounted to $30,000 annually. He put the seminary on notice that it would be responsible for making up the budget gap each year (between $65,000 and $80,000) and raising an extra equal amount each year to pay back the $900,000. Carnell's first response to this depressing news was to write Ockenga and suggest a "patient, orderly transition" to a president "who can give himself completely to the problem of making the Seminary solvent.''[48] During the next two weeks, a good bit of educating and persuading went on behind the scenes, for on October 10, Carnell sent a telegram to Ockenga's Belmont, Massachusetts home saying, "WE HAVE BROUGHT DOCTOR FULLER TO THE PLACE WHERE THE FOUNDATION WILL CANCEL ALL SEMINARY DEBTS" and urging him not to let Dr. Fuller "REVERSE THIS PROMISE OR WE SHALL BE IN SERIOUS TROUBLE WITH THE ACCREDITATION AGENCY."[49] Carnell anticipated – accurately, it turns out – that the seminary's financial dependency on the Foundation would trip a warning signal in the accrediting association over a potential academic freedom issue. If one of the faculty members, for example, were to espouse views in his classes that the Foundation board judged heretical, might they not withhold funds until the seminary either disciplined or dismissed the offending teacher? To Carnell this was no abstract theoretical matter. Dr. Fuller was a man of broad theological sympathies and irenic spirit. But how much longer would he be around? "We cannot imagine what possible demands may be made upon us by the Foundation after the death of Dr. Fuller. Miss Baessler [Dr. Fuller's longtime secretary] has repeatedly warned that if the Seminary ever departs from the purposes set down by Dr. Fuller, the Foundation money will go elsewhere."[50]

The seminary's indebtedness to the Foundation was canceled, but the organizational dependency remained unchanged. Exactly as Carnell had expected, the initial AATS report in December 1956, while not a rejection, delayed action pending the receipt of further information. Given the seminary's roots in the fundamentalist movement, the examining committee wanted further evidence of a spirit of ecumenical cooperation. But they were also obviously troubled about the Foundation's continuing role in seminary affairs. The official communication read as follows:

Voted: that we receive the report of the inspection team that visited Fuller Theological Seminary, that we note the progress of the institution with interest and satisfaction, but that we postpone action regarding its request for accreditation until a significant amount of endowment has actually been transferred to the institution, and its relationship to the churches and to neighboring theological schools has been explored more fully by the Executive Director and other representatives of the American Association of Theological Schools who may be appointed by the President of the Association.[51]

Dr. Fuller had decided the previous September to put all the Foundation's assets under the seminary board. But because the bond market was low at the time, he delayed implementing the decision.[52] Apparently what finally satisfied the accrediting team, as Carnell explained to Ockenga early in January, was an arrangement whereby the seminary's name would be put on all the securities as joint owner until such time as they were actually transferred. This move did not, however, solve the more serious long-range problem of actual financial control of the institution.

All of this wrangling about money wore Carnell down. Three weeks after informing Ockenga that the organizational question involving the seminary and the Foundation had been at least partially resolved, he sent another letter submitting his resignation, to take effect at the end of the school year. The decision, he said, had not been made rashly but over a period of months. Furthermore, it was "final and irreversible."[53]

Thus began a six-month tug of war, Ockenga and the Fullers seeking to change Carnell's mind, Carnell gradually shifting his position from unconditional to conditional and finally agreeing to stay on in view of certain promised changes. He made it clear all along that money was the chief problem:

If the Trustees will not take seriously my decision to be relieved, then I shall have only one course left. It will be the radical one of leaving the institution. I am prepared to take this step. All my energies are exhausted in leading the faculty, guiding the students, teaching, writing, and keeping the public happy. I simply cannot accept this burden of raising money.[54]

Even Ockenga, to whom Carnell had always been completely courteous, even deferential, in correspondence over the years, was subjected to some angry words:

You think I am inconsistent in naming the reason why I am leaving this office. Think what you want, I don't care. To me your attitude is only further proof of how really *little* you know of the actual cause of my unhappiness. And I suspect that the reason why you don't know is that you have never made any real effort to find out what was wrong.[55]

The ending of this brief note contains a clue we should not overlook. "I wish I could go to a ranch somewhere for a month or so. I am completely exhausted."

One evening that spring Dr. Fuller invited Carnell to his home to discuss the presidency. After a two-and-a-half hour conversation, during which (as Fuller later reported to Ockenga) Carnell "opened his heart and revealed some things I had never realized were there," Fuller concluded that the resignation was never as final and irreversible as Carnell had claimed: "Although writing to us as he did 'plain as the English language can make it,' yet I think he was hurt that we did not *urge* him to stay, did not consider him 'the indispensable man.'" Declaring that he could back Carnell's philosophy of education one hundred percent, Fuller said, "I feel it would be tragic to let him slip through our fingers."[56]

At their annual May meeting, the trustees poured healing balm on the wounds by expressing sincere appreciation for Carnell's work, and on July 31 he sent each of them a letter announcing withdrawal of his resignation. Internal evidence, however, suggests that a power struggle had been going on:

If the Board members choose to retain my services, I shall interpret this as a sign that they not only accept the philosophy of education which I am trying to develop, but that they will wholeheartedly back me up in all its details – and especially as it involves a crusade for new friends and donors. I cannot bear the burden alone. Only a close teamwork between Board, administration, and faculty will bring Fuller Theological Seminary into line with the classical evangelical tradition.[57]

We shall return to this tension between Carnell and the trustees. For now let us simply note that the decision to remain in the presidency meant that Carnell was still at the helm to accept congratulations when in December the American Association of Theological Schools notified the seminary that its application for accreditation had been approved. Accreditation unquestionably ranks as the major achievement of the Carnell regime, with immediate and long-range effects on academic prestige, student recruitment, expansion of program, and fund-raising possibilities. In his congratulatory telegram, Ockenga was careful to give equal credit to President Carnell and Dean Lindsell.[58] LaSor, in his account, did the same, explaining that "Ed Carnell was not the man for handling such vast quantities of detail, but Harold Lindsell was." He added that "without Ed's leadership and statesmanship, we could never have convinced the accreditation team that we were anything more than what we had often been labeled – a Bible school calling itself a seminary."[59] The members of the accrediting team itself clearly found Carnell the pivotal figure. One of them was Robert Rankin, later to become Vice-President of the Danforth Foundation. Acknowledging that neither then nor subsequently has he identified himself with Fuller Seminary's evangelical position, he says he was impressed in 1957 and, through continuing contacts over the years, has "developed an increasing respect for the character of its evangelical witness and the quality of its educational programs."

The accomplishments of the Seminary are sound measurements, I believe, of the distinguished leadership which Dr. Carnell gave to it during those formative years of his Presidency. Perhaps the most admirable quality of the institution, from my liberal point of view, is its amazing ability to maintain very strong evangelical commitments on one hand, and on the other to remain open and imaginative and flexible so that it can learn from persons and groups of different convictions. It strikes me that Fuller Seminary has achieved this quality of greatness because of the splendid leadership Dr. Carnell gave to it during an earlier time. As I need not explain to you, this combination of spiritual depth and commitment to broad public service requires a rare quality of Christian statesmanship. In my view, this began in the ministry of Edward J. Carnell and is being continued through the distinguished leadership of David Hubbard and his colleagues.[60]

The new appointments the seminary made during Carnell's presidency strengthened the legacy to which Rankin refers. Paul Jewett arrived in the fall of 1955 to take over Carnell's responsibilities in Systematic Theology. Geoffrey Bromiley was persuaded to leave his native Scotland to teach Church History beginning in the fall of 1958. Both of these men, as David Hubbard puts it, "have been anchors for us ever since."[61] One more appointment of a different kind during the Carnell years proved to be of great importance, not only for the remainder of his own administration but beyond. While talking with his brother-in-law, Donald Weber, during a family outing in Illinois in the summer of 1955, Carnell realized that Weber might have some interest in becoming a field man for the seminary. Credentials were never a question, only availability. Weber at the time was living in Wheaton, representing the Dennison Manufacturing Company in the Midwest. To Carnell's delight, he was ready for just such a step. By the end of the year he was traveling for the seminary; by summer he and his family had moved to the Pasadena area, and he was working full-time in development and public relations. To quote David Hubbard once more: "If Carnell is the most important man in setting the course of this seminary, then Don Weber has to be number two. In the four years between Carnell's resignation and my own appointment, Weber virtually ran the school."[62] Carnell let Weber know right away how important he was:

Whether my presidency is to succeed or not will depend in a large part on whether I can keep the financial wolf away from the door. With you on the field I have had great peace of heart this year. I know that this is the first realistic step we have taken toward solving a difficult problem here.[63]

Carnell and Weber made an effective team, especially after Weber settled in with the formal title Assistant to the President.

Nevertheless, even with all these plus factors, the presidency continued to be an almost intolerable burden for Carnell. He faced two other constantly nagging problems that neither the thrill of achieving accreditation nor the supporting presence of Don Weber could overcome. One was his continuing inability to find adequate time for scholarship; the other was an effort within the seminary itself to undermine his administration.

When he became president in 1954, Carnell had thrown out a challenge to his colleagues on the faculty: he would continue to produce scholarly work in spite of his heavy load of administrative duties; he would expect them to do the same.[64] It was not the sort of commitment a proud man like Carnell could back away from. As a matter of fact, he did fulfill his pledge – quite brilliantly in a way, or at least so it seemed for a while in the fall of 1956. In the previous year he had found enough time to finish and revise a third major book on apologetics, this one called *Christian Commitment*. In October he received word that The Macmillan Company had accepted it for publication. One must not underestimate the significance of this bit of news to Carnell. His regular publisher, up to that point, had been the William B. Eerdmans Company in Grand Rapids, Michigan. Carnell owed a lot to them (they had, after all, started him off with a $5,000 prize for *An Introduction to Christian Apologetics*) and indeed he would return to them for the final two books of his career. But he had long chafed under the realization that, for whatever reasons, evangelical writers were not getting published by secular houses. So Macmillan's acceptance of a book defending conservative Christianity elicited much satisfaction. Perhaps a touch of cockiness too. Before the book came out in the spring, Carnell confidently told the faculty that it would change the way apologetics is done.[65] Alas, *Christian Commitment* did not come close to fulfilling expectations. It was reviewed here and there in religious magazines, with mixed reaction, but sold poorly and was quickly remaindered by the publisher. Carnell surely never expected it would hit the best-seller list, but inasmuch as he considered it his best work, its failure to make the theological world sit up and take notice was the greatest disappointment of his professional life. He said as much in correspondence and in his classes.[66] Lest we think of him as totally humorless in the face of such numbing disappointment, we might add that the situation gave him a focus for his particular brand of sour, deadpan humor. He walked into class one day and matter-of-factly announced that he had just received a telephone call from his publisher: "They've sold another copy of my book."[67]

The failure of a given book, however traumatic, occurs within a certain relatively brief chronological period. Losing touch with one's scholarly field is a slower and more subtle process. During the years of his presidency, Carnell could not escape the increasingly persistent fear that he would never be able to get back on the main track of scholarship. "I am suffering, I guess, from the insecurity of knowing that my academic career is gradually eroding away."[68] Although that particular comment did not pop to the surface until March 1959, its wording clearly suggests that Carnell's troubled awareness of the problem had been building for some time.

Equally troubling to Carnell was the growing opposition to his leadership within the seminary family. We noted earlier the resentment with which some faculty members greeted Carnell's inaugural. On the part of one of them, Professor of Church History Charles J. Woodbridge, the spirit of criticism intensified as the months passed. Early in his presidency, Carnell pegged Woodbridge as one who "has not characteristically risen to the research opportunities given him here at the school."[69] A year later he identified him as the "number one offender" in the faculty tendency to accept too many speaking engagements in the area. ("I really believe that he spends more time in the Lake Avenue Congregational Church than he does in his classes here at the Seminary."[70]) A far more serious problem came to a head in the fall of 1956. According to Carnell, Woodbridge, while still on the seminary faculty, was spreading the word that Fuller Seminary had in certain significant ways departed from orthodoxy. With his contacts nationwide, especially through Jack Wyrtzen, a youth leader and evangelist at whose resort in upstate New York Woodbridge was a resident summer Bible teacher, this subversive campaign could not be casually ignored. "I have documented evidence," Carnell wrote to Ockenga, "that Dr. Woodbridge has deliberately poisoned the mind of Jack Wyrtzen and that both of these men feel it their calling from God to damage the health and the security of Fuller Theological Seminary."[71] He saw no mystery in Woodbridge's motivation:

The issue, of course, is the struggle between fundamentalism and the new evangelicalism. Dr. Woodbridge is a straight-line fundamentalist. He has been an enemy of your philosophy of the new evangelicalism from the very inception of the institution. My being appointed president crushed his hope of seeing the institution come under the control of his position.[72]

Carnell expected some criticism. He had the wisdom to see that "the school would not be a great school if it were not subject to resentment, public criticism, and endless misunderstanding."[73] In one sense the Woodbridge matter was handled with tact and dispatch. By early November 1956, Woodbridge handed in his letter of resignation, which Carnell immediately accepted on behalf of the board of trustees.[74] Neither Carnell nor the seminary, however, were destined to escape the repercussions of the Woodbridge affair that easily, for before he left, Woodbridge (according to Carnell) shrewdly sowed seeds of discord where they would have the greatest effect: within Fuller's governing board of trustees. Carnell, writing to Ockenga some fifteen months later, trying to explain to him why things had gotten so bad early in 1957 that he had submitted his resignation, cited the Woodbridge problem as a major contributing cause:

Third, when Dr. Woodbridge left the Seminary, he won the sympathies of Trustees Taylor and Johnson, and principally those of Johnson. This meant that I had to fight a theological battle with two members of my own board. Their contention was that if I had been true to the purposes of the Seminary, Dr. Woodbridge would never have resigned in the first place. In other words, they named Dr. Woodbridge's resignation as prima facie evidence that there was malfeasance, if not heresy, in the present administration. Well, this was frightfully serious. And before I finished the altercation, I was so weary that I had no interest in continuing as president.[75]

As the year 1959 rolled around, Carnell had to reckon with one more besetting difficulty not unrelated to all the others – his deteriorating health. Actually the pattern was not totally new: He had often referred to exhaustion, and in *Christian Commitment* he wrote that since high school days he had been bothered by insomnia. This time, though, there was a difference, and it would profoundly affect his life. By December 1958, he was seriously hooked on sleeping pills, a self-labeled barbiturate addict.[76] In February he was ordered by a doctor to cut back on his duties, but, as he explained to Ockenga, "the teaching and administrative obligations here at the Seminary go on relentlessly."[77] When Carnell had submitted his earlier resignation, the status quo had hardly budged, even with all the declarations of finality and irreversibility. This time, when Carnell passed the word, things began to happen fast. To Ockenga went a telegram:

1959 APR 25 PM 2 46

PLEASE DO ME A GREAT FAVOR AND PERSUADE DR FULLER TO RELEASE ME FROM THE PRESIDENCY. THE PRESENT FINANCIAL WAR OF NERVES IS MORE THAN I CAN SUFFER A CONTINUATION OF THIS STRESS MAY LEAD TO THE RUINATION MY HEALTH AND MY WITHDRAWAL FROM THE SEMINARY ALTOGETHER. I DESPERATELY WANT TO RETURN TO THE QUIETNESS AND PEACE OF THE PROFESSORIAL LIFE. BEST WISHES.

Thinking perhaps that Ockenga might delay (or even resist) persuading Dr. Fuller, Carnell at the same time sent an unequivocal letter to Dr. Fuller, concluding with the plaintive declaration, "I simply do not have the strength to continue in office." Ockenga's reply came in the form of a day letter. It did not minimize the seriousness of Carnell's request, but neither did it treat the resignation as inevitable. In part it read: "Please take an immediate vacation of three or four weeks. Turn administrative duties over to Lindsell and teaching duties to Jewett for that time. Take a complete rest in the mountains or desert. Leave the worrying to me."[78]

We do not have Dr. Fuller's response, but its substance is apparent from Carnell's April 29 reply to his "kind note": "I am glad you are not going to pressure me into staying with the presidency. Such pressure would only have the effect of forcing me to resign from Fuller altogether. My course is clear."[79]

On commencement evening early in May, after Carnell had handed out Fuller's five hundredth diploma, Ockenga announced that Carnell had resigned because of failing health and that he had been granted sabbatical leave until January 1960, at which time he would return to full-time teaching. Harold Ockenga once again took up the post of president-in-absentia. Harold Lindsell, Don Weber, and Business Manager Richard Curley ran things day to day on campus. And Edward Carnell slipped off temporarily into limbo.

E. Breakdown and the road back: 1959–1967

"I do not shrink from this threat."
Edward Carnell
Preface to *The Case for Orthodox Theology*

In William Faulkner's *The Sound and the Fury*, Quentin Compson says that "Christ was not crucified" but was "worn away by a minute clicking of little wheels." Bringing those little clicking wheels to a stop, however, does not guarantee an instant cure for the victim. So it was with Carnell. He could relish eight months of freedom. Thorough medical examinations dispelled concern over possible serious organic disease. The Board of Trustees voted him a five hundred dollar salary increment. But his reply to their question as to how he wanted to divide the increment between present salary and retirement betrayed his broken spirit: "I believe I shall accept the $500 in cash, for present needs seem more pressing than those of retirement. Whether I shall ever see 65 is highly doubtful." One does not sense the envisioning of new horizons: "It is ironic, but now that I have a sabbatical leave, I don't know what to do with myself. I guess I would be better off teaching."[80]

Inevitably, perhaps, given the particular nature of Carnell's problems, sabbatical leave proved to be a mixed blessing. To be sure, it was an enormous relief to be out from under the oppressive burden of administrative duties. Conversely, however, he was inclined to feel even more acutely the pressure to turn out new writing now that he did not have those responsibilities to hide behind. By late fall, new controversy dampened somewhat his enthusiasm for continuing scholarship. The publication of his new book *The Case for Orthodox Theology*, almost simultaneously with his resignation, should have been an unalloyed triumph for Carnell. In 1958, he had been asked by Paul Meacham of Westminster Press to join with two other scholars in producing a trilogy of short books expounding sympathetically the conservative, liberal, and neo-orthodox theological positions. The other two authors were L. Harold DeWolf (second reader of his dissertation at B.U.) and William Hordern.[81] The series was designed to provide for laypersons, students, teachers, and clergy "a clear statement of three contemporary theological viewpoints by convinced adherents to these positions. Each was given perfect freedom to state his case."[82] Meacham offered to tell Carnell who the other contributors were, but he declined on the grounds that it would be more interesting if the authors remained unknown to each other until manuscripts were submitted. That was the plan Westminster Press followed.[83]

So far so good. Carnell was assured instant access to a new segment of the reading public and instant recognition on a par with two more widely accepted scholars. But in fulfilling the charge, he faced a delicate problem. He had begun his career defending the "trinitarian-theistic faith," which he explicitly identified with "fundamentalism."[84] In the intervening years, however, he had put considerable distance between himself and fundamentalism, even contributing a two-page essay on the subject to *A Handbook of Christian Theology* in which he defined fundamentalism as "an extreme right element in Protestant orthodoxy."[85] Although possessing orthodox theological truth, fundamentalists "failed to connect their convictions with the wider problems of general culture," got bogged down in a misguided effort "to maintain status by negation," and cut themselves off from "the wisdom of the ages." His problem as of 1958, obviously, was how to write a book that would effectively say Orthodoxy Yes, Fundamentalism No. Put another way, could he conscientiously write the case book without probing orthodoxy's weaknesses? And if he probed the multiple weaknesses subsumed under the label fundamentalism, could he do so without unleashing the Furies? The answer to both questions was no.

All of the trouble focused on two chapters called "Difficulties" and "Perils." In the former he raised a number of issues that exemplified a continuing tension between science and history on one side and the concept of biblical infallibility on the other. One would have thought that Carnell's conclusion would be considered unassailably orthodox. After acknowledging certain "inductive difficulties in the text," he brushed them aside: *"But in no case is the doctrine of inspiration accommodated to the difficulties. If orthodoxy were to tolerate such accommodation, it would forfeit the principle by which any Christian doctrine is established. This would banish theology to the wastelands of subjectivity."*[86] To the fundamentalist mentality, however, the damage is done once one has made the heinous mistake of admitting there are "difficulties." Carnell also stepped on sensitive toes in the "Perils" chapter. Not only did he define fundamentalism with the catchy but inflammatory phrase "orthodoxy gone cultic," but he identified orthodoxy's gravest peril as the ease with which it converts to fundamentalism.[87] He attacked the ecclesiastical separatism of J. Gresham Machen, intellectual hero of the theological conservatives and one of the founders of his alma mater Westminster Seminary. He ridiculed apocalyptic demagogues, money-begging evangelists, and zealots who paint "Jesus Saves" on rocks in the park.

At about this time, Carnell made another strategic decision that backfired: He published two candid and controversial articles in *Christian Century*, long considered to be the chief journalistic voice of conservative Christianity's liberal antagonists. The first, appearing in the summer of 1959, shortly after his resignation, was titled "Post-Fundamentalist Faith."[88] It sought to explain to a more or less uninitiated audience "that anxious breed of younger men who are conservative in theology but are less than happy when they are called 'fundamentalists.'" Fundamentalism, he said, fought a legitimate battle against modernism but in time shifted from affirmation to negation, often taking on "the mannerisms of a pugnacious cult." It made the "pompous theological error" of confining the true church to those in possession of true doctrine. Orthodoxy (the term he preferred despite some unfortunate connotations) "does not affect a monopoly on truth" but has the great advantage of indicating "assent to the great doctrines of the faith." He declared that the pilgrimage for these post-fundamentalists is far from easy, having learned from personal experience that "to one reared in the tyrannical legalism of fundamentalism, the recovery of a genuine theology of grace is no insignificant feat."

The second article, along much the same lines, appeared the following March under the title "Orthodoxy: Cultic vs. Classical."[89] Again drawing on personal experience, he reflected on the painful insight that orthodoxy suffers from "a serious illness":

The symptoms were too clear to be missed. Orthodoxy has at times denied modernists the most elementary civil courtesies; it has subtly evaded Christian social action and cooperative church ventures. But I could not accuse orthodoxy without accusing myself, for I was a direct offspring of orthodoxy. I soon found that my own heart was hardened. I forgot that Jesus names *love*, not possession of doctrine, as the sign of a true disciple. I corrupted the communion of the saints by refusing to hold friendly, exploratory conversation with Christians of other traditions; I was more anxious to correct than to be corrected. This was a painful admission, but it served as a spiritual catharsis. It prepared me for the delicate task of judging my own heritage. I knew what was wrong with orthodoxy because I knew what was wrong with myself.[90]

He expanded then on the distinction he had drawn in *The Case for Orthodox Theology* between classical and cultic orthodoxy. Whereas he applied the former term to historic orthodox Christianity, the latter he equated with fundamentalism, which like a cult "lives by mores and symbols of its own devising" and "makes no effort to join fellowship with the church universal." Making at least a gesture toward even-handedness, Carnell pointed out that "when liberalism dismisses orthodoxy as a refuge of ignorance, it manifests the same signs of cultic thinking that protrude so conspicuously in fundamentalism." This was not enough, however, to balance the scales for the fundamentalist readers, who saw only that one of their own had betrayed the cause within the stronghold of the enemy. Admittedly, Carnell brought on much of the calumny himself by being needlessly abrasive. Here, for example, is how the article ends:

> Perhaps the day will come when the fundamentalist will temper his separatism by the wisdom of the ages. Perhaps not. But in the meantime let us not be too disturbed by his vanity. The fundamentalist means well. He wants status in the church, but he errs in the way he goes about getting it. Having missed the way, he needs our pity, not our scorn.[91]

It is difficult to imagine a more scornful ending to a purportedly irenic paragraph.

One of the early blasts in retaliation to *Case* appeared in *The Sword of the Lord,* a fundamentalist newspaper published in Wheaton, Illinois, but sent to a national constituency. The frontpage headline accurately set the tone of editor John R. Rice's lengthy "review": "Fuller Seminary's Carnell Sneers at Fundamentalism."[92] Accusing Carnell of being "very anxious to please modernists, unbelieving scientists, and the men of this world," it ran out of specific criticisms after 4,000 words and ended with a challenge to the seminary:

What will Fuller Seminary do about Dr. Carnell? If the seminary does not repudiate this volume, then it may properly be counted officially in favor of it. I do not believe that out-and-out Bible believers can safely send students to Fuller Seminary or send any money to support the seminary as long as Dr. Carnell and men like him are in places of authority and responsibility in the school, and as long as they openly repudiate the great principles and doctrines and standards dear to Bible believers.

There is a good deal of truth to the observation that neither Carnell nor the seminary were surprised by the kind of response that came from pockets of fundamentalist resistance like *Sword of the Lord.* In the Preface Carnell frankly acknowledged that in calling attention to orthodoxy's faults he was "bound to incur censure from those who are too sure of their own perfection. I do not shrink from this threat."[93] He did not at first appear to take the hostile responses very seriously. Before publication he wrote to Ockenga, who had read the book in manuscript and had let Carnell know he thought it would be bitterly attacked.[94] Said Carnell:

It will be interesting to follow reactions to the book. I have observed, in the past, that fundamentalists can't read. Although I have come out with very bold statements in my previous books, not once, to my knowledge, has my stuff been attacked. For example, I have used the R.S.V. in all my books. Fundamentalists, I am convinced, become frightened when close reasoning is required. They feed on the carrion of rumor, scare-type headlines and opinion.[95]

In this case it was Ockenga who knew better which way the wind was blowing. As an outspoken New England preacher and a national evangelical leader, Ockenga never shied away from controversy. In fact at this very time he was under fire himself for having publicly proclaimed what he called "the new evangelicalism."[96] Ockenga was saying nothing different from what he and other post-fundamentalists had been saying for years – namely, that evangelicalism must regain leadership in American Protestantism and make an impact on intellectual, cultural, and social issues – but by giving their approach a name, he provided the right-wing fundamentalists a convenient point of attack. Then, when Carnell's *Case* appeared, it became a lightning rod for the hostility that had been building up against "new evangelicalism" generally.

While he was still president, Carnell realized that Fuller Seminary was being gradually identified as the intellectual center of "new evangelicalism," with considerable adverse effect in its public relations. Without in any sense backing away from the substance of the movement, he made sure that the label would no longer be used in any seminary literature. His December 1958 directive to staff and faculty included the following instructions:

The term "New Evangelicalism" was originally chosen because Fuller Seminary felt it might stimulate an interest among God's people for a fresh approach to the eternal gospel. This approach includes a dedication to the great doctrines which unite, rather than divide, us. It includes an attempt to restore scholarship in the preparation of ministers, teachers, and evangelists. It includes the goal of bringing Bible-believing Christians into a new spiritual unity, with Christ as the head. It includes an effort to develop the social implications of the gospel – justice, mercy, etc.

Because the term "New Evangelicalism" has caused no small misunderstanding on the field, the Seminary will henceforth not use it when describing its goals. Instead, the Seminary will refer to itself as the "Home of Historic Christianity."[97]

Ironically, the shift in terminology did not have much effect. If anything, the barrage of criticism intensified.

It would serve no useful purpose to survey here the numerous fundamentalist pamphlets, newspapers, and magazines that attacked Carnell in his post-presidential years. One book, however, takes on special importance: Charles Woodbridge's *The New Evangelicalism*.[98] Although it was not published until 1969, two years after Carnell's death, its message had been disseminated for several years. Dr. Bob Jones, Jr., says in the Foreword that he first heard Woodbridge speak on the new evangelicalism "some years ago." Furthermore, Jones points out that these lectures have been given "all across America and in the Antipodes, and recordings of these messages have been heard all around the world." The book is representative of the full spectrum of hostile criticism. Woodbridge addresses his comments to "genuine heart-mind-and-will believers in the Word of God, to those who are willing to stand fearlessly for that Word, no matter what reproach or obloquy may be heaped upon them by champions of the new evangelical point of view" (10). There is surely no dearth of obloquy in this little book, but it all emanates from Woodbridge. He unmistakably clarifies his extreme ideological position when he instructs the reader, "Wherever *liberal* is used in this context, read *infidel*" (7). This strategy enables him to attack the new evangelical emphasis on preparing seminary graduates for service within the major denominations as nonseparation from "evil" and "the enemies of the Lord" (7). He singles out Carnell for special attention because he has gone on record in print, because he carries a lot of weight with "many oncoming theological neophytes," and because his Fuller Seminary colleagues have not protested his writings. As a prime example of the new mood of tolerance toward heresy, he cites Carnell's inaugural address (although in this case he identifies the speaker only as Fuller's president). Objecting to the call for love toward those who disagree doctrinally, he sniffs, "I am growing weary of pious sentimentalism" (24). He criticizes Carnell for participating in the 1962 seminar with Karl Barth at the University of Chicago ["Did the Apostle Paul enter into dialogue with the Galatian legalizers?" (25)] and rejects the very idea of dialogue as "spiritual flirtation with the enemy" (33).

One is tempted to assume too hastily that Carnell and Fuller Seminary were beyond being bothered by such critical barbs. But Woodbridge was an indefatigable campaigner and could flash, after all, some impressive credentials: He had been Carnell's colleague, a Fuller insider for some six years. Moreover, negative responses to *The Case for Orthodox Theology* and the *Christian Century* articles were by no means confined to the likes of Woodbridge, Wyrtzen, and *Sword of the Lord*. Ockenga relayed to Carnell critical feedback he had been picking up from leaders in the evangelical movement – that is to say, from "people who are our friends."

He cited, for example, an Inter-Varsity convention in Paris at which "the unanimous opinion" was "that you are lost to the evangelical cause." Ockenga himself, usually completely supportive of Carnell, chided him for "waging a running battle against fundamentalists when our real enemy is the modernist" and urged him to submit the manuscript of his next book to his colleagues for criticisms and suggestions prior to publication.[99]

At the above-mentioned Barth Seminar, Carnell experienced the most disturbing rejection of all. In the spring of 1962, as a featured segment of Karl Barth's visit to America, Carnell was invited to join with five other young American theologians in a dialogue with Barth at the University of Chicago Divinity School.[100] Carnell's mentor, Gordon Haddon Clark, covered the proceedings for *Christianity Today*. Clark was deeply disappointed with what he considered damaging admissions by Carnell on the biblical inerrancy issue in his interchange with Barth, a judgment he expressed frankly in his *Christianity Today* report. But his harshest words were saved for an otherwise amiable breakfast meeting when he told Carnell to his face that he could not forgive him for his criticism of J. Gresham Machen in *The Case for Orthodox Theology*. As Carnell put it when he reported on the Chicago events in a subsequent Fuller chapel session: "Professor Clark thinks that Saint Machen could do no wrong."[101] Many of his colleagues at the time felt that the encounter with Clark in Chicago was devastating to Carnell – almost like a disowning.

By the time of the Chicago conference, Carnell was bearing one additional burden, perhaps the most debilitating of all. During the period since his resignation, he had suffered a series of severe psychological problems to which the term "breakdown" can fittingly be applied. Sometime, probably in late 1960, Carnell began seeing Dr. Harlan Parker, the Los Angeles psychiatrist who had successfully treated a similarly troubled Fuller colleague, Dr. Clarence Roddy.[102] Letters from that period reveal that in his therapy sessions he did considerable reflecting on the distant as well as the immediate past. "I have inherited," he said, "a nervous temperament from my mother."

My anxieties were brought to a head by the fears which I faced in the presidency, of course, but I want you to know that I am fully aware that the root of my anxieties goes back to childhood. I am a minister's son who was raised in a highly legalistic and emotionally erratic atmosphere. The scars of these early childhood experiences remain with me. I mention this so you will understand that I hold no grudges against the Board of Trustees on the matter of the presidency. The fault was altogether an emotional problem beyond our control.[103]

Breakdowns cannot always be pinpointed exactly in time. But when a sudden escalation of symptoms leads to hospitalization and a radical change in treatment, perhaps it is justifiable to single out that occasion for special attention. Carnell himself describes the moment in time when his gradually evolving personal struggles took an acute turn. It was the summer of 1961.

My hospital stay came about in this manner: I was asking my psychiatrist, Dr. Parker (the man who pulled Dr. Roddy out), if my wife would be free to go to Hawaii with her mother and several friends in August – and then I burst into tears, for I was suffering from severe depression. Dr. Parker called up Dr. Wells and made arrangement for me to be hospitalized in the Methodist Hospital, there to receive shock treatment for depression. I was in the hospital ten days, during which time I received five shock treatments. The depression abated a good deal, and I was released. Since then I have been an outpatient with the Wells Medical Group of Arcadia, having received my 6th and 7th shock treatments. Right now I am feeling quite good. I hope it keeps up.[104]

The new physician was Dr. Philip H. Wells, a medical doctor who had developed a special emphasis in psychotherapy, had been Associate Professor of Psychiatry at Stanford University during the early 1950s, and had set up a private practice in Arcadia, California, under the name Wells Medical Group. In this final phase of Carnell's life, Dr. Wells took on an importance quite the equal, in its own distinctive way, of Gordon Clark's and Harold Ockenga's. After the hospitalization, Carnell projected a decidedly upbeat attitude. He proudly informed Ockenga that since leaving the hospital he had not taken any sleeping pills, "the first such victory in at least 6 years."[105] Unfortunately, the euphoria was only temporary. He would see Dr. Wells regularly for the remaining six years of his life, he would never be free of barbituric dependence, he would have many more electroconvulsive treatments to deal with the recurring dark cloud of depression, and he would be hospitalized again – notably for six weeks prior to the Barth Conference in the spring of 1962.

Through all of this, he also managed to cope with the responsibilities of teaching. Because of these multiple adversities, Carnell's resumption of classroom teaching, on a more or less full-time schedule, was far from the cure-all he once imagined it would be. Part of the problem involved the definition of his new role at Fuller. He had been hired in 1948 as Professor of Apologetics and Systematic Theology. With the appointment of Paul Jewett as his successor in Systematics, a shift in title was made necessary. In the years since the seminary's beginning, apologetics had become increasingly less prominent as a distinct academic discipline. Nevertheless, even though Carnell himself had changed his apologetical approach,[106] he still thought of himself as professionally committed to a philosophical defense of the Christian faith. The problem was solved by conferring on him the title Professor of Ethics and Philosophy of Religion, with apologetics subsumed under the philosophical side. The new field for Carnell was ethics. It was not totally new, of course, but he had never been a specialist in ethics – a situation made all the more difficult by his perfectionist tendencies. In September 1962, a little more than two years after stepping down from the presidency and resuming his position on the faculty, he sent a brief note to his brother-in-law, Don Weber, at that time a major figure at Fuller in the interim period between the Carnell and Hubbard administrations. He reneged on a previous agreement to contribute a chapter to a book and suggested another faculty member in his place. Then he said: "Remember I lost five years as president. I also lost the field I had prepared for – systematic theology. All my free time must now, of necessity, go into ethics. I literally have hundreds of books and articles with which I must make peace – and soon."[107]

In the summer of 1961, Carnell wrote Ockenga that he was looking forward to teaching again, "for here is where I can unleash expressive powers which lie dormant within me."[108] The reports, though, are mixed. The lowest point seems to have been in 1961 and 1962, after the acute phase of the breakdown occurred and he began receiving electroconvulsive therapy. In the spring of 1962, he was seeing Dr. Wells twice a week, with one of the appointments used for shock treatment.[109] Whatever good those treatments did him – and he unequivocally maintained that they temporarily dispelled the intolerable black cloud of depression[110] – they crippled his classroom performance by ravaging his prodigious memory. Students recall uncomfortable occasions when Carnell would pause in midsentence, search for a word, wait for a moment or two, walk to the window and wait longer.[111] Sometimes the pause would stretch out to two or three minutes, long enough to awaken in them the unnerving fear that maybe he would not find his way back. Many students were also disturbed that Carnell often became embarrassingly confessional in his classes; in his most seriously affected period, initially respectable class enrollments sometimes dwindled to a handful by the end of the term. Without necessarily being judgmental, many students simply decided they had not enrolled in seminary to listen to a faculty member's personal problems. Other students had the opposite reaction: In their privileged exposure to the existential probings and emotional anguish of a genuine human being – as opposed to a traditional, impersonal, analytical approach – they sensed a priceless enrichment of their academic preparation.[112]

Even in the last years, when he was generally coping better with his responsibilities, he never fully regained his accepted status as a master pedagogue. A student in his Ethics class during the semester in which Carnell died says that he "stood head and shoulders above any professor that I had had in my academic career," but also observes that "it was grievous at times to see the man heavily sedated by medication."[113] Another student in the same class refers to Carnell as "a great teacher," commends him for adding personal involvement to scholarly rigor, but acknowledges that he "had really lost a great deal of his teaching abilities by the time I was taking the ethics course from him and in reality the course was not very good."[114]

The strength and the weakness of his approach to ethics shows up clearly in student notes from the course. On the positive side, he constructed a wholesome antidote to the system of repressive moralistic legalism that characterized his own background. One student writes, for example:

He startled the Ethics class (me anyway) at the start of the course by commenting on the therapeutic effects of masturbation in relieving life's tensions (not only sexual tensions), and by advocating it as a release when pressures – academic and otherwise – built up. This may be something everyone knew – but it wasn't something one expected an evangelical professor of theology in an ethics course to come out and advocate.[115]

However, inasmuch as he allowed his pietistic background to set the agenda for his ethics course, its very strength became also its weakness. Whereas Carnell did not ignore the larger issues, he did tend to deal with them in personal terms. As one student put it, "I was always impressed with the fact that he refused to just deal with these big issues in ethics without seeing how deeply implicated he was as an individual in them and how very complex they really were." That same student, however, cannot recall (in the spring semester of 1967) any mention of either the civil rights struggle or the war in Southeast Asia.[116]

A glance at Carnell's ethical writings in the sixties confirms the narrowness of his approach. His 1963 *Christian Century* article entitled "A Christian Social Ethic" stresses the Christian mandate for social justice but assigns it to the individual Christian, as a divinely nurtured result of redemption, rather than to the church.[117] The church's duties "include the preaching and defense of the gospel, the comforting and edifying of believers and the providing of help for the needy." Nor is there any indication in the article that the duties of the church "include" anything else – certainly no hint of any institutionalizing of the role of the Old Testament prophet in the cause of social justice and collective morality. Finally the individual Christian who seeks to advance the cause of justice gets a pat on the back and a dash of cold water in the face: "Let him seize this opportunity with all of his might. But let him never be deceived into thinking that a citizen's crusade for justice will result in such pleasant utopian conditions that society can dispense with the church's preaching of the gospel." Perhaps the most revealing clue to Carnell's stance on the Christian social ethic is in this statement: "Justice is a child of love, and love is the queen of the Christian virtues."[118] There is no denying Carnell's whole-souled commitment to the supremacy of Christian love, but to make the birth of justice contingent on the queen of Christian virtues being crowned in the human heart is to guarantee the perpetuation of injustice. One is reminded of Carnell's admission in the mid-fifties that he had "never devoted an entire sermon to the 'sins of the white man'" because of his "failure to find a final way to measure and defeat racial pride in my own life."[119] Leaving aside the dubious value of "the sins of the white man" as a sermon subject, we must question whether the prophet is enjoined from addressing the collective conscience on the personal and structural evil of racial injustice until he is first satisfied that love has removed every vestige of racial pride from his own heart.

Whatever the limitations of his theoretical ethical system, Carnell became a more compassionate, more magnanimous person in these difficult years. He candidly reflected on that recognition in a letter to a former student from his Gordon days:

I still have periodic visits with my psychiatrist, and now and then I have an electric shock treatment (when I suffer from a build-up of anxieties and my brain feels like it is going to split; and when I feel like going to the top of Mt. Wilson and screaming with all my might). I sincerely am resting in the Lord and his providence, trusting that this terrible experience will make me a more compassionate and humble teacher; for I now know a bit more about the complexity of human nature, for I know a bit more about the complexity of Carnell.[120]

Carnell's widow, Shirley Carnell Duvall, says that his therapy made him realize that his own clergyman father had neglected the Carnell children in favor of his ministerial duties; consequently, he determined that he would not make the same mistake himself. Edward Carnell's own children, Jean and John Paul, who were twenty and sixteen years old respectively when their father died, convincingly portray life with a father who was every bit as loving and demonstrative and outgoing with the family as he was reserved and withdrawn outside. Both children warmly recall more or less ritualized activities: family television with their father making the popcorn, Bible reading and discussion every evening around the table after dinner, a cross-country automobile trip the summer before their father died – across the south, up the Atlantic coast to New England for a nostalgic revisiting (for their parents) of the scenes of earlier years, and then back via the northern route. Both gratefully acknowledge their parents' unconditional acceptance of them as individuals, their reluctance to pressure them unduly toward academic achievement or toward particular occupational goals, but their unfailing availability for help when needed. Carnell was a devoted letter writer to both children – three times a week to John Paul away at summer camp, to Jean when she enrolled at Westmont College. The letters were invariably single-spaced typewritten chatty accounts of everything going on at home that would interest them. When Carnell reached the bottom of the page, he would pull out the sheet, write "Love, Dad," and send it off.[121]

The letter he sent to Jean on April 15, 1967, mentions an upcoming conference at which he is scheduled to deliver a lecture. He is apparently relaxed, even a bit flippant, about the prospect: "I have finished the speech I am going to give to the Catholics in Oakland on the 25th of April. I am getting really ecumenical!" He did not live to fulfill that speaking engagement.

F. Death in Oakland: 1967

"I find death undetermined whether ACCIDENTAL OR SUICIDAL."

Verdict of Coroner
State of California
County of Alameda

Eleven years after Edward Carnell's death, his psychiatrist Dr. Philip Wells, retired and living in British Columbia, summarized Carnell's case in this brief paragraph:

It has been over ten years since I worked with Doctor Carnell, and I do not have my records. He was troubled during the years with severe and persistent obsessive thoughts and dreams which he could not prevent. They made him feel very guilty, because of his strict upbringing, and very depressed. He was often angry at the rigidity of creedal and moral codes in which he was trapped by his connection with Fuller Theological Seminary, which was his life work. He got some satisfaction in working some of this out with his students, especially in his ethics class. He was much more gentle and forgiving with others than with himself.[122]

In the absence of both official records and medical expertise, I shall refrain from second-guessing what little I have learned from hearsay about the therapy Dr. Wells prescribed for Carnell, which included electroconvulsive treatments in significant numbers, perhaps approaching as many as fifty.[123] What I will do, however, is convey some of the impressions shared by those who observed what was going on at the time. While friends and colleagues knew that under Wells's care Carnell had been restored to a certain level of everyday capability, some of them harbored serious misgivings. A few at the seminary saw Wells as a rather orthodox Freudian who tended to allow Carnell to see himself as a victim of his past. They felt that a doctor from the post-Freudian existentialist school of psychotherapy might have given him more tools to cope more effectively with his present conflicts.[124] Dr. Wells himself says: "His therapy was not an orthodox Freudian analysis. While there was some analysis, therapy was mostly supportive."[125] Others were suspicious of the dependency apparent in a doctor–patient relationship lasting some six years – and still very much in effect at the time of Carnell's death.[126]

Carnell himself expressed profound gratitude for Wells's help. Although occasionally he would come home from a session and complain that he had just spent good money retelling the same things he had told many times before, his more reflective judgments were unambiguously favorable. On the dedication page of his final published book, *The Burden of Sören Kierkegaard*, he summed up the debt he felt to Dr. Wells and made a clear and candid personal statement to his readers on the value of psychotherapy:

Affectionately dedicated to Dr. Philip H. Wells, chief psychiatrist of the Wells Medical Group, Arcadia, California; without whose personal encouragement it is unlikely that I would have attempted to write this book.

It was surely no small accomplishment for Carnell in the year 1965 to break into print once again with a book on an important philosophical and theological figure. But a closer look indicates that the very nature of the achievement suggests limitations as well as reawakened possibilities. The wording of the dedication obscures the fact that most of the book had been written seventeen years earlier as his Boston University Ph.D. thesis. Very little is new; most of the writing is revision, some of it only minor. But these comments obviously do not undercut the subjective significance of the achievement in the context of Carnell's troubled life.

Whatever the nature of Carnell's dependency on his relationship with Dr. Wells, one fact is certain: He never was able to overcome his addiction to sleeping pills, and that dependency finally proved his undoing. Here is how events developed in the spring of 1967: That year the Bishop's Ecumenical Commission for the Roman Catholic Diocese of Oakland was acting as host for the Fourth National Ecumenical Workshop, to be held in the Claremont Hotel in the hills between Oakland and Berkeley. One member of the organizing committee was a former Fuller Seminary student, Reverend Duke Robinson, then minister at the Montclair Presbyterian Church in Oakland. When Monsignor John Cummins asked whether anyone on the committee knew a likely candidate for leading a seminar on "Evangelicals and Ecumenicity," Robinson immediately recommended Carnell, who in turn accepted the Monsignor's invitation.[127]

The workshop was scheduled to run from Sunday evening through Wednesday, with several hundred delegates and sixty-two speakers delivering formal talks. Carnell was one of three keynote speakers. Dr. Robert McAfee Brown, Professor of Religion at Stanford University, delivered the opening Sunday evening address; conference host Bishop Floyd L. Begin gave the final address; Carnell's address on "Conservative Protestantism" was slated for Tuesday noon.

Before Carnell accepted the invitation, he discussed the matter with his wife and Dr. Wells. By that time they had arrived at a mutual agreement that Mrs. Carnell would dispense the sleeping pills as needed, because of Carnell's occasional unreliability in keeping track of dosage. He had settled into a steady pattern, however, and all three agreed that he was up to making the trip. Mrs. Carnell considered accompanying him, but at the time had a part-time job that conflicted with the conference schedule. At first everything went as planned. Carnell flew to Oakland on Sunday, checked into Room 413 at the hotel, and called home to assure his wife that he was fine.[128]

At that point the situation started to unravel. Duke Robinson went to the opening banquet on Sunday evening hoping to renew his acquaintance with Carnell, who was assigned to a seat at the head table with some twenty-five dignitaries. There was one empty seat, however, and no Carnell. Robinson tells what happened next:

As we were leaving, however, I spotted him in the crowd; for some reason, perhaps because he was not feeling well or because he did not want to be in the spotlight, he had eaten at a regular table. My wife and I approached him. I immediately introduced myself, and while it had been 12 years or so since we had been at Fuller, I expected some recognition. I got very little, and a rather strange reaction, even for him (he had never been most comfortable in social situations); he rather quickly and coldly, although politely, excused himself. As he walked away it seemed to my wife and me that he was dragging a foot, as if he had suffered some kind of paralysis.[129]

Robinson did not see Carnell at either the morning or afternoon sessions on Monday. Monsignor Cummins did not seem disturbed, thought perhaps that Carnell was taking the assignment a bit too seriously, and guessed that he might be working on his speech. We know, of course, that Carnell had finished writing the speech at least by April 15 when he wrote his daughter to that effect. But in retrospect we know also that he was feeling considerable anxiety nonetheless. Monsignor Cummins had received a letter from Carnell during the previous week, expressing some doubt as to whether he should come to the conference, minimizing the contribution he would be able to make, and offering to back out if they had someone else to ask. Cummins had immediately written back reassuring him that they wanted him to come.[130]

On Tuesday morning, with Carnell still conspicuously absent and with the time for his noon address fast approaching, one of the conference officials went with the hotel manager to his room. They found him on the floor, dead. The time of death was estimated to be Monday evening. He had been last seen alive by a hotel maid who opened the door to clean the room at four P.M. She reported later that Carnell was in bed and sat up and assured her he was all right when she asked why he had not answered the telephone. The Alameda County Coroner declared that "death was caused by pulmonary congestion and edema due to barbiturate intoxication, suffered at an undetermined time, on the estimated date of April 14, 1967, at the Claremont Hotel, Oakland, California."

Edward Carnell ingested an unknown amount of barbiturates.
Alcohol determination——Absent
Barbiturate determination——3.5 MG% (Calculate as Mixed). (Secobarbital and Amobarbital)
Salicylates—Absent
I find death undetermined whether ACCIDENTAL or SUICIDAL.[131]

Shirley Carnell identified the body, which was then flown back to Los Angeles. President Hubbard called the faculty together on Tuesday afternoon, read a portion of Second Corinthians, Chapter five, and broke the news to them. On Wednesday morning, faculty member Carlton Booth led a short chapel service consisting of scripture reading, prayer, and a few quietly sung hymns. On Friday, April 28, funeral services were held at the Lake Avenue Congregational Church, with interment at Rose Hills Memorial Park in Whittier.

Dying alone in a hotel room, Carnell never had a chance to share any carefully chosen last words. And yet, in a sense, he did. We have the text of the speech he never gave to the conference delegates: "The Conservative Protestant: Who Is He and What Is His Relation to the Ecumenical Movement?"[132] In answering those questions, Carnell managed to touch on many of the themes that had absorbed his attention throughout his career, some of which we will explore in Part Two of this book: the infallibility of the Bible, the forensic explanation of salvation, the nature of faith as belief based on sufficient evidences, fundamentalist status by negation, and the danger of "the swamps of subjectivity." More germane to the subject at hand, however, are several passages that, while primarily meant to explain why some Protestants and Catholics are fearful of ecumenical dialogue, reveal more of Carnell's own insecurities than he perhaps intended. For example, he referred to "the conscious or unconscious threat to personal security that an individual often experiences when he is confronted with reasons why he must re-examine what he comfortably believed was beyond need of re-examination." "It is not easy," he said, "for any person to become flexible about convictions that he has somehow identified with his worth as a person." And "we shall only delude ourselves if we think we can easily persuade a rigidly structured mentality to realize that the rigidity, in large part, is merely a gratification of psychological needs." His final words, though, strike a chord of hope and courage:

> But all is not lost. Otherwise I would not have had a deep, spiritual motive to come and share your fellowship. I retain a glimmer of hope, though candidly it is no more than a glimmer. This hope emerges out of the very elements of courtesy and personal respect that bind us together. It may be that if we act humbly and consistently within *general* revelation, God in his loving mercy may grant us new illumination as we strive for unity in our interpretation of *special* revelation. I fully realize that our ignorance of divine truths surpasses our understanding. But perhaps this is not as serious as that strange form of ignorance which denies its ignorance. If we once rally courage to accept our limits, we may not find it quite so painful to admit that we know in part.
>
> In any event, thank you for the invitation to be with you.

In an attempt to sift out conflicting evidence, make some interpretations, and gain some perspective, I shall have to find some last words of my own concerning the life and death of Edward Carnell. First, however, something else makes a rightful claim on our attention.

In his *life*, Carnell went public with considerable ambivalence, much preferring (as he often declared) the cloistered life of the scholar. In his *writing*, however, he emulated the spirit of Milton's "Areopagitica," distrusting "a fugitive and cloistered virtue" and believing that "in a free and open encounter" the truth would not finally be defeated. No responsible discussion of Carnell can avoid a conscientious examination of the books and articles that resulted from this public commitment. We turn, then, to the arena where this struggle took place – the printed word where, said Milton, resides "the breath of reason itself."

Part two

CHAPTER VII

Apologetics of the mind:
toward the penumbral zone

In his novel *Beecher,* Dan McCall has the Reverend Henry Ward Beecher counsel his younger brother Tommy, who has been reexamining his theological beliefs: "If you wish to compute your doctrinal latitude you may discover much more than you wish to know, Tommy. Evade exact definition, and keep the fruits of faith."[1] Whatever whiff of practical wisdom we sense in Beecher's statement, the advice exudes more pervasively the sweet prudential smell of worldly success. At all costs "keep the fruits of faith" – whether internal or external. And if that means ignoring the hard questions, or pirouetting around them like a dancing bear, so be it.

Tommy would never have received that kind of advice from Edward Carnell. Hard questions about the Christian faith were not to be evaded. By nature and profession he was more like another character from contemporary fiction. In Frederick Buechner's novel *The Final Beast,*[2] Rooney Vail, an offbeat and strikingly attractive young married woman, joins the Reverend Theodore Nicolet's church more to please her husband than out of any personal conviction. In fact, she is quite outspoken about her lack of interest: "If I were God," she says, "I'm damned if I'd be so interested in religion and churches. I'd be interested in making things. I'd always be making marvelous new worlds, and marvelous new kinds of people to put in them . . . babies." Nevertheless, as often happens, it is she rather than her husband who comes regularly to church. She makes light of her faithfulness, telling Nicolet that "she was no good at praying and the hymns were too high for her and that she could never remember what his sermons were about." So she adds up the hymn numbers. "Somebody's got to do it. And if they come out even, that's good.") But then the suppressed anger rises to the surface: "There's just one reason, you know, why I come dragging in there every Sunday. I want to find out if the whole thing's true. Just *true.* That's all. Either it is or it isn't, and that's the one question you avoid like death."

From the time his mind was awakened, in Gordon Clark's philosophy classes, until the last night of his life, in an Oakland hotel, the lodestar of Carnell's life was the insistence that the most difficult question of all be faced head-on: Is it true? The Reverend Theodore Nicolet found it impossible to shake off the brooding figure of Rooney Vail sitting in the next to last pew, "usually in black with her red hair in a bun tucked under her broad-brimmed black hat, a witch or a nun." In Carnell's case, what is most compelling and, finally, more revealing is that the person who inevitably backed him into a corner was himself.

In a new preface he wrote in 1952 for the fourth edition of *An Introduction to Christian Apologetics*,[3] Carnell acknowledged that apologetics is not for everybody. God, he said, has given people different types of minds and interests. Whereas there are Christians who experience a "direct, intuitively grasped acceptance" of Christianity and are not troubled by rational objections to the faith, he classes himself with the questioners whose hearts cannot believe what their minds reject as false. It is this latter group for whom he writes. "My concern is to encourage those who, like myself, feel a burning within them to know if Christianity can be accepted with the consent of all our faculties." Carnell asked questions and gave answers. Whether Rooney Vail would have been satisfied is something else again. And that is what apologetics is all about.

A. "Always be prepared to make a defense"

Apologetical effectiveness, like beauty, is in the eye of the beholder. If your mind has an apologetic bent at all, whether C. S. Lewis speaks to you more convincingly than Paul Tillich or Hans Kung or James Orr will depend just as much on a complex interplay of subjective factors as on the chain of evidential argument. This natural tendency can be overdone. Even as some people subconsciously define an alcoholic as "anyone who drinks more than I do," those who take Christian belief seriously sometimes hear voices whispering words of advice: "Anyone more conservative than you is an irrelevant reactionary" or "Anyone to your left is a dangerous heretic."

Furthermore, the entire apologetic enterprise has fallen on bad times even in evangelical circles. In his recent book *After Fundamentalism: The Future of Evangelical Theology*, Bernard Ramm (long an evangelical spokesman himself) goes so far as to sound the death knell: "Traditional apologetics has lost its case to the children of the Enlightenment, and a reading of evangelical literature on Christian apologetics shows that this message has not been heard very clearly in evangelical circles."[4]

One difficulty is that apologetic systems seek to "prove" too much. Exiled Polish philosopher Leszek Kolakowski may not have had apologetics specifically in mind when he made the following statement, but the net of his language clearly is wide enough to take it in: "I rather tend to accept the law of infinite cornucopia which applies not only to philosophy but to all general theories in the human and social sciences; it states that there is never a shortage of arguments to support any doctrine you want to believe in for whatever reasons."[5]

Sören Kierkegaard, writing in the nineteenth century, saw apologetics not only as useless but counterproductive. Its devotees "did not observe that the more reasons one adduces, the more one nourished doubt and the stronger it becomes, that to present doubt with reasons with the intent of slaying it is like giving to a hungry monster one wants to be rid of the delicious food it likes best."[6] Carnell disagreed with Kierkegaard, commenting on this very passage: "The apologist firmly believes that it is easier to become a Christian when the weight of probable evidence is more in his favor than against him, while Kierkegaard vehemently disagreed."[7] So much for that. The drummer to whose beat Carnell marched was the Apostle Peter: "Always be prepared to make a defense to any one who calls you to account for the hope that is in you, yet do it with gentleness and reverence" (I Peter 3:15).

Carnell repeatedly cited the First Peter reference as his biblical authority for doing the work of apologetics. It is a mighty leap, however, from that apostolic counsel to a full-blown systematic philosophical theism. Whereas Carnell considered it *necessary* to include a biblical component in the foundation underlying the apologetic superstructure, he knew it was not *sufficient*. Even adding the subjective need of people like himself for rationally convincing arguments was not enough of a justification. Apologetics needed a third pillar of support, and Carnell found it in church history. In every age critics have hurled potentially damaging accusations at Christianity.

Is there nothing that the Christian can do? Must he sit by idly and allow skeptics to ridicule his faith? The church has risen to the challenge by commissioning apologists to answer critical questions.[8]

That being true, the agenda for apologists cannot be entirely controlled by Christianity's defenders. They must answer the questions that are being asked at a given time, said Carnell. His illustration was Augustine, who faced the charge that Christianity was hostile to the state and in a sense responsible for the destruction of Rome. Finding an area of common agreement between the Christian gospel and the Roman culture, Augustine showed that "Christ is the absolute embodiment of whatever relative virtues were celebrated in the national heroes of Rome." And then Carnell added: "I think that Augustine went at things in the right way." He looked back over his own career in apologetics and isolated the particular point of contact between the gospel and culture in each of four books. In *An Introduction to Christian Apologetics* it was the law of contradiction; in *A Philosophy of the Christian Religion* it was values; in *Christian Commitment* the judicial sentiment; and in *The Kingdom of Love and the Pride of Life* the law of love.[9]

Carnell considered these varying approaches incremental, not mutually exclusive. He did not think of himself as having come on a journey in which the earlier stages had to be sloughed off. Each new apologetic approach represented a new way to make the gospel credible to the modern secular mind. One characteristic remained constant, however, in Carnell's effort to fulfill the apologetic mandate in First Peter: the double criterion of verification, which he called *systematic consistency*.

Systematic consistency is the combination of formal and material truth. It is a *consistency* because it is based upon a rigid application of the law of contradiction, and it is a *systematic* consistency because the data which are formed into this consistent system are taken from the totality of our experience within and without. (ICA 59)

This affirmation, in turn, is a theoretical outgrowth of an even more fundamental enduring conviction:

In the contest between the rational and the empirical schools of thought, a Christian must pitch his interests somewhere between the two extremes. If he surrenders the *rationes aeterne* (the norms by which we judge), he ends up with a high and dry philosophy. I have not retreated one millimeter from this conviction.[10]

We shall look, then, at both elements of Carnell's test for truth: nonviolation of the law of contradiction and devotion to all the facts of experience. As we do so, we shall come back now and then to Rooney Vail, that brooding figure in the next to last pew of Theodore Nicolet's church – taking for granted, of course, that when she asks the question "Is it true?" she is willing to make a certain commitment to the search and is not merely looking for some benign ecclesiastical paterfamilias who will stroke her gently on the head and say, "Yes, Rooney, God's in his heaven and all's right with the world."

B. "The most perfect philosophical argument ever devised"

In Book Four of the *Metaphysics*, Aristotle developed the law of contradiction, which declared that "the firmest of all principles is that it is impossible for the same thing to belong and not to belong to the same thing at the same time in the same respect." He demonstrated that the Skeptics, in their very effort to deny the law, confirmed its validity. Carnell repeatedly endorsed this law as the bedrock of his own apologetics – indeed of *any* valid philosophical system and of all significant speech.

Significant speech *must* obey the law of contradiction. It seems to me that this is the most perfect philosophical argument ever devised. A skeptic establishes the law of contradiction by his very effort to deny it. There is no meaningful way to escape the force of this demonstration. (CC 40)

As an absolute, the law of contradiction does not itself demand proof. "The only demonstration of any absolute is this: Without the presupposition of its existence nothing else has meaning – not even the denial of that absolute" (PCR 186).

These statements might lead one to guess that the law of contradiction is something on which the confraternity of traditional Christian apologists agree. They do not. Two of Carnell's professors – Gordon Clark at Wheaton College and Cornelius Van Til at Westminster Seminary, both unembarrassedly dogmatic in their Calvinistic theology – nevertheless differ significantly on this very issue. Their differences may help us to define Carnell's own position more precisely. In Clark's system, the task of apologetics is primarily negative – to lay bare the contradictions and inconsistencies in all non-Christian positions through application of the law of contradiction. Positively, the only position that comes through this process unscathed is biblical trinitarian Christianity. Farther than this, apologetics cannot go. As Van Til sees it, for Christianity to go even this far is suicidal. To use the law of contradiction as a criterion – that is, to require that the Christian faith have a rational foundation – is tantamount to demanding that the Creator pass a test set up by the creature.[11] "The only 'proof' of the Christian position is that unless its truth is presupposed there is no possibility of 'proving' anything at all."[12] Or to put it another way, "The Christian is bound to believe and hold that his system of doctrine is certainly true and that other systems are certainly false. And he must say this about a system of doctrine which involves the existence and sovereign action of a self-contained God whose ways are past finding out."[13]

Carnell rejected both of these positions. As I have earlier pointed out, he and Van Til discussed the problem at length on a Boston visit Van Til made during Carnell's Harvard years. As Van Til recalls the conversation, "He was sure, as he told me during a whole day we spent together discussing these matters, that since I did not do justice to Aristotle's fourth book of the *Metaphysics*, my faith must be a blind faith. He was sure I could make no intelligible contact with the unbeliever."[14] The break with Clark's position was less definitive. In contrast with Van Til's unquestioning acceptance of the biblically revealed Christian position as a starting point, both Clark and Carnell, although accepting that same Christian position, do so as a *hypothesis* that must be subjected to epistemological verification. For Carnell especially, the initial presupposition of the triune God Who has revealed Himself in the Bible is a sort of heuristic device to get all the right issues out in the open where they can be put to the test of consistency. Carnell differs from Clark in his insistence that the law of contradiction by itself does only half the job of apologetics. It can knock out the underpinnings of false views and demonstrate Christianity's internal self-consistency. But the apologist must also demonstrate that Christianity squares with the full range of external and internal facts – with fewer difficulties than any other position.

To put it as succinctly as possible: (1) in Clark's apologetics, the law of contradiction is both necessary and sufficient; (2) in Van Til's, it is neither necessary nor sufficient; (3) in Carnell's, it is necessary but not sufficient.

One has to admire Carnell's courage. Not only was he not content with Van Til's Fideism (the unquestioning acceptance on faith alone of Christianity's ultimate and absolute truth); neither was he willing to remain in the privileged sanctuary of Clark's self-contained rational consistency. The apologetical triumphs made possible by such strategies fall critically short of what the truly questioning mind demands. Mere internal coherence does not guarantee the truth of any thought system.

Now what of Rooney Vail? By this time her attention has probably strayed and she is back at her old self-imposed task of adding up the hymn numbers. With good reason, one is tempted to add. Perhaps we can recapture her attention if we leave behind these esoteric theoretical distinctions and look instead at how Carnell puts the law of contradiction into practice. The fact that he does not cite many specific violations should not surprise us; it does, after all, take some effort to imagine world-class philosophers and theologians blundering into a situation in which they declare, even implicitly, that the same thing belongs and does not belong to the same thing at the same time in the same respect. This is not to minimize the importance of the principle. It is every bit as fundamental to rational discourse as Aristotle said it was. But not every alleged violation of the law of contradiction holds up in court.

Our first example comes from *An Introduction to Christian Apologetics*. Carnell claims that the Reformation resulted from an application of systematic consistency to the teachings of the Roman Catholic Church.

The Reformers, one and all, saw that the Bible teaches we are saved *solely* by grace through faith, while the Romish Church says we are saved by grace *plus* the merit

which accrues by our own good works. In a rational universe these two propositions cannot simultaneously be true. (ICA 73)

We should acknowledge first that except for the pejorative label "Romish," this is hardly a low blow at Roman Catholicism. Carnell correctly
argues that the Reformers singled out a difference that really did make a
difference. But are the teachings of the Bible and the Catholic Church on
this particular point *logically* contradictory? Considering that various
biblical passages discuss good works as the necessary fruits of salvation
that give evidence that regeneration has actually taken place – and that the
Epistle of James declares that "by works a man is justified, and not by
faith only" (James 2:24) – we might better class these statements not as
logical contradictions but as generalizations that oversimplify nonetheless
real historical differences.

As we have already seen, Carnell often staked out his own positions in
contradistinction to those held by Reinhold Niebuhr. He quotes a passage from *Human Destiny* in order to show how in Niebuhr's theology
logical consistency plays second fiddle to religious experience. The subject of the Niebuhr passage has to do with the disturbing recognition that
even the recipients of divine saving grace are not exempt from the tendency to continue sinning:

"It is not easy to express both these two aspects of the life of grace, to which all
history attests without seeming to offend the canons of logic. That is one reason
why moralists have always found it rather easy to discount the doctrine of 'justification by faith.' But here, as in many cases, a seeming defiance of logic is merely
the consequence of an effort to express complex facts of experience." (PCR 492)

Niebuhr thus carefully makes it clear that he is not defying "the canons of
logic." But that is not enough for Carnell. He says:

A "seeming" defiance of logic lies so perilously close to an actual defiance, that it
serves as a flag of warning for philosophers of religion to proceed with caution.
The actual difference between a seeming, and real, defiance might be skillfully
obliterated by a dictator armed with an intention to rule the world. (PCR 493)

If we examine these two statements closely (eliminating the red herring of
a hypothetical world dictator), we can see a troublesome issue: "the
canons of logic" versus "the complex facts of experience." In another
passage, exactly the same tension shows up. Carnell first lets Niebuhr
make his point:

"Formally there can be of course no conflict between logic and truth. The laws of
logic are reason's guard against chaos in the realm of truth. They eliminate contra-

dictory assertions. But there is no resource in logical rules to help us understand complex phenomena, exhibiting characteristics which seem to require that they be placed into contradictory categories of reason. Loyalty to all the facts may require a provisional defiance of logic, lest complexity in the facts of experience be denied for the sake of a premature logical consistency." (TRN 93)

In a footnote, Carnell underscores his disagreement: "A veritable nest of difficulties will emerge as a result of this sweeping methodological concession." There surely are difficulties. But they are not essentially caused by a methodological concession. Many of the difficulties that trouble Carnell can be attributed to the fact that, when it comes down to a question of whether a violation of the law of contradiction has occurred, there is ample room for honest disagreement.

If we think back to Carnell's *systematic consistency*, the twofold principle of verification, we can see that the logic–experience tension is not merely a matter of Carnell versus Niebuhr or evangelicalism versus neo-orthodoxy. It goes to the heart of the Carnellian verification principle itself, for if "consistency" concerns the canons of logic, "systematic" has to do with the complex facts of experience. To the formal validity of logic, Carnell insists on adding the material validity that comes only from exposure to "the concrete facts of history." As we shall see, however, it takes more than courage to develop a convincing Christian apologetic in the implacable face of historical reality and empirical fact.

C. "A devotion to all of the facts of experience"

In one of the passages Carnell quoted from Niebuhr's *Human Destiny*, Niebuhr faced the troubling persistence of sin in the redeemed person's life. In the very next sentence, he sought to do justice to the complexities of experience by resorting to paradox: "It happens to be true to the facts of experience that in one sense the converted man is righteous and that in another sense he is not."[15] But Carnell cut off the Niebuhr quotation right at the point where this sentence begins, probably because he knew that to include it would have seriously compromised his argument. For this sentence explains precisely why Niebuhr's view is only a "seeming defiance of logic," not a logical contradiction. Paradox does not violate logic; it is only an apparent contradiction for the sake of effect. In this case, when one sorts out the different meanings of "righteous," the apparent contradiction disappears.

Carnell's discomfort with the language of paradox runs through all his writings. It erupted to the surface in an illuminating way in connection with the Barth seminar. One of the questions Carnell directed at Barth concerned the ontological reality of evil, but because of the way the question was worded, Barth's answer finally focused down on the objective reality (or unreality) of the devil. Here is the relevant portion of that answer:

To go on to the next point, my answer is that sin and evil have an ontological being of their own kind. A kind of being which can only be described in purely negative terms. As, for example, I should say sin and evil, and the devil himself, are impossible possibilities. Or, if you prefer, unreal realities. It cannot be helped – that is their nature because sinning means living a lie. You can describe a lie only in terms of a lie.[16]

When Carnell gave his report on the seminar to the Fuller faculty and students (a talk reprinted in slightly different form in *Christian Century*), he offered these comments on Barth's answer:

I was disturbed by the ease with which he employed the language of paradox. When I inquired, for example, about the metaphysical status of the devil, Barth was satisfied to speak of him as "an impossible possibility." Perhaps I need another course in logic, for the language of paradox strikes me as plain "weasel-wording."

Let me illustrate. Suppose my wife, on returning from a weekend trip, were to ask if I had fed and clothed the children according to our agreement, and suppose I were to reply, in a mood of detachment, "It is an impossible possibility." I am sure that my wife would look me in the eye and demand that I answer with a plain Yes or No. To violate the law of contradiction, whether in marriage or in theology, is no innocent matter. (CBC 153, 154)

Granted that the language of paradox can be used as an evasion, granted that there are other ways to treat the issue of a personal devil – nevertheless, equating the question "Is there an objective devil?" with "Have you fed the children?" and identifying Barth's paradoxical phrase "impossible possibility" as a violation of the law of contradiction were unworthy tactics that demeaned both Barth and Carnell himself.

What is it about the language of paradox that made Carnell so uncomfortable? Niebuhr, I think, has already given us the clue in his reference to "complexity in the facts of experience." The facts of real existence are so inescapable and so messy that we cannot reduce them to the neat categories of logic. We need to draw on the complete range of resources available to us in language – not just paradox but myth, metaphor, parable – if we hope to get some sort of conceptual handle on the chaos of reality. Carnell was no fool; he had eyes to see and ears to hear the complex data of existence. But he faced a dilemma. Having committed himself irrevocably to "all of the facts of experience" as part of his verification principle, he could not retreat to the more secure apologetic home bases of Clark and Van Til. On the other hand, having opened the floodgates of empiricism, he faced the threat of drowning in the turbulent seas of history and life experience.

The irony is inescapable. When Carnell opted for the strategy of appealing to experience as a validation of Christianity, he had to devise (both consciously and unconsciously, I should say) counterstrategies to keep the facts of experience at a distance. His strategy at this point was to force the issues of apologetics into Procrustean twin beds of either/or. He settled for a two-valued orientation in which one must opt for either *this* or *that*.

Fortunately, he had an inner voice that kept whispering to him that life is not that simple. In his generally level-headed book *Television: Servant or Master?* (the polarized title of which belies its basic approach), Carnell argues convincingly that all of life is mixture, that nothing natural or human is either wholly good or wholly bad, and that television's future will depend on how human beings sort out its perils and potential. Even here, however, he slips into an unjustified dichotomy that does not do justice to the actual conditions in the modern mass media. "There is no satisfying alternative," he says. "Either God is the captain of the television industry, or man is" (TSM 20). Whatever happened to mixture?

Carnell adds a touch of class to this either/or response by giving it (or, to be more accurate, its opposite) a venerable Latin term, *tertium quid*, which he defines as "A third somewhat. A mediating alternative which one may choose when pressed into a dilemma" (ICA 368). There could hardly be a better illustration of how Carnell uses the "no *tertium quid*" strategy than the passage in *An Introduction to Christian Apologetics* where the phrase itself appears:

> One of the easiest yet surest ways to test a man's allegiance to the Christian faith is to pose one question: What is the relation between God and the process of history? He will either aver that the Almighty originally created the world out of nothing by free, sovereign power, and presently decrees the movement of history according to the counsels of His own will, both majestically to display His infinite perfection and glory, and to bring many sons to salvation through the free grace merited by the redemptive work of his beloved Son, Jesus Christ, or he will not. There is no *tertium quid*. (ICA 276)

Note the only two alternatives we are given. On one side, a list of specific criteria that summarize "the Christian faith"; on the other side, only negation. One is not inclined to dispute Carnell's claim that this is an *easy* way to test a person's allegiance to the Christian faith. Whether it is a *sure* way (as he also claims) or a *fair* way is another matter. This particular game of apologetics is being played with loaded dice. By what right does

Carnell say there is no third way? Or a fourth way? Or a fourteenth? It is simply not true to our experience that "there are two sides to every question"; there are innumerable sides to most questions. But by arbitrarily disqualifying all options except Yes or No, Carnell sloughs off the responsibility to examine a whole array of possible positions on the complex middle ground of ambiguity. He uses a comparable strategy in the argument of *A Philosophy of the Christian Religion*, where his stated objective is to establish "a dialectic of despair as *the* alternative to the Christian option" (PCR 45, italics added). Either Christianity (as Carnell defines it) or despair. Take your choice; there are no other options. Whatever else we may think of "no *tertium quid*" as a debating technique, we must judge it ill-suited to an apologist who claims "a devotion to all of the facts of experience" and an insistence on finding out "if Christianity can be accepted with the consent of all our faculties."

Carnell did change his apologetic approach in some ways as he grew older, but he used variations on the "no *tertium quid*" maneuver even in the late writings. In *The Case for Orthodox Theology*, he argues that "when orthodoxy is called on to verify its claims, it appeals to the axiom that undergirds a decent society: *namely, that in all matters where a good man is competent to judge, his word should be accepted unless sufficient reasons are found for rejecting it*" (COT 82). In this case, the good man whose word we should accept is Jesus.

> Jesus is a good man because he verified everything that a decent society means by goodness. Not doctrinal teaching alone, not superior intellect, but a consistent exhibition of self-giving love – *this* is what holds us. Love is the substance of rectitude, and Jesus loved God with all his heart and his neighbor as himself. He healed the sick, raised the dead, comforted the sorrowing, and shed his blood for sinners. Therefore, if we can trust the word of any man, we can all the more trust the Word of Jesus Christ; for he is the absolute embodiment of whatever relative goodness we acknowledge in one another. (COT 82)

Some Christians might quibble about how that testimony is worded in one or two places, but most will accept it pretty much at face value. We should note, however, that Carnell is reaching for much more than an affirmation of the goodness of Jesus. The larger claim is that we can accept as truth whatever he has said. Here is where Carnell introduces the either/or:

> This conclusion can be voided only by an egregious disregard of elementary logic and morals. Either it must be proved that the axiom of a decent society is not true, or it must be proved that Jesus Christ is not a good man. The first proof, if successful, would do more than invalidate this or that decent society; it would invalidate the very *possibility* of a decent society. And the second proof can only

succeed by repudiating the most firmly established evidences: "For this thing was not done in a corner" (Acts 26:26). Nineteen centuries of critical scholarship support the claim that Jesus Christ lived a sinless life. If we reject the goodness of Christ, despite this weight of scholarship, we court incredulity. In such a case we invalidate the possibility of *truth*, let alone a decent society. (COT 82, 83)

Here, then, is orthodoxy's first line of proof: "The gospel is true because Jesus Christ, the Lord of the church, says it is true." Setting aside the worrisome recognition that good men and women have often been wrong about one thing and another, let us ask only whether at this point Carnell is showing "a devotion to all of the facts of experience." I suggest not. Although he blithely cites "nineteen centuries of critical scholarship," his "no *tertium quid*" strategy effectively slams the door on anything modern scholarship might have to say about the historical Jesus and the reliability of the New Testament record.

The Case for Orthodox Theology is crucial in any attempt to take the measure of Carnell the apologist. For one thing, by the time he wrote it, as a veteran writer of five published books, as a teacher whose ideas had been tested in the classroom for over a dozen years, and as an administrator whose idealism had been tempered by institutional realities, he must be thought of as having attained his maturity. If he had tasted success, he had known too the bitterness of failure – most especially seeing what he considered his best work ignored (when Macmillan in unseemly haste remaindered his book *Christian Commitment*). Consequently, the request from Westminster Press to participate in the *Case* trilogy was a welcome tonic. We know too, from conversations he held at the time with close associates, that he did not take the responsibility lightly.[17]

As *the case* for orthodox theology, however, the book leaves much to be desired. A clue to its fundamental shortcoming appears on the first page of the Preface. On the one hand Carnell declares that apologetics changes with the times: "Since attacks on the faith are being constantly revised, each generation must formulate its own defensive strategies" (COT 13). That is not the shortcoming to which I refer; indeed, one suspects that the Westminster editors selected Carnell because they believed he would do exactly that – develop an orthodox apologetic for our time. But on the same page he also says this: "The theology of orthodoxy looks to a long tradition of exegetical and confessional labor. I have made a heavy draft on this tradition. There is no other way, short of outright plagiarism, to bring orthodoxy's case before the modern mind." This statement also makes a good deal of sense. By definition, one should expect the case for orthodox theology to stress the unchanging validity of historic Christian truth and thus to rely somewhat on sources from the past. The problem to which I refer surfaces in the implementation of the declared dual purpose: the apologetic defense of a *traditional* faith against *modern* objections. The result is an anachronism. A pre–twentieth-century mentality dominates the entire book. The authority figures, quoted repeatedly and often at great length, are men such as William Paley, Charles Hodge, William G. T. Shedd, William Cunningham, Matthew Henry, Horatius Bonar – all of them theologians, apologists, or Bible expositors from another era. Even the more recent authorities, such as B. B. Warfield, James Orr, and Abraham Kuyper, are figures from a world gone by. Furthermore, the quotations are so lengthy and so frequent that at times Carnell seems almost to disappear from his own book. In one chapter, for example, out of 541 lines of text, 295 (or fifty-five percent) are quoted from these sources. It is not my purpose to devalue certain theologians because they wrote in another century. However, this book is a work of apologetics that explicitly claims to formulate a strategy appropriate to its own generation. On its own terms it must be judged a failure. It would have been a vastly different book if Carnell had seriously adhered to the empirical part of his verification principle: "a devotion to all of the facts of experience." As it is, too much has been left out. It is not sufficient, for example, to annotate the names of Joseph Butler and William Paley, on a collateral reading list, with the brief observation that "when examining these sources, however, due allowance should be made for the intellectual climate that prevailed in the seventeenth and eighteenth centuries" (COT 90, 91). Yes indeed. That is exactly what we would like to read about. What are Carnell's thoughts as to how the mid–twentieth-century intellectual climate differs from theirs? Of what significance are those differences to a traditional orthodox religion? Has the orthodoxy of 1959 found some better answers to the old questions? And what of the new questions Butler and Paley could not even have guessed? The kinds of questions in Rooney Vail's mind? Of all this we get almost nothing.

Rooney Vail again. It is time we returned to her persistent question that is the testing ground of any apologetic effort: Is it true? But in order to do that, there is one more fact that we must know about the woman herself. Fictional characters admittedly sometimes get loose from their creators and go their own way; critics with particular axes to grind have been known to track them even farther afield. Fortunately, when we ascribe theological significance to Rooney Vail, we can be sure we are not piling on a burden her creator never intended her to bear. She is not the caricatured bored suburban woman who, in her susceptibility to the latest spiritual fad, got tired of TM, is now flirting with Christianity, and next year will be primed for a fling with EST. Frederick Buechner, the author who created her, has said that he purposely developed the character

Rooney Vail as the fictional embodiment of the question that Karl Barth says people have in mind when they come to church.[18] Barth articulates the question in *The Word of God and the Word of Man*. In the face of all that threatens Christian faith – "the impenetrable muteness of the so-called nature that surrounds us, the chance and shadowy existence of every single thing in time, the ill fortune and ill fate of nations and individuals, the basic evil, death" – "the question will no longer down, but breaks out in flame: *is it true?*" We are misled, says Barth, when we think that people will be satisfied with "secondary utterances," when their "last and profoundest questions" are given "next-to-the-last and less profound answers."

The serious meaning of the situation in our churches is that the people want to hear the *word*, that is, the answer to the question by which, whether they know it or not, they are actually animated, *Is it true?*[19]

So when Rooney Vail says to the Reverend Theodore Nicolet, "There's just one reason, you know, why I come dragging in there every Sunday. I want to find out if the whole thing's true," we should be hearing not just her voice but also the voice of the twentieth-century's most dominant theologian giving expression to the most profound question the men and women of modern times can ask of the Christian preacher and apologist.

Carnell's apologetic approach may be flawed, but not because he avoids Rooney's Barthian question. If Rooney were to express dissatisfaction with Carnell, it would more likely be on the grounds that he had not listened hard enough to the many subtexts of the one basic question. As Barth said, people are not listening for "mere assertion."

Whether the objections are fair or unfair, shrewd or silly, ought we not in a way to accept them, as David did the stone-throwing of Shimei, the son of Gera, with the thought that there is a reason behind them – rather than to rush to defend ourselves against them in the armor of a subtle but questionable apologetic? Would it not be wiser to let certain storms which threaten quietly work out upon us their purifying strength than to meet them at once with an ecclesiastical counterstorm?[20]

"A subtle but questionable apologetic." In this discussion what I have found most questionable in Carnell's apologetics is an unimaginative propensity toward the canons of logic, not only on the rational side of his "systematic consistency," where he claims far too wide an application for the law of contradiction, but also on the empirical side, where he tries to force the complex facts of experience into an either/or straitjacket. It can hardly have escaped the reader's notice, however, that after Rooney Vail asks "Is it true?" she tacks on an either/or comment of her own: "Either it is or it isn't." What makes the two-sided alternative all right for Rooney but all wrong for Carnell? The answer, of course, is that Buechner intends Rooney's question finally to be Barth's. And Barth's way is that of the dialectic. In discussing how the minister ought to go about answering the churchgoer's most profound question in terms of Christianity's most profound affirmation – namely, that God has become man – Barth suggests "three ways we might take in the direction of finding such an answer, and they all three end with the insight that we cannot reach it." The three ways are dogmatism, self-criticism, and dialectic. He chooses the last as intrinsically the best:

The great truths of dogmatism and self-criticism are presupposed by it, but so also is their fragmentariness, their merely relative nature. This way from the outset undertakes seriously and positively to develop the idea of God on the one hand and the criticism of man and all things human on the other; but they are not now considered independently but are both referred constantly to their common presupposition, to the living truth which, to be sure, may not be named, but which lies between them and gives to both their meaning and interpretation.[21]

In other words, the "living truth" lies somewhere in the tension between the Either and the Or. For this reason, the life of faith is an enormous risk even for the one who proclaims from the pulpit, "It *is* true."

But how now shall the necessary dependence of both sides of the truth upon this living Center be established? The genuine dialectician knows that this Center cannot be apprehended or beheld, and he will not if he can help it allow himself to be drawn into giving direct information about it, knowing that *all* such information, whether it be positive or negative, is *not* really information, but always *either* dogma *or* self-criticism. On this narrow ridge of rock one can only walk: if he attempts to stand still, he will fall either to the right or to the left, but fall he must. There remains only to keep walking – an appalling performance for those who are not free from dizziness – looking *from one side to the other*, from positive to negative and from negative to positive.[22]

That is to say, Barth's use of either/or in *The Word of God and the Word of Man* is not in the least reductive. Consequently, although he may not have thought of himself as an apologist in the narrow sense, if we broaden our understanding of what an apologist does – if, for example, we set aside logical terminology and (following Stephen Toulmin's lead) think rather of "the soundness of the claims we make"[23] – we can justifiably maintain that Barth all along was doing apologetics in the best sense of the word.

D. "One must preserve a penumbral zone in his theology"

Until the eighteenth or nineteenth century, as Robert Bellah points out, religious unbelief was confined to intellectual elites. "The masses," he says, "have been afflicted not with nonbelief but with overbelief, at least from the point of religious orthodoxy, in a dismaying variety of magical notions, superstitions, and taboos."[24] We can see a particularly vivid example of this tendency in the people's reaction to a devastating extended drought in Sicily in 1893. As John Steward Collis tells it, none of the usual religious rituals did any good: prayers, vigils, masses, even scourgings and fireworks.

At last all patience was exhausted. Some saints were banished. At Palermo St. Joseph was put outside to observe the state of the weather himself. Other saints were turned with their faces to the wall, like naughty children. Others were ducked or insulted, while St. Angelo was put in irons and threatened with drowning or hanging. "Rain or the rope!" roared the mob, shaking their fists in his face.[25]

This is not 1893 and we are not Sicilian peasants; such credulity is almost beyond our ken. And yet we are repeatedly taken aback by what supposedly sophisticated people believe in modern times. Witness the extraordinary popularity of Hal Lindsey's *The Late Great Planet Earth*,[26] with its fantastic, intricately detailed vision of the end-times based on selected apocalyptic passages from the Bible, mechanistically interpreted as history written down before the fact.

It would be unfair to tar Carnell with that particular brush. He did, after all, spend his entire adult life trying to show that orthodox Christianity is intellectually respectable. Moreover, among those for whom intellectual respectability is not a prime value, he made countless enemies with his criticism of fundamentalism as cultic. One of the hallmarks of the cultic mind, he insisted, is that it courts credulity, believing where it should doubt (COT 28). Nevertheless, as we have seen, the Carnellian apologetic has credulity problems of its own. It too easily brushes aside serious objections, too quickly declares difficult questions answered. Symptomatic of this tendency – perhaps even partly a cause – is Carnell's definition of faith (*generic* faith, not *saving* faith) as "the resting of the mind in the sufficiency of the evidence." Whether one consults early, middle, or late Carnell, the definition is an unqualified constant.

When one comes across this definition on rereading various passages in his books, the mind registers a small click, the subconscious warning that a mistake of some kind may accidentally have crept into the text. What one expects to read is something like this: Faith is a resting of the mind in spite of *insufficient* evidence. If the evidence is *sufficient*, why call it faith?

Theologian Van Harvey says: "Religious belief, in the nature of the case, seems to involve either the believing of propositions with no evidence or, more often, an intellectual commitment incommensurate with the evidence to which it appeals."[27] But what kind of evidence is admissible, and how does one locate the line between insufficient and sufficient? Carnell expands on these important issues in his late book *The Kingdom of Love and the Pride of Life,* where he maintains that the criterion of sufficient evidence is no different from the standard by which we judge *anything* meaningful:

> For example, cultured people believe that Socrates was tried by an Athenian court. But why do they believe? They believe because they are satisfied with the sufficiency of the evidences. They not only presume that Plato was honest in reporting his facts, but no countervailing testimony has successfully called his report into question. Cultured people know that a rejection of sufficient evidences is a sign of incredulity. And incredulity is bad business, for by its refusal to proportion assent to evidence it leaves a person free to accept or reject whatever happens to suit him. This spells the end of all critical investigation. (KLPL 148)

Note the clever switch that has taken place within a single paragraph. In the process of defending his definition of *faith,* Carnell finally portrays his view as a bulwark of protection for *critical investigation.*

The New Testament incident that precipitates a good deal of this discussion in *Kingdom* is the raising of Lazarus from the dead by Jesus. To be sure, there are intelligent, well-educated, modern Christians who have no difficulty believing Lazarus was raised from the dead. Nevertheless, it seems clear that giving intellectual assent to such a claim qualifies as a clear example of a leap of faith in the absence of sufficient evidence. Carnell will have none of this. "If the raising of Lazarus was not an event that could be judged in the same way that an upright man judges any other event in history, then the senses were no longer trustworthy and meaningful distinctions between fact and fiction could no longer be made" (KLPL 143). And then, to drive the point home: "The Scriptures witness to a body of redemptive events that are as much a part of history as the voyage of Columbus."

If Carnell means that the biblical record makes historical claims that the historian must evaluate on the same grounds applied to all other historical claims, then one need take no exception to the statement. What comes into play under these ground rules, as Van Harvey puts it in *The Historian and the Believer,* is "the texture of assent," which involves degrees of probability rather than true–false categories:

> It reflects the trained judgment of the historian, the degree to which he is prepared to stake his authority on a certain utterance. He communicates his own estimate

of the matter, the quality of assent it deserves, by a careful and judicious placement of qualifications. He indicates what he believes can be affirmed with practical certainty, what can be asserted only with caution or guardedly, and what is to be asserted as possible, given the present state of his knowledge. The historian's assent, so to speak, possesses a texture. He does not traffic in mere claims but in qualified claims ranging from tentativity to certitude.[28]

But this is clearly not what Carnell is getting at. He means quite plainly that the raising of Lazarus from the dead is just as reliable a historical fact as the voyage of Columbus.

Claims like this are open to the same charge of cultic credulity that Carnell levels at the fundamentalist. What is missing from his approach is not only Van Harvey's "texture of assent" but Stephen Toulmin's "the soundness of the claims we make" and the creative tension of a Barthian dialectic. Along with the resoundingly faithful *Yes*, we need to sense the presence of a *No* whose threads are woven inextricably throughout the whole tapestry of faith and certify both its vulnerability and its authenticity. Only once in a while, within the *Yin* of Carnell's often overconfident apologetics, do we find a sentence that opens the door to the *Yang* of doubt and mystery.

One such passage appears in *Christian Commitment*. In the final stages of his argument, Carnell appropriately titles the chapter "The Finality of Jesus Christ." But he recognizes the need for some words of caution. Christianity, he says, is not an airtight system that forces itself upon us. What *is* forced upon us is the necessity of choosing; which particular system we place our trust in is up to us. Furthermore, despite Carnell's repeated assurances that faith is the resting of the mind in the sufficiency of the evidence, it turns out that in the journey of faith the pilgrim may have to walk through the valley of shadows. Here is the passage:

Revelation is fragmentary. "The secret things belong to the Lord our God; but the things that are revealed belong to us and to our children forever" (Deuteronomy 29:29). Whenever a systematic theologian becomes too systematic, he ends up falsifying some aspect of revelation. It is extremely difficult, if not impossible, to coax all the data of Scripture into neat harmony. One must preserve a penumbral zone in his theology; new exegetical possibilities should be welcomed. "Now I know in part; then I shall understand fully, even as I have been fully understood" (I Corinthians 13:12). (CC 285)

With this insistence that one's theology must allow for "a penumbral zone," Carnell created an opening of no small significance. If there is such a zone, we want to know how wide it is. How extensive is the shadowy area in which we cannot see things clearly? In his conscious intent, the perimeters of Carnell's shadow zone are rather well defined. He needs to reserve a place for the unpredictable intervention of the supernatural. In such a system, however rationalistic, not everything that happens can be filed in human reason's manila folders. Moreover, some basic Christian doctrines transcend the powers of human rationality. In the same chapter of *Commitment*, for example, Carnell acknowledges that the substitutionary atonement is beyond human inventiveness and describes it, in scriptural terminology, as a "mystery hidden for ages and generations but now made manifest to his saints" (Colossians 1:26). In *Kingdom*, Carnell posits the dimension of mystery as a sort of escape hatch for the Christian rationalist in dealing with the problem of evil. He assures us first that God deals patiently with people who have difficulty reconciling their faith in a sovereign and good deity with the pervasive presence of radical evil in the world. But God does not go so far as to answer all their questions. Providence will always retain an element of mystery, and "a pious heart is ready to accept mystery, for we are men and not God" (KLPL 67, 70). If that seems like an excuse for sweeping tough problems under the rug, another sentence from the same book puts mystery in a more positive context: "We have alienated ourselves from the ground of our being by divesting the universe of its sense of mystery" (KLPL 25).

The concept of mystery has taken on much importance in the religious thought of this century. Rudolf Otto's *The Idea of the Holy* (1917)[29] introduced the terms *mysterium tremendum* and *mysterium fascinosum* to describe two complementary religious attitudes experienced by the worshipper in the contemplation of the sacred being. The former stresses dread, the latter enchantment, but both preserve at the heart of the religious experience a fathomless mystery, beyond rational analysis. In 1935, Gabriel Marcel, in *Being and Having*,[30] developed an important distinction between problem and mystery. Whereas problems are solvable by the operations of the detached intelligence, mystery involves the participation of the human subject and does not yield to problem-solving techniques. "A mystery," says Marcel, "is a problem which is entrenched upon its own givens, which invades them and by that token goes beyond being a problem."[31]

Thoughtful contemporaries have extended these provocative insights. Annie Dillard, doing the work of a philosopher-theologian-naturalist while writing behind the mask of a "pilgrim at Tinker Creek," seems always very much aware of both the *tremendum* and the *fascinosum* in Rudolf Otto's *mysterium*. On one occasion, in the dead of winter, she locates a woodpecker in the sky after first seeing its giant shadow on the ice of Tinker Creek:

It flew under the neighborhood children's skates; it soared whole and wholly wild though they sliced its wings. I'd like a chunk of that shadow, a pane of freshwater ice to lug with me everywhere, fluttering huge under my arm, to use as the

Eskimos did for a window on the world. Shadow is the blue patch where the light doesn't hit. It is mystery itself, and mystery is the ancients' ultima Thule, the modern explorers' Point of Relative Inaccessibility, that boreal point most distant from all known lands. There the twin oceans of beauty and horror meet.[32]

Perhaps the most surprising contemporary references to mystery come from members of the scientific community. The time is long past, of course, when the public optimistically expected science to usher in a golden age for mankind and when most scientists themselves acquiesced in the assumption that any question to which science could not promise an answer at some future point probably was not worth asking in the first place. Now, after old paradigms have been shattered and new ones have promised (and produced) awesome results that are both life-enhancing and life-threatening, we hear scientists speaking in accents that are unmistakably religious. Although Lewis Thomas is not explicitly religious in his approach, the sense of wonder and mystery pervades much of his work. In *Late Night Thoughts on Listening to Mahler's Ninth Symphony,* Thomas acknowledges that "there can be no promise that we will ever emerge from the great depths of the mystery of being."[33] He still retains some of the scientist's old self-confidence: "Indeed, I cannot imagine any sorts of questions to be asked about ourselves or about nature that cannot sooner or later be answered, given enough time" (159). But he admits that science will need help in this effort:

We have a wilderness of mystery to make our way through in the centuries ahead, and we will need science for this but not science alone. Science will, in its own time, produce the data and some of the meaning in the data, but never the full meaning. For getting a full grasp, for perceiving real significance when significance is at hand, we shall need minds at work from all sorts of brains outside the fields of science, most of all the brains of poets, of course, but also those of artists, musicians, philosophers, historians, writers in general. (150)

It is interesting that in Thomas's list of contributors from outside the sciences there are no theologians or professional religious figures. Their absence, however, is of little consequence. For one thing, if the poets and artists and the others who did make it onto the list have a respect for both the *mysterium tremendum* and the *mysterium fascinosum* (as Lewis Thomas himself clearly does), then the religious sensibility will go along on the journey through the "wilderness of mystery." Conversely, any theologians or religious leaders who (to borrow Carnell's words) have no "penumbral zone" in their theology or whose hearts are not "ready to accept mystery," probably would have little or nothing to contribute anyway.

Would Carnell himself qualify for the journey? We have to acknowledge, I think, that Carnell does not strike out boldly for the uncharted territory of mystery. The boundaries of his own penumbral zone are disappointingly narrow. For Carnell as apologist, the most crucial issues converge right at this point, issues that inextricably mesh with the problem of language. To discuss Carnell's apologetics is to discuss theism, and to discuss theism is to raise the question of God-language.

Of all the young radical theologians of the 1960s, Paul Van Buren was most deeply concerned with problems of language. His contribution in that decade was *The Secular Meaning of the Gospel*,[34] in which he argued that analogical as well as literal language about God makes no sense to the empirically minded secular "believer." Instead he shifted attention to the man Jesus of Nazareth, about whom certain statements can be made that can be explored and clarified by linguistic analysis. Then, in 1972, in *The Edges of Language: An Essay in the Logic of a Religion*,[35] Van Buren pushed the question of religious language to yet another stage. Still drawing heavily on Wittgenstein, he found solid ground on which to base the use of the word "God": "The logic of God, then, is the logic of the edges of language, and the man who says 'God' in a serious way is engaging in the farthest extremities of the linguistic behavior that is religion" (130, 131). The tendency of Hebrew religion, he said, was to stop short of that frontier; Christianity's temptation has always been to go right to the brink and still presume to speak clearly and give definitions of God.

The mistake is to think that the word "God" either falls well within the edges of language, where religious claims about God would be meaningful but would appear to be false, or else lies outside language altogether. It seems evident to me now that the word had never had much life in either of those foreign soils. Planted in its own ground, however, right on, and marking, the boundary of language, the word can be as alive and flourishing today as in the past. If saying "God" is an acknowledgment that one has come to the end of language, if it is a religious way of indicating that one longs to say all that could possibly be said on some matter of great concern, then that is a role which lies just barely but legitimately within our language. (144)

It seems to me that Van Buren could not have identified more precisely the major flaw in the Carnellian apologetics and the apologetics of traditional theism. Carnell theoretically recognizes the limitations inherent in the philosopher-theologian's task, but as a writer he seems always to be doing his work in the clean well-lighted rooms of a confident rationalism. He may talk about the penumbral zone of mystery, but for him it is not friendly territory. Hemingway's hero Nick Adams absorbs the healing power of fishing for trout in a wilderness stream, but he is aware that downstream the river narrows and heads into a dark swamp.

In the swamp the banks were bare, the big cedars came together overhead, the sun did not come through, except in patches; in the fast deep water, in the half light, the fishing would be tragic. In the swamp fishing was a tragic adventure. Nick did not want it. He did not want to go down the stream any further today.[36]

Nick Adams and Ed Carnell may seem unlikely kin, but they share the same apprehension, for reasons not totally dissimilar, with regard to entering the mystery zone of their respective "Big Two-Hearted Rivers." Carnell too chooses to remain on safer territory, restating traditional positions and interpreting biblical passages not as genuine efforts to clothe with words the all-but-ineffable data from the edges of language but as detailed road maps to eternity. The key difference between the two situations is that in the work of apologetics the dark mysterious swamp is everywhere. There is *only* the penumbral zone. Recognizing this fact is not equivalent, however, to giving up, saying there is nothing to believe in, nothing to which we can legitimately commit ourselves.

Before bringing this chapter to a conclusion, we must return one more time to Rooney Vail's question: "Is it true?" Rooney never does get her answer from the Reverend Theodore Nicolet. Her help comes instead from an unlikely source, an eccentric but deeply spiritual woman by the name of Lillian Flagg, who has the gift of healing. Rooney acknowledges, when she first meets Mrs. Flagg, that she was apprehensive about coming to her country retreat, afraid she would get a reputation she did not deserve, "for believing in something enough to come here. I don't really believe very much in anything." To which Mrs. Flagg replies: "Well, that doesn't matter a bit, at least not at first." She cites the man in the Gospels who said, "Lord, I believe. Help Thou mine unbelief."

"That's it, you see. The man who said that didn't really believe very much in anything either, and it made no difference. His boy was healed. You believe in spite of not believing . . . It's the best any of us can do at first, and it's enough."

If that is enough for Lillian and for Rooney, it is not quite enough for Frederick Buechner, who as the novel's author is perhaps more interested in how the question of belief and truth is settled in Nicolet's ministry. Rooney's question, you remember, was put into her mouth by Buechner, who got it from Barth, who had declared that this is the one question modern churchgoers want answered: "Is it true?" Does Buechner's young minister ever come to the point where he can answer Yes? Nicolet tracks Rooney to Lillian Flagg's home and meets the healer himself, but he is not ready, as Rooney was, for this "guardian of Christian mysteries." He keeps her at a distance. But Nicolet is a man with his own deep needs. Most especially he needs some sign of divine blessing on his ministry. Is it true after all, this evangel he is supposed to preach? Rooney's question has got under his skin. In the novel's central scene, Nicolet is lying on his back at daybreak, out behind his father's barn. "Please . . . please," he whispers, and reaches out his arms as far as they will extend, not really knowing what he is asking for. "Please come," he says, then "Jesus" –

> Two apple branches struck against each other with the limber clack of wood on wood. That was all – a tick-tock rattle of branches – but then a fierce lurch of excitement at what was only daybreak, only the smell of summer coming, only starting back again for home, but oh Jesus, he thought, with a great lump in his throat and a crazy grin, it was an agony of gladness and beauty falling wild and soft like rain. Just clack-clack, but praise him, he thought. Praise him. Maybe all his journeying, he thought, had been only to bring him here to hear two branches hit each other twice like that, to see nothing cross the threshold but to see the threshold, to hear the dry clack-clack of the world's tongue at the approach of the approach perhaps of splendor. (177)

The moment is interrupted by the arrival of Denbigh, Nicolet's assistant pastor, completely loyal and large-spirited but hardly in tune with Nicolet's real needs. Nicolet's elaborations of the clack-clack experience are as much for his own sake as Denbigh's. He picks up the rung of a broken ladder and raps it twice against the tree, suggesting cryptically that if life is a dance of faith, then perhaps this is the rhythm.

I think the dance that must go on back there . . . way down deep at the heart of space, where being comes from. . . . There's dancing there, Denbigh. My kids have dreamed it. Emptiness is dancing there. The angels are dancing. And their feet scatter new worlds like dust. . . . If we saw any more of that dance than we do, it would kill us sure. . . . The glory of it. Clack-clack is all a man can bear. (182)

It is a mystical experience, of course, a revelation direct from the penumbral zone, and it carries the subjective certitude of all such experiences. So Nicolet has the answer he needs. It *is* true. But he realizes soon enough how difficult it is to communicate mystery. He thinks of his congregation and how little, in a sense, he has to give them – "like the sprig of olive in the beak of Noah's dove, only a scrap of splendor from a derelict orchard to bear witness to the presence of a land, a hope, beyond the grey sea-swells." This, I submit, is an authentic, reverent, compelling word from the realm of mystery, the penumbral zone of theology and apologetics. Given the audacity of Christianity's claims and the radical objections it faces, it may be the Christian religion's only defensible apologetic defense.

E. Some concluding words: mostly Mozart

At a particularly intense moment in Peter Shaffer's play *Amadeus*, Mozart's nemesis, the mediocre court composer Salieri, holds in his hands the original manuscripts of several Mozart compositions. Looking back on this incident as an embittered old man, he says: "I was staring through the cage of those meticulous ink strokes at an Absolute Beauty." What makes the experience especially galling to Salieri is that he knows this divinely gifted young man Mozart to be a lewd and obscene fool, whereas he, Salieri, who has committed his musical talent to God, alas, has not all that much talent to give. But if he cannot himself produce greatness, at least he can recognize it in others. In fact, as Shaffer portrays Salieri, his religious faith rests on what we might call an apologetics of natural theology. At one point in the play he says, "It is only through hearing music that I know God exists."[37]

Carnell saw Karl Barth as appealing to the music of Mozart in much the same way. In his report on the Chicago Barth seminar, he argued that in *Church Dogmatics* "Barth does not hesitate to use the word 'proof' when pressing the achievements of Mozart into apologetic service" (CBC 155). This tactic bothered Carnell for two reasons: (1) if Barth were consistent in his often repeated rejection of natural theology, the music of Mozart would be disqualified as evidence; (2) even if Mozart's music is allowed entrance into the discussion, Barth's praise does nothing more than give vent to his own feelings.

Let us look at the passage Carnell singled out as "the most glaring example" of Barth's use of an argument from natural theology. It is from a chapter in *Church Dogmatics* entitled "God and Nothingness" in which Barth discussed the difficulties caused by creation's having a negative as well as a positive side. "Viewed from its negative aspect, creation is as it were on the frontier of nothingness and orientated toward it. Creation is continually confronted by this menace." According to Barth, it is a slander, however, to suggest that the shadowy side of creation belongs to the nothingness that is opposed to God. "When Jesus Christ shall finally return as the Lord and Head of all that God has created, it will also be revealed that both in light and shadow, on the right hand and on the left, everything created was very good and supremely glorious."[38]

At this point Barth interposed more than a full page of fine print on the "incomparable" Mozart, whose music, he said, demonstrated that "he knew something about creation in its total goodness that neither the real fathers of the Church nor our Reformers, neither the orthodox nor Liberals, neither the exponents of natural theology nor those heavily armed with the 'Word of God,' and certainly not the Existentialists, nor indeed any other great musicians before and after him, either know or can express and maintain as he did." The specific passage to which Carnell referred comes from the final paragraph of this interposition: In the music of Mozart we have "clear and convincing proof that it is a slander on creation to charge it with a share in chaos because it includes a Yes and a No, as though oriented to God on the one side and nothingness on the other."[39]

Were Carnell's criticisms of Barth's alleged use of natural theology justified? Was Barth actually using Mozart as evidence in the service of apologetics? We should note first that in one of the passages I have quoted he explicitly dissociates Mozart's contribution from those made by "the exponents of natural theology." Moreover, in the sentences following the one Carnell quotes, Barth clearly removes Mozart's role from the realm of logical proof: "Mozart has created order for those who have ears to hear, and he has done it better than any scientific deduction could." What about Carnell's second criticism, the charge that Barth's praise of Mozart tells us nothing more than his feelings and preferences, "just as he would in declaring that he considers a pipe a greater delight than a cigar"? In this passage on Mozart, it seems clear that whereas Barth intended to convey considerably more than his musical preferences, he was making considerably less of an apologetic claim than Carnell implied. Admittedly some of the ambiguity is attributable to Barth's too casual use of the phrase "clear and convincing proof." Only in the full context does the more modest apologetic function of Mozart's music come clear. As Barth put it, the light of Mozart's music "shines all the more brightly because it breaks forth from the shadow." In the terms we have been using in this chapter, Mozart is incomparable because his music, more than any other, comes to us from theology's "penumbral zone," creation's realm of mystery. It is not clear and convincing proof of anything; Carnell was right to challenge Barth on that point. But by the same token, Carnell was tone deaf to the mysterious harmonies that Barth's sensitive ear picked up in Mozart's music.

Annie Dillard suggests a category for this kind of achievement. She calls Shakespeare's King Lear, like Melville's whale, "an aesthetic or epistemological probe by means of which the artist analyzes the universe."[40] When apologetics gets to its own bottom line, perhaps that is all it can do. But that is no small achievement when one is reckoning with ultimate mystery.

Emily Dickinson would have understood. No stranger to either the *mysterium tremendum* or the *mysterium fascinosum*, she distilled much of what I have been trying to say about Carnell and apologetics and the penumbral zone in a little-known four-line poem. More than likely the genesis of the poem can be found in the Apostle Paul's sermon on Mars Hill, as recorded in Acts 17. Most of Paul's hearers rejected his message and turned away, but a few believed, including one Dionysius the Areopagite. It is to him that Emily Dickinson addresses these lines:

> Lad of Athens, faithful be
> To Thyself,
> And Mystery –
> All the rest is Perjury – [41]

CHAPTER VIII

Apologetics of the heart:
the perspective of inwardness

In *The Temptation to Exist,* the French philosopher E. M. Cioran said, "We never follow the consistent rationalist for long; once we pluck out his mystery and know where he is headed, we abandon him to his system."[1] After the cold and somewhat sterile rationalism of *An Introduction to Christian Apologetics,* Edward Carnell seemed to experience this sort of dissatisfaction within himself. His second major work of apologetics, *A Philosophy of the Christian Religion,* published in 1952, developed a defense of Christianity based on the broader category of values and began with the claim that "religion starts whenever an individual is willing to name a value for which to live and die."[2] He designated clearly the limited role of reason and logic in this quest:

It is the scholastic, not the Biblical writer, who is responsible for the definition that man is a rational animal. Scripturally, *man is a sentient creature qualified to worship God.* Man releases his best powers when he enjoys communion and fellowship, not when he perceives rational connections in a formal syllogism. (179)

Put another way, for the whole person satisfaction must involve more than reason's "knowledge by inference"; it also entails "knowledge by acquaintance," a category that includes knowledge of persons as well as places and things, and that enjoys its ultimate fulfillment in knowledge of God. Carnell called this angle of vision "the perspective of inwardness" and said that Kierkegaard taught him how to use it:

Without the stimulation of the Danish gadfly, I probably would never have learned how to ask questions from the perspective of inwardness. It is a pleasure to acknowledge my indebtedness to Kierkegaard. (CC 73)

151

To be sure, Carnell never became an irrationalist, never backtracked from his insistence that Christianity does not ask the heart to trust values that reason cannot embrace, never relinquished the didactic dogma of biblical inerrancy. But the realities of everyday human experience, inner as well as outer, pressed him to widen the scope of his apologetic effort. In the bargain he opened himself up to new tensions and a serious division within his apologetic approach that he never happily resolved and that intensified the divisions we have already noted in his personal and professional life.

A. "The heart has its reasons"

Perry Miller said of Jonathan Edwards, "Protestantism had not yet seen, though it had often aspired to, so perfect a union of the hot heart and the cool head."[3] As far back as 1947, before he had finished graduate school, Carnell saw in that combination the prescription for evangelical success. In his letter of application to teach at Fuller Seminary (which was just about to open its doors to its first entering class), he commended President Harold John Ockenga for combining a commitment to Reformation Christianity with a love for present-day fundamentalists, "an attitude which, I believe, by uniting a tear in the heart [by which he meant a teardrop, not a rip] with the law of contradiction in our logic, will, in the long run, win."[4]

We are not surprised by mention of the law of contradiction, since we know that Carnell had just finished writing *Apologetics*, in which he called it "the most perfect philosophical argument ever devised." But the "tear in the heart," although not totally new, strikes a jarring note. Not a pietistic person by nature, Carnell at times gave the impression of calculated condescension when he used the language of fundamentalist spirituality. Moreover, in this statement we listen in vain for gentle irony and look unsuccessfully for the slightest evidence of the tongue's presence in the cheek. Carnell was serious here. He was writing to a respected authority figure asking to be considered for a job he knew could change the entire course of his life. Nevertheless, while the choice of words is blatantly sentimental, we must not doubt the substance of what he was saying. The "tear in the heart" indicates that he was already in the early stages of putting distance between his own views and those of Gordon Clark, for whom the law of contradiction is all one needs to separate truth from error. Although Carnell continued to condemn subjectivism in religion, he turned his own gaze inward, tentatively at first, then with more assurance. The more he espoused inwardness – that is, the more attention he gave to values, to the moral sense, to the emotions – the farther he strayed from the criteria of pure logic and the more inevitable became a serious break with Clark's ideas.

We do not have to guess about this. For a time in the early 1950s, Carnell and Clark conducted a correspondence. When it began, Carnell had just published *Philosophy* and inside of two years would be elevated to the Fuller presidency. Clark was chair of the Philosophy Department at Butler University in Indianapolis. Although the two men focus most of their attention on the inerrancy question, the tension between logic and inward response, between head and heart, plays an important secondary role. The thirty-four-year-old apologetics professor boldly challenges his own revered mentor, arguing the limitations of the law of contradiction and contending that "inspiration is far more dynamic than you are willing to concede."

On your view a person can have the infallible assurance that the chronologies in the Old Testament or the dimensions of the temple or the endless Levitical laws are true, and then yawn and go to sleep; on my view this truth must be probed until it blesses the heart, moves, and convicts: *then* inspired truth has been found. Our consolation in the Bible is more than that which comes from a rational assurance that it is infallibly true; it is a spiritual response based upon a source of life. (1/5/53)

He says he senses a "scholarly sterility" in Clark's position and even suggests that the rise of neo-orthodox teaching (i.e., "the other extreme of denying the objective truth") may be in part a reaction against views like Clark's that, in Barthian eyes, might seem to "allow a dynamic text to become *geometrized*." A brave charge, indeed, to level at Gordon Haddon Clark. The key to their differences, he says, is the definition of truth.

Apparently your view means that if science could develop an electron machine capable of employing the law of contradiction perfectly, it could see the truth of the Bible. On my view only a man of a humble and contrite heart can see it. Biblical propositions are truth only (so far as the *receiver* is concerned; I do not refer to the objective state of the text) when they transform. (2/23/53)

If we were to miss the tone of these letters, it would be easy to make too much of them. Two friendly scholars, on a "Dear Doc" and "Dear Ed" basis, are playing an intellectual game, testing ideas, not at all reluctant to use sharp debating techniques and accuse each other of the same tactics. Reading the letters, one at times feels lost in a wilderness of split hairs. At one point Carnell sticks the knife in and gives it a little twist: "I detect the familiar Clarkean impatience cropping out in the last letter. I really had looked for it to appear long before this" (3/24/53). Throughout the correspondence, Clark, who according to all reports was rarely bested in such intellectual byplay, gives as good as he gets.

We would be just as mistaken, however, if we saw all this as *merely* a scholarly game. For Carnell especially, the dialogue is important. He assures Clark that he puts the letters on file and occasionally rereads them: "Do not think, therefore, that you are wasting your time. As usual, I have the profoundest respect for your judgment" (2/17/53). Respect yes, but not agreement. All the banter notwithstanding, Carnell's stress on inwardness represents a significant difference between his own views and Clark's.

But turning inward involves risk. In this respect, as we shall see, the watershed book in Carnell's career was *Christian Commitment*. But the strains had already begun to show in *A Philosophy of the Christian Religion*. Although it was his fourth book, it was in some ways a new beginning. In *The Theology of Reinhold Niebuhr* he had reworked his Harvard doctoral thesis. In *Television: Servant or Master?* he had dealt with a popular although by no means unimportant subject, hoping to make enough money for a down payment on a house. With *Philosophy*, however, he was making his second foray into his major field of expertise, five years after the auspicious appearance of *Apologetics*. Then he was an unknown; at this time he had an established reputation in the evangelical world.

Basing his argument on axiology, the study of values, Carnell first makes clear the parallel with logic: "*Foolishness is to axiology as inconsistency is to logic*" (21).

Whereas wisdom is tested by consistency, values are judged by their power to increase or decrease happiness. When a man rushes into a burning house and rescues his collection of cigar bands, while allowing his own children to perish in the flames, he is properly branded a fool. He is juxtaposing himself – a seeker after happiness – with a decision which can only result in the long run in the decrease of that happiness. (21)

Carnell's strategy, then, is to compare conservative Christianity to other religions and philosophies on the basis of how satisfactorily they fulfill our universal human needs. The process, however, will not yield logical proof: "The nearest that proof will be enjoyed is in the establishing of a dialectic of despair as the alternative to the Christian option" (45). The head can take the inquirer only that far; the heart must move him or her over the threshold into the salvation offered by Christ.

Therein lies an important clue. Ostensibly, Carnell has neatly parceled out the duties of head and heart, but his attempts at evenhandedness reveal an inner tension:

There is something very strange about Christianity. Whereas the great philosophic systems are fortified by immense arguments to justify both their procedure and their goal, the Scriptures start off point-blank to discuss some of the profoundest topics conceivable to man: God, creation, the relation between time and eternity, the nature and destiny of man. The procedure seems almost naive in our eyes, we are so used to proceeding along other lines of method. (26, 27)

It is not clear why there is anything at all strange about this procedure; indeed, it would be far stranger if the Bible were to start out with definitions and major and minor premises. To be sure, that is exactly Carnell's point. Then why does he bring up strangeness at all? Perhaps because the Bible's "almost naive" approach *is* a bit of a surprise to an indoctrinated Clarkean rationalist trying to see things with a fresh inner eye, and he has to spell it out – for himself as much as for his readers. He argues that the Bible's interlarding of poetic insights with formal doctrinal consistency "is what we should expect if the *whole* man is being addressed" (38). The Bible is "quite conscious of the fact that the most lasting and abiding joys in life are never so purely rational that they engage only the mind" (38). Who (we might ask) but an unreconstructed rationalist could ever doubt that? These comments are redolent of the *repentant* rationalist who is beginning to see the light. That the heart is still subservient to the mind, however, is quite clear from Carnell's italicized emphasis: "The heart knows a depth of insight which, *while it may never be separated from rational consistency,* is yet not univocally identified with such consistency" (39).

In the last few pages of the book, Carnell returns to the head–heart issue, this time in the familiar terms of knowing and believing. Which do we do first? Both, he answers. "First we know in order that we might believe; then we believe in order that we might know" (515). He asks us to imagine a man deciding whether to leap into a swimming pool. First he has to be rationally convinced that the blue patch below is actually water and not painted concrete. Only then is he ready to commit himself. So knowledge comes first. But when he acts on his belief and jumps into the water, he experiences what it is like to get wet, thus gaining "a body of knowledge which could never be gained by an eternity of rational anticipation." As Pascal said, "The heart has its reasons that the reason knows not of."

However, Carnell's assertion that both knowing and believing come first is misleading. According to the illustration, *rational* knowledge comes first, followed by intellectual belief; this in turn leads to commitment, which produces *experiential* knowledge. Inwardness or heart-knowledge is the goal (he argues that point with great conviction), but the sequence begins with necessary prior head-knowledge. In this regard his swimming pool illustration is problematical. There knowledge clearly and rightfully assumes priority. Before we dive, we had better possess knowledge (with a 99.9 percent probability) that the patch of blue is water of a certain depth rather than painted concrete. But can we have the same kind of knowledge before the leap into religious faith? Carnell's illustration clearly implies we can. Anthropologist Clifford Geertz disagrees.

In tribal religions, authority lies in the persuasive power of traditional imagery; in mystical ones in the apodictic force of supersensible experience; in charismatic ones in the hypnotic attraction of an extraordinary personality. But the priority of the acceptance of an authoritative criterion in religious matters over the revelation which is conceived to flow from that acceptance is not less complete in tribal religions than in scriptural or hieratic ones. The basic axiom underlying what we may perhaps call "the religious perspective" is everywhere the same: he who would know must first believe.[5]

In *A Philosophy of the Christian Religion*, Carnell is still very much of a rationalist. He acknowledges that Christianity is not without problems, but he is confident that he has shown it to be the best available alternative: "Is not a rational man satisfied with that system which is attended by the fewest difficulties?" In his appeal to the heart, however, he has tempered somewhat the unbudging rationalism of his first book on apologetics.

B. Completing the moral cycle

We have noted in an earlier chapter that the failure of Carnell's next book, *Christian Commitment*, published in 1957, was his greatest professional disappointment, but there we focused our attention mainly on the ill-advised decision to publish with a major commercial house. What went wrong, however, cannot be totally blamed on the Macmillan Company, although one does wonder how much success they ever anticipated for the book. *Christian Commitment* is an enigma. Purportedly autobiographical in method, it is curiously impersonal. Aimed at a secular reading audience, it is often pedantic in style and (finally) parochial in approach. Called by its author a "pilgrimage into inwardness," it is every bit as rationalistic in its methodology as his *Apologetics* and *Philosophy*. Carnell's unresolved conflict between head and heart had, if anything, grown more serious.

Because readers and critics invariably note the allegedly personal quality of the book, let us begin with that. They are quite correct in one respect; Carnell does make an unequivocal autobiographical claim: "I am lifting the veil from *my* experiences in order that others might be guided into a more accurate understanding of their own."

It is not easy for one to use his own life as a paradigm in the development of apologetical method. Yet, I am quick to confess that a sense of pleasure preponderates my fear. Although it is painful to unbosom the self, such uneasiness is more than balanced by the feeling of cleanness that comes when the self is honest with the self. (3)

When one examines the book itself, it is difficult to take this statement at face value. The veil is lifted very gingerly. Only rarely do we sense anything that deserves to be called a painful attempt to "unbosom the self." Carnell gives us a glimpse of the deleterious effects of the insomnia he says has plagued him since adolescence. He recalls narrowly avoiding a serious farm accident. Some of the personal references involve the routine activities of everyday life: feeding pigeons in the park, standing in line at a local store. Most are hypothetical situations ("Suppose we are walking along the bank of a muddy river . . .") which illustrate abstract points. Carnell may argue theoretically that "the real man is not the rational man; the real man is the moral and loving man," but except for intermittent flashes of personal authenticity the "I" whose experiences are traced in *Commitment* is an abstraction, not a real living human person.

As a book of apologetics, *Commitment* must stand or fall on the soundness of its claims, the cogency of its argument, not on whether it succeeds or fails to deliver on its promise of confessional candor. The superstructure of the book is built on a foundation Carnell neatly schematizes for us:

The three kinds of truth: ontological truth, truth as propositional correspondence to reality, and truth as personal rectitude. *The three methods of knowing:* knowledge by acquaintance, knowledge by inference, and knowledge by moral self-acceptance. *The three conditions of knowing:* direct experience, the conceptual ordering of reality, and moral responsibility.

These three elements, in turn, form three separate concatenations. *The first chain:* ontological truth, knowledge by acquaintance, and direct experience. *The second chain:* truth as propositional correspondence to reality, knowledge by inference, and the conceptual ordering of reality. *The third chain:* truth as personal rectitude, knowledge by moral self-acceptance, and moral responsibility. (29)

We are familiar with the first two chains from *Apologetics* and *Philosophy;* it is the third chain that Carnell develops at length in *Commitment.* If I understand his reasoning process correctly, he begins with the assertion that all persons conduct their affairs in a moral and spiritual environment every bit as binding in its own sphere as is the law of contradiction in logic and communication (41). There are certain things we take for granted in our relationships with other people. If the dignity of our person is violated, our judicial sentiment is aroused, and we expect some kind of adjustment of the moral balances. When we respond this way, whether we realize it or not, we are involving ourselves in a set of necessary implications. Honesty demands acknowledgment that our judicial sentiments are part of a moral cycle that requires an administrator of justice.

> The very manner of our existence commits us to the reality of a God who is occupied with what is vastly more dignified business than eternal self-knowledge. God is the author of the moral and spiritual environment; he is the sleepless monitor of our dignity; he completes the moral cycle by answering to the judicial sentiment. He is, in short, our only reason for believing that human values, and the ultimate values of the universe, are metaphysically continuous; and that we are not alone in our moral stand. (121)

Carnell's move toward the perspective of inwardness has put him in touch with what is arguably a universal human experience: the need for assurance that the values and standards we accept as givens on the human level do not conflict with the way things are in the essential fabric of the universe – whatever one's metaphysical assumptions. Others have made similar points. In their interpretation of the ethic of Jesus, Waldo Beach and H. Richard Niebuhr put it this way: "The man who is merciless, unforgiving, and unloving is going *against the grain of the universe*, is trying to violate the inviolable law of nature, society, history, of God."[6] On an even wider scale, Clifford Geertz says this way of looking at the world is at the heart of the religious perspective: "the conviction that the values one holds are grounded in the inherent structure of reality, that between the way one ought to live and the way things really are there is an unbreakable inner connection."[7]

But in *Christian Commitment* Carnell is reaching for more than that. Recall that just prior to the book's publication he confidently predicted at a Fuller faculty meeting that it would change the way future apologetics is conducted. Perhaps what he meant by that statement can be deduced from one paragraph of the Preface:

> Hence, I am careful to speak of a "spiritual approach to God" rather than a "rational proof of God's existence." Although both approach and proof presuppose critically assessed evidences, they differ in the moral attitude of the investigator himself. An approach to God calls for an exercise of spiritual as well as rational faculties, while a proof of God's existence calls for an exercise of only the rational. A wretched man can intellectually assent to God's existence, but only a man of character can spiritually approach God's person. (ix)

That declaration leaves no room for doubting Carnell's intention to leave rationalistic apologetics behind for a more inward perspective. At several points in the text he repeats the assertion that he is not trying to prove the existence of God but merely delineating "a procedure by which one acquaints himself with the realities that already hold him," including "the fact that man lives and moves and is in God" (109). The disclaimers are not completely convincing. It is one thing to speak of "the grain of the universe" (Beach and Niebuhr) or "the inherent structure of reality" (Geertz); it is quite another thing to name God as the necessary completion of the moral cycle. There is no clearly discernible and substantial difference between rationally proving God (which Carnell rejects) and developing an argument that culminates in postulating God as "our only reason for believing that human values, and the ultimate values of the universe, are metaphysically continuous" (121).

The thread of the book's argument leads not just to the person of God as guarantor of the entire moral cycle but to Christianity as its most plausible elaboration: "Existence itself raises a question to which the righteousness of Christ is the only critically acceptable answer. Hence, Christianity is true" (286). Furthermore, the Christianity that is declared true is one particular interpretation of the New Testament record: the orthodox tradition with the dogma of substitutionary atonement and all its forensic implications. This, I suggest, is a leap too far. Kierkegaardian inwardness may have succeeded in moving Carnell's apologetics along a promising new path (although not so radically new as he seemed to think), but Clarkean rationalism has grabbed the reins and dug in the spurs. Carnell saw the problem. A footnote alerts the reader to a shift in method:

Rather than proceeding to reality by way of the third method of knowing, we are dogmatically reviewing the Christian doctrine of salvation. This must be accepted as a literary convention. In the final chapter an effort will be made to show the relation between moral self-acceptance and our present appeal to Scripture. In the meantime we simply ask, how *can* one decide whether Christianity answers to reality, unless he acquaints himself with the essence of Christianity? Even if a man rejects the way of the cross, he at least ought to have an accurate understanding of what he is rejecting. (249)

If we set our suspicions aside and agree to this "literary convention," what do we find when we get to the final chapter? Carnell repeats there the double criterion he earlier called systematic consistency: "*Systems are verified by the degree to which their major elements are consistent with one another and with the broad facts of history and nature.*" He doubly underscores the first half of that claim by adding that "a consistent system is a true system." With considerable justification, he claims to have shown this kind of internal consistency. The moral cycle he develops in his philosophical reasoning fits perfectly with the forensic soteriology of his conservative theology and completes an unbroken circle. But then he adds: "Were a person to demand a higher or more perfect test than this, he would only show his want of education" (286). If the reader can at this point set aside the intimidating and specious appeal to the amount of his or her education, it is not only possible but justifiable to ask for something more. Inner consistency verifies nothing outside the boundaries of the system itself. As Geertz vividly puts it in a different context, "There is nothing so coherent as a paranoid delusion or a swindler's story."[8]

Carnell's recognition, throughout his apologetic writings, that one must move on to the second half of the double criterion – namely, consistency with the broad facts of history and nature – is at least a tacit admission of the deficiency alluded to by Geertz. The problem is that he *shows* internal consistency but only *declares* consistency with history and nature. He confesses the obvious shortcoming in the latter category but offers a rationale:

My excuse is twofold: first, the really crucial elements in the system have been established, and this is the main thing; second, books on Christian evidences are in great abundance. The findings of archaeology have been conveniently catalogued. If the reader is interested in discovering whether Christianity vertically fits the facts, the sources are available. (286)

The appeal to archaeology and the alleged plethora of presumably satisfactory books on Christian evidences does not have the ring of conviction. It has instead the sound of someone who senses he is swimming too far from shore and had better yell for help. But as we have seen in discussing Carnell's earlier efforts, the insistent voices of history and nature cannot be dismissed in such a cavalier manner.

I suggest, then, that the rationalistic methodology of *Christian Commitment* failed to resolve the book's argument in a convincing fashion. However, we are also considering the book as in certain respects a departure from rationalistic apologetics and a step along the path toward a greater inwardness. Among the few critical responses *Commitment* elicited were some comments relative to Carnell's appeal to inwardness as a starting point. One reviewer, writing in the conservative *Westminster Theological Journal*, criticized the book's overconfidence in the spiritual understanding and responsiveness of unregenerate persons.[9] Following the same tack, a reviewer in *Christian Century* went even farther, ironically noting that Carnell's perspective of inwardness had much in common with the traditional liberal confidence in the innate human ability to know and do the divine will.[10] Thus, *Christian Commitment* reveals that whereas Carnell, in this journey inward, has not sloughed off rationalistic methodology, he has departed more radically than ever before from the rigorous Calvinistic theology of his Westminster Seminary training.

C. "Except ye become as little children . . ."

I have called *Christian Commitment* Carnell's watershed book. Before its publication his career was steadily on the rise; after publication the curve turned downward. Reports on the dismal sales figures were bad enough, but the lack of critical attention was even harder to take. As he wrote to Harold Ockenga, "I know how disappointing it is to say provocative things and yet inspire small interaction."[11] That disappointment intensified the disillusionment that haunted his administrative duties in spite of occasional notable achievements, the most triumphant of which was academic accreditation. His chronic insomnia worsened and led to increased dependence on sleeping pills. A growing tendency toward serious depression complicated his general feeling of physical malaise and finally forced his resignation from the presidency in the spring of 1959. Although it is true that Carnell would never regain the stature and influence he enjoyed during his first two years as Fuller's president, it does not follow that in the years from 1959 until his death in 1967 he careened ever faster down a toboggan slide to destruction. He learned to cope. He did not kick the barbiturate habit, but on his doctor's advice and with the help of his wife, he stabilized within a carefully controlled daily quota. Although electroconvulsive therapy ravaged his short-term memory, he resumed classroom teaching. He was invited to participate in the prestigious 1962 Barth seminar. He wrote articles and revised his Boston University Ph.D. thesis on Kierkegaard (published in 1965 as *The Burden of Sören Kierkegaard*). And in the spring of 1967 he was invited to address a Roman Catholic Ecumenical Congress in Oakland. Clearly he was not totally a burnt-out case.

One of the more interesting achievements of this period – and in some ways the most significant – was the book *The Kingdom of Love and the Pride of Life*. *Commitment* had explicitly declared itself to be different, a new way of doing apologetics, and in certain relatively circumscribed ways it *was* different. Fundamentally, however, it was a product of the same Carnell who wrote *Apologetics* and *Philosophy*. If we were to delete the author's name, the preface, and the "semi-autobiographical" references (which on examination prove to be not very personal at all), readers of his earlier books would have little trouble identifying it as Carnell's. Not so with *Kingdom*. It comes on the scene quietly but it strikingly departs from its predecessors. I feel sure that if the publisher had sent the original manuscript of this book around anonymously to members of its editorial board, they could not have confidently attributed it to Carnell.

They might have detected Carnellian mannerisms and expressions here and there ("the convictions of the heart," "the testimony of sufficient evidences"), but those transparencies are embedded in a larger context so non-Carnellian that they would probably have dismissed them as coincidental or as some other writer's unconscious borrowings.

What exactly is different about *Kingdom*? For one thing, its organizing principle. The writer who in *The Case for Orthodox Theology* had argued not only that the New Testament epistles are hermeneutically more significant than the gospels but that Romans and Galatians are didactically most significant of all here structures a serious work of apologetics around an incident in the life of Jesus, the raising of Lazarus as recorded in the eleventh chapter of the Gospel According to John. This choice inevitably leads to other methodological changes. In each of the earlier books, Carnell had built into the work a chain of logical reasoning. One might question the validity of any given link in the chain or disagree with the apologetic conclusions, but one was assuredly dealing with a logically patterned progression. In *Kingdom* the objective is the same – a defense of the orthodox Christian faith – but Carnell takes a different route to get there. Although he claims in the Preface to have constructed "a chain of arguments," one is hard put to trace it link by link. The book is more accurately seen as a series of meditations circling around the theme of the New Testament law of love, each one individually evoked by or somehow related to a detail in the Lazarus account, and all together intended to form "a new base for Christian apologetics." In the absence of his usual logical pattern, Carnell adopts one other device to unify the book, a sort of touchstone against which he tests all of his ideas: "the manners of a happy child." He acknowledges that this new strategy "may strike critics as being either odd or trivial."

> But before my arguments are dismissed, let the critics make a serious effort to discover just what Jesus *did* mean when he said that we should humble ourselves and become like a child. It is possible that we are too sophisticated to perceive the relationship between the kingdom of heaven and the beautiful world of childhood. (10)

The most striking difference of all is the simple style. As the mature Carnell looked back on his first book, written while he was a graduate student at Harvard, he was not inclined to defend it as a model of good prose style. He worked hard to improve subsequent books, especially *Christian Commitment,* which (according to his secretary at the time) "he typed and had retyped innumerable times, trying to make it 'cellophane clear.'"[12] Nevertheless, although the style of *Christian Commitment* may be clearer than that of *Introduction to Christian Apologetics,* compared to *Kingdom* it is a linguistic thicket.

Contrasting two paragraphs out of context from two different books cannot qualify as proof of thoroughgoing stylistic renovation. However, if in each case the paragraph is the first in the initial chapter, we can at least get a sense of how the writer ushers the reader into two separate worlds of language. Here is how *Commitment* begins:

When formulating a philosophy of life, I contend that the least accessible fact, and thus the most baffling to isolate and classify, is the complex moral and spiritual environment of the philosopher himself. Most efforts in abstraction fail to impress the common man because sages seldom take time to interpret life from within the center of their own perspective as individuals. The more carefully I have meditated on this, the more convinced I have become that a world view remains truncated to the degree that a thinker fails to deal with data gained by a humble participation in the moral and spiritual environment.(2)

And here is the beginning section of *Kingdom* (two short paragraphs, actually, that add up to the same number of words as the paragraph just quoted):

The Apostle John begins his story on a sad note. "Now a certain man was ill, Lazarus of Bethany, the village of Mary and her sister Martha" (John 11:1). We do not know what was wrong with Lazarus, but we soon learn that he was ill unto death.
  A pious heart is disturbed by this. Lazarus trusted God. And from all we can discover, he was in the perfect will of God. Still, he was ill unto death. What about the people in Bethany who did not trust God, and yet went right on living? Was it fair that Lazarus should suffer and die? (13)

Statistics bear out the initial impression that these are two different linguistic worlds. The average sentence length in the *Commitment* paragraph is thirty-four words; in *Kingdom,* eleven words. In *Commitment* 16 percent of the words have more than two syllables; the figure for *Kingdom* is 8 percent, which is surely enough lower to make a point, but if we delete the names of persons and places (Apostle, Lazarus, Bethany), the figure drops to 1 percent (the single word *discover*). As for syntax, all three sentences in the *Commitment* paragraph are complex; five of the nine sentences in the *Kingdom* paragraphs are simple. We must also ask, however, whether these passages are representative of their respective books. To be sure, there are relatively complicated passages in *Kingdom* and relatively simple ones in *Commitment,* but the contrast evident here holds up with remarkable consistency throughout the two books.

What happened stylistically in *Kingdom* is more than a greater effort to be clear. The entire book has an air of self-conscious simplicity, an almost studied naiveté. Up to this point, Carnell's most cherished professional objective had been to present orthodox Christianity in such a way as to win the respect of the modern scholarly world for the evangelical point of view. For a man who was perhaps much too conscious all his post-graduate school life of being "a Harvard man," *Kingdom* was indeed apologetics in a new key. Carnell's purposely unsophisticated style in *Kingdom* should be seen, I suggest, against the backdrop of his bitter personal disappointment over the failure of *Christian Commitment* to impress the academic community. He turns away from academia and moves on to what he hopes will be a more receptive audience. But there is more to it than that. He has not given up on an educated readership but has (intuitively, I think) developed a strategy for sneaking up on their blind side. He still does the work of an apologist – seeking to demonstrate that the Christian gospel is worthy of acceptance on any and all criteria – but since too much sophistication has hindered the ability of modern readers to see the truth, he attempts to break through that pseudo-intellectual resistance ("the pride of life") by the very simplicity of his approach.

Inwardness has influenced theme as well as style. In choosing to expound the apologetical importance of love, he is reacting to a series of deeply disillusioning personal experiences related to the constant barrage of criticism and heresy-hunting aimed at him, both as a writer and as president of a progressive (and therefore controversial) evangelical seminary. This is not to say that adversity introduced him to the law of love. In his inaugural address as Fuller's president he had pointed to the love of self as a mysterious given of our humanity that not only serves as our criterion for the moral quality, the degree and the consistency of our love for others, but should keep us from passing final judgment on the heart of another. If loving others as we love ourselves means anything, he said, "it follows that even as we never allow either ourselves or others to approach the heart apart from a humble, loving acceptance of the mystery of the heart, so we must approach others with an equal sense of mystery and with equal humility and love."[13]

Ironically, while under Carnell's presidency the ambience at Fuller became more tolerant of dissent, the institution itself became the object of mounting adverse criticism. Carnell was appalled not just at the constant sniping at Fuller but at what he observed in evangelicalism at large. Speaking in the fall of 1958 to a large audience of seminary supporters in the Chicago area, he stressed the contradiction between the admonition of Jesus that the disciples should "love one another" and the disgraceful spectacle that people see today when they look at the evangelical churches: "a knot of quarreling sects."[14] Having been victimized inwardly by the destructive effects of love's antithesis, he can see more clearly its indispensability. "I believe," he says in the preface to *Kingdom*, "that if Christian apologists would rally their wits and make better use of love as a point of contact, great things might be accomplished for the defense of the faith."

"Love as a point of contact": There, of course, is *Kingdom*'s use of inwardness as a starting point. Carnell maintains that today, through the insights of psychotherapy, we know more surely than we have ever known before that as human beings we crave the unconditional acceptance of love. Christianity has always known this. Juxtaposing these two facts puts in one's hand the key to Carnell's method in *Kingdom*. We are made a certain way, he says: We desire and need love. This is what life is all about. And Christianity, with its message of redeeming divine love and its command that in return the redeemed ones love not only friends but enemies, fits our human condition like Cinderella's slipper, even though in actual practice Christians are far from perfect in their implementation of the ideal. Whereas *Commitment* had also begun with inward evidence – the universal human recognition of the judicial sentiment – its argument proceeded by carefully delineated logical steps. While *Kingdom* is by no means an irrational book, it eschews linear logical development in favor of impressionistic homilies, each of which deals with a variation on the love theme.

Further examination reveals that the specific characteristics that differentiate this book from its predecessors all bear a family resemblance because they emanate naturally from the initial choice of a theme. Why the story of Lazarus, Mary, and Martha? Because there is no better way to introduce the subject of love than to see it in action, on levels both human and divine, in a simple gospel narrative. Why the touchstone of the happy child? Because Jesus himself identified childhood metaphorically with the kingdom of love. And how does one write about such a kingdom? Asking the fact for the form, Carnell turns away from adult logic and linguistic complexity toward a childlike simplicity, a manner much more in keeping with his subject matter.

D. A "second naiveté"

All of life is mixture, said Carnell in *Television*, and that includes the scorecard on *Kingdom*. An author who writes a calculatedly simple book on a complex subject takes a great risk. If he or she can manage to ignore existing paradigms, define the problem in new terms, and attack it with determination, it is at least conceivable that complexity can be reduced to simplicity with no loose ends left hanging. The writer then earns the reputation of a Great Simplifier. If the effort falls short of its goal, however, *simple* easily slips over into *simplistic*. If we interpret *Kingdom* as an effort to reduce to simplicity the imposing complexities of apologetics, it must be judged to have fallen short of its goal. Nevertheless, we should not dismiss the book as inconsequential. Carnell's increasing reliance on the perspective of inwardness opened new channels in his thinking and liberated some genuine intuitive insights that at the time gave cause for anticipating further changes in new directions.

His new approach served him well in some respects. Tackling the difficult question of ecumenism, he first deftly describes the unique historical contribution of each major Christian group, along with its most distinctive shortcoming. As an evangelical, he cannot condone the prospect of institutional unity achieved at the price of relinquishing doctrinal integrity, but he is even more uncomfortable with the scandal of separation. He locates an authentically pluralistic still point at the center of Protestantism's spinning fragmented world:

We should not be ashamed of our theological differences. They are signs that we are taking the work of exegesis seriously. Furthermore, a genuine Christian fellowship can exist *within* the framework of denominational plurality. Love can hurdle existing barriers. (119)

His premise that psychotherapy has lent modern support to the Christian view that love is the law of life elicits from him words of theological commendation for Freud, who had received few such affirmations from evangelicals over the years:

He restored the symbolism of common grace by accepting the unacceptable. Neurotic behavior evoked scorn from society, judgment from the church. Freud rejected both attitudes. He refused to believe that neurotics were either odd or perverse. They were sick, that was all. (59)

Ironically, as he says, the church often plays the opposite role, turning into "a neurosis-producing agency by substituting legalistic attitudes for the freedom of grace in Christ Jesus" (93). We find evidence also that Carnell's combined move toward the perspective of inwardness and the strategy of simplicity has sharpened his awareness of the importance of mystery:

In our zeal to interpret and control nature, we have lost sight of the kingdom of love, and thus of the kingdom of heaven. We are afraid to dream; we are critical of religious symbolism; and we live in the thin world of statistics. We have alienated ourselves from the ground of our being by divesting the universe of its sense of mystery. (24, 25)

No one will have much success trying to sell these ideas as revolutionary, but it would be even more ill-advised to argue that in 1960 they were the common intellectual currency of evangelicalism.

Kingdom stands or falls, however, on Carnell's appeal to "the manners of a happy child" as spiritual and moral touchstone. If the strategy of simplicity involves risk, using childhood as evidence elevated the risk considerably. The traps are many, but one kind predominates. Says a prominent psychologist, "Children spend all their time walking around inside adult scripts."[15] In Wordsworth's script, the child was the "best Philosopher," coming from afar, "Not in entire forgetfulness, / And not in utter nakedness, / But trailing clouds of glory." Nineteenth-century America revered the saintly child as hero of hundreds of popular stories with a similar pattern: "the confrontation between an innocent child and a corrupt society, and the demonstration of the ultimate power of innocence."[16] Playing a less sentimental but nonetheless romantic variation on that theme, Emerson, in his essay "Self-Reliance," extolled the child's nonconformity:

The nonchalance of boys who are sure of a dinner, and would disdain as much as a lord to do or say aught to conciliate one, is the healthy attitude of human nature. A boy is in the parlor what the pit is in the playhouse; independent, irresponsible, looking out from his corner on such people on their merits, in the swift summary way of boys, as good, bad, interesting, silly, eloquent, troublesome.

Carnell's script for the representative child bears a family resemblance to all of these. According to his interpretation of the gospel narratives, when Jesus counseled his followers to become like children, he cut through all sophisticated moral rationalizing and founded the kingdom of love on an elemental standard of goodness: "Every happy child knows that a man is good when he is kind and truthful, and so does every person who is a child at heart." Furthermore, the child has an intuitive knowledge as to who measures up and who does not – and, like Emerson's self-reliant boy, "is forthright in saying so" (30, 31).

Fairy tales (to which Carnell often alludes, most frequently to Cinderella) parallel the child's standards of good and evil. Far more significant than mere entertainment, they project (he says) an image of general history that assures children that the convictions of the heart are trustworthy. The ending of a fairy tale, therefore, is serious business: "A bad ending would threaten the values that the child already takes for granted" (19), the most important of which is that "in the end a good person has nothing to fear" (17).

At this point, I think, warning lights flash on in the mind of even the sympathetic reader. To commend the refreshing candor of children is beyond cavil. One can justify placing considerable credence in their intuitive awareness of who is good and who is bad. But even granting for the moment the assumption that fairy tales do clearly imply that for good people everything works out right in the end, is that article of childhood faith legitimately transferable to the adult world? When Jesus said, "Except ye become like little children, ye shall in no wise enter the kingdom of heaven," was he requiring that adult sensibilities and standards be checked at the gate?

Carnell, of course, says no – and at one point he uses as a daring test case Anne Frank, the young Jewish girl barricaded with her own and another family in a secret Amsterdam apartment in an ultimately unsuccessful effort to escape capture by the Nazis. We certainly have no trouble accepting Anne Frank as a good person, but from an adult perspective do we perceive her as in the end having nothing to fear? As a child, did even Anne herself have that faith?

To answer both yes and no is not to waffle on the issue, for Anne Frank acknowledged that she was "a little bundle of contradictions." As Carnell sees Anne, "the convictions of the heart united with the promises of the Old Testament" to assure her that the brutality that surrounded their clandestine existence would not have the last word. "Anne Frank was too busy enjoying herself to worry about cosmology. She was quite content to let the Lord run the universe" (72, 73). Happy children, he says, would agree, and so should adults who have learned to "live by the wisdom that illuminates the heart of a child." There is something to be said for this reading of Anne's diary. Entry after entry makes it clear that Anne is irrepressibly happy in the most trying of circumstances. Her hope never dies. She makes plans for the postwar years, and when she hears over British radio the news of D day she entertains the possibility of being back in school by fall. Her unquenchable optimism, however, exists side by side with an unblinking realism that matter-of-factly records the "talk, whispers, fear, stink, people breaking wind, and always someone on the pot," and survives under the constant threat of imminent discovery and death. After one especially close call, she reflects on the larger implications of what they are experiencing:

Who has inflicted this upon us? Who has made us Jews different to all other people? Who has allowed us to suffer so terribly up till now? It is God that has made us as we are, but it will be God, too, who will raise us up again. If we bear all this suffering and if there are still Jews left, when it is over, then Jews, instead of being doomed, will be held up as an example. Who knows, it might even be our religion from which the world and all peoples learn good, and for that reason and that reason only do we have to suffer now. We can never become just Netherlanders, or just English, or representatives of any country for that matter, we will always remain Jews, but we want to, too.

Be brave! Let us remain aware of our task and not grumble, a solution will come, God has never deserted our people. Right through all the ages they have had to suffer, but it has made them strong too; the weak fall, but the strong will remain and never go under![17]

So in some ways Carnell's purpose is well served in using Anne Frank as an illustration. But there is something wrong. As readers we know too much. Inevitably we approach the optimistic diary entries with full awareness of their tragic irony, knowing that on August 4, 1944, Nazi authorities discovered the secret hiding place, arrested all the occupants, and sent them off in cattletrucks to Auschwitz. Subsequently, Anne Frank was transferred to Bergen-Belsen where she died in March 1945. "In the end," Carnell assures us, "a good person has nothing to fear." If the child Anne Frank had such faith, was it justified? More important, does her faith constitute a valid model for adults to follow? Anne, I suggest, is much too potent an example for Carnell's purposes. By using her, he gains support for a particular point in his discussion, but he also opens the door to "the terror of history."[18] Anne provides what is otherwise missing in *Kingdom* – a real flesh and blood child – and her very presence calls into question the use Carnell makes of the child analogy throughout the book. If Wordsworth's child philosopher came into the world "trailing clouds of glory," Anne Frank enters the pages of *The Kingdom of Love and the Pride of Life* trailing the stench of the gas ovens of Auschwitz, and the abstraction Carnell calls "the happy child" can never again look quite the same.

Even Anne Frank is more than one child. The sensitive wise fifteen-year-old, on the brink of adult womanhood, who was captured by the Nazis in 1944 is a far different person from the child who began writing the diary shortly after her thirteenth birthday. Her developing character and personality remind us that children come in different ages, in all shapes and sizes, and obstreperously resist convenient categorization. Carnell cannot be faulted for taking seriously and trying to understand Jesus' counsel to his followers to humble themselves and become like little children. He does lay himself open to criticism, however, when he creates *ex nihilo* an all-purpose platonic Ideal Child who presumably behaves as all children do (or should) and therefore represents a model of life in the kingdom of love. Evidences of such generalizing crop up on almost every page: "ask any child," "every child knows," "try telling that to a child." In the most blatant example of this pervasive tendency, Carnell confidently extols the child's ability to analyze the problem of evil, refute philosophical pantheism, and dispatch Spinoza in the bargain:

Philosophical pantheism views the universe as either an emanation from God, or as God considered under various modal aspects. But both possibilities are unacceptable, and every child knows why. If God and the universe are the same thing, then human beings are not human beings at all. They are aspects of God. But this is false. Human beings are sinners, and sin has no place in the divine being.

Spinoza argued that we have no right to believe that the universe is friendly to human values. He defined the universe as a vast order of necessary being, something like a huge triangle.

This is all well and good, but just try telling it to a child. A child knows that if nature is like a huge triangle, then Spinoza himself is part of this triangle. (69)

The introduction of the real person Anne Frank into the text reminds us not only of childhood's infinite variety but of life's monumental suffering and the presence in our world of radical evil. The kingdom of love confronts formidable forces of darkness. Except for the reference on two pages to that little group of people huddled in their Amsterdam attic, one would hardly know that *Kingdom* is a product of the brutal twentieth century. There are passing references to Naziism and Communism, a chapter on anxiety, some words on the problem of alcoholism. For the most part, however, the level of evil confronted in *Kingdom* does not go beyond violating the royal law of love – that is, not doing unto others as you would have them do unto you. "Discourtesy," Carnell tells us, "is the first sign that a person is unwilling to honor the dignity of man. All other evils begin with this evil" (52). To be sure, he is tracing sin and evil and all kinds of injustice to their roots. Nevertheless, the book's failure to portray the depth of the world's real evil creates hollow places that cry out for the voice of the Old Testament prophet.

On the positive side of the moral equation, Carnell argues that love also starts with small gestures: courtesy, tact, timely words of encouragement, treating others as one would like to be treated. Love's two criteria, he says several times, are kindness and truth; those two virtues spell out the primary duties in the kingdom of love. "As long as the small duties of love are honored, the large duties will take care of themselves" (52). The single example of Anne Frank and all that her experience represents should have been enough to disabuse Carnell of that misplaced confidence. If history has taught one single lesson with near perfect clarity, it is that the larger mandates of love and justice do not "take care of themselves" as a natural outgrowth of personal moral rectitude. Without the compelling and continuing presence of the larger world in all its overwhelming ambiguity, the apologetic appeal to Christianity's royal law of love is shallow at best.

In summary, then, the book's methodological problem is not so much in the metaphor of childhood but in the abstract "happy child" who exists only in the writer's mind. How different the book would have been if Huck Finn and Holden Caulfield had put in an occasional appearance, or even Carnell's own two children, to whom he dedicated the book. It may well be important to understand what Jesus meant when he urged his followers to humble themselves and become like little children, but surely the adult disciple needs a better exemplar than the child for whom "a puppy is proof that God is sovereign, for who but God could have created a puppy?" (105). To use this child as spiritual and moral touchstone is to turn childlike into childish, simple into simplistic. Reacting to the silence that greeted *Christian Commitment*, a more sophisticated philosophical treatise that he considered his best work, Carnell in *Kingdom* made a conscious effort to be simple; reacting to the disappointing behavior of fellow adults, he turned to the child as model; reacting to years of carping criticism, he explored Christianity's law of love as a basis for apologetics. But the result was fundamentally regressive.

Only a year later, Carnell himself left behind the drastically limited view of childhood that dominates *Kingdom*. In the summer of 1961 he published an article in *Eternity* magazine that dealt with an aspect of the same general subject – "The Secret of Loving Your Neighbor" – but the references to children sounded an entirely different note. The article cites psychotherapy's support for the view that "many of our adult anxieties trace to the persistence of feelings that are conditioned in childhood." In the contrast between childhood and the adult life, no longer does the adult emerge second best. In fact, when adults go wrong it is precisely because they regress: "We revert to the manners of childhood by substituting competitive relationships for the adult responsibilities of sharing and serving. Children gratify their love needs by *getting*, adults by *giving*" (CBC 137).

We are passing through a time of great social change, for a prophetic judgment is being leveled against tribal injustice, colonialism, caste privilege, racial discrimination, and denominational pretention in the church. The resulting disintegration of form can be ruinous for a person who is plagued by persisting childhood emotions, and who continues to imagine that he is a child in an adult world. He cannot cope with the feeling that he must stand mobilized against a hostile and changing social order. He desperately craves reassurance from those whose emotional maturity releases them to do as they would be done by. (CBC 139)

Three specific differences are worth noting: (1) Carnell has reverted to a more complex writing style; (2) the frightening ambiguities have come trooping in through a wide open door; and (3) the exemplary "happy child" by whose hypothetical response everything was judged in *Kingdom* has apparently fallen from grace. "The beautiful world of childhood" can turn sour: "An insecure childhood is the seedbed of an insecure adulthood." Why the sudden significant change?

Kingdom was published in the fall of 1960. Given the necessary leadtime for book publication, it is safe to assume Carnell had finished the manuscript by the previous spring. Between the spring of 1960 and the appearance of the *Eternity* article in July 1961, he experienced his psychological breakdown, was hospitalized for ten days, and received seven shock treatments. We know from Carnell's letters during that period and from the statement by his psychiatrist, Dr. Philips Wells, that Carnell's attention had been drawn to certain anxiety-producing circumstances of his childhood.[19] Bernard Ramm remembers a conversation, shortly after one of those sessions with Dr. Wells, in which Carnell shared some new and troubling insights he had gleaned concerning his childhood – the sort of perspective that was totally absent from *Kingdom* in spite of its stated indebtedness to Freud. He said to Ramm: "I have never been able to put my Saturday father together with my Sunday father," a reference to his childhood perceptions of a father who he felt tyrannized the family on Saturday when he was preparing his sermon and then was all sweetness and light in the pulpit on Sunday.[20] And lest we conclude that he focused all this retrospective attention on his father, we recall his observation to Charles Fuller that he had inherited a nervous temperament from his mother. In Carnell's subsequent writings we read no more references to "the happy child"; that abstraction evaporates into nothingness, victim of all too real personal troubles, a few new insights, and an open-eyed look into his own past.

Why then do we take *The Kingdom of Love and the Pride of Life* seriously? If the book is so badly marred by its use of "the happy child" as moral and spiritual touchstone, should it not be left alone in its oblivion? Maybe it should. I argue only that in *Kingdom* Carnell was traveling in a new direction, grasping at some genuine insights on the intuitive level even though he was not succeeding very well in his conscious intent. There was nothing inherently contradictory or invalid in his move toward the apologetics of the heart; simplicity is not an unworthy ideal, and the emphasis on love of God and neighbor is theologically unimpeachable. Even the metaphor of childhood should not be disparaged as a strategic error. In *Toward a Psychology of Being*, Abraham Maslow refers to "a healthy regression without fear in the service of the greatest maturity, a true integration of the person at all levels."[21] If Carnell had had a different sense of what truths lay sleeping in the childhood metaphor, he could have significantly transformed this odd book. He might have found in his purposeful strategy of studied naiveté something akin to an idea developed by Paul Ricoeur in the final pages of *The Symbolism of Evil*.[22] Ricoeur begins with the assumption that we are thoroughly modern men and women who "are in every way children of criticism" and have left behind "primitive naiveté." Having lost "immediacy of belief," we can "no longer live the great symbolisms of the sacred in accordance with the original belief in them." But that is not the end of it. "Beyond the desert of criticism we wish to be called again," says Ricoeur. We must not relinquish our birthright of modernity, but we can "seek to go beyond criticism by means of criticism, by a criticism that is no longer reductive but restorative."

In our use of language, says Ricoeur, we find the means to accomplish this. The critical use of language has been partially responsible for our modern tendency to forget the signs of the sacred. We have achieved technological mastery partly because "our language has become more precise, more univocal, more technical in a word;" we are "the heirs of philosophy, of exegesis, of the phenomenology of religion, of the psychoanalysis of language." But precisely because language has bestowed on us this modern gift, it makes possible remembering, recharging, restoring, re-creation. Our objective – completely consistent with our modernity – is a "second naiveté" at which we can finally arrive only by going *through* criticism.

Thus hermeneutics, an acquisition of "modernity," is one of the modes by which that "modernity" transcends itself, insofar as it is forgetfulness of the sacred. I believe that being can still speak to me – no longer, of course, under the precritical form of immediate belief, but as the second immediacy aimed at by hermeneutics. This second naiveté aims to be the postcritical equivalent of the precritical hierophany. (352)

In the Preface to *Kingdom*, you remember, Carnell issued a challenge to prospective critics of his strategy: "before my arguments are dismissed, let the critics make a serious effort to discover what Jesus did mean when he said that we should humble ourselves and become like a child." Ricoeur does not explicitly relate second naiveté to the analogy Jesus drew between childhood and the true spiritual kingdom, but I suggest that his concept fulfills admirably Carnell's demand for a "serious effort" to interpret that analogy. An effective defense of Christianity's viability in our times must maintain the tough-minded critical mentality of adult modernity but at the same time recapture the child's naive openness to the symbolism of the sacred.

The Kingdom of Love and the Pride of Life is an important book not because of what it actually achieves but because with all of its flaws it nonetheless shows that Carnell had at least an intuitive glimpse that he must go forward by going back. He thought of his child-as-touchstone strategy as a return to a less sophisticated approach from what he considered a critical philosophical stance that had proved to be deficient. ("It is possible that we are too sophisticated to perceive the relationship between the kingdom of heaven and the beautiful world of childhood.") What he considered his critical stage, however, was not critical enough. One legacy of fundamentalism that Carnell never completely sloughed off was a resistance to the influence of modern criticism. Among his friends within the evangelical constituency, he gained the *reputation* of having slain the beast of modern criticism. However, he achieved that reputed victory without having fully experienced the *reality* of the journey through the labyrinth. *The Kingdom of Love and the Pride of Life* can best be described as Carnell's "song of innocence," but one listens in vain for something comparable to William Blake's "song of experience." Without any "Tyger! Tyger! burning bright / In the forests of the night," the "Little Lamb" with its "tender voice" and "Softest clothing, wooly, bright" can represent little more than a return to a primitive naiveté.

E. Conclusion: the great river and the first ape that became a man

The process of learning to be a pilot of a Mississippi riverboat, as Mark Twain describes it in *Life on the Mississippi*,[23] offers a striking parallel to the tension between primitive naiveté and the critical stage in almost any educational process. Twain says he had always been enchanted by the river's beauty. Its "graceful curves, reflected images, woody heights, soft distances" he drank in with "speechless rapture." But then Horace Bixby took him in hand and taught him the river. No modern field of learning could make more meticulous demands. Virtually every inch of the entire river had to be memorized – every dead tree, every reef, every sandbar. Every ripple on the water's surface was part of a language that had to be understood, with special attention to the unexpected detail that might signal possible disaster for boat and passengers. However, gaining this formidable array of functional knowledge and technical expertise exacted a high toll.

Now when I had mastered the language of this water, and had come to know every trifling feature that bordered the great river as familiarly as I knew the letters of the alphabet, I had made a valuable acquisition. But I had lost something too. I had lost something which could never be restored to me while I lived. All the grace, the beauty, the poetry, had gone out of the majestic river.

His mind fixed at one point on an analogy he says has stayed with him through the years:

Since those days, I have pitied doctors from my heart. What does the lovely flush in a beauty's cheek mean to a doctor but a "break" that ripples above some deadly disease? Are not all her visible charms sown thick with what are to him the signs and symbols of hidden decay? Does he ever see her beauty at all, or doesn't he simply view her professionally, and comment upon her unwholesome condition all to himself? And doesn't he sometimes wonder whether he has gained most or lost most by learning his trade?

Twain drops the discussion at this point, implying the inevitability of a trade-off: When you seriously enter the detailed, technical, critical stage of any learning process – whether it be mastery of the Mississippi, the human body, the piano, the Bible, contemporary physics, or contemporary theology – you will lose much of the sense of wonder and reverential awe you experienced when you were still able to approach the subject in your primitive naiveté. No hint of a second naiveté here. Is Paul Ricoeur perhaps too sanguine in his hope that criticism can be restorative rather than reductive? that one can break through to a "postcritical equivalent of the precritical hierophany"?

I do not think this is Twain's line of argument at all. I think rather that he is playing a more subtle language game with the reader. *Life on the Mississippi* is the product of a mature writer – the artist from Hartford, Connecticut, who had revisited the scenes of his youth along the great river. When he projects himself backward in time to his pre-riverboat days and reminisces about how he used to revel in the river's beauty, we should pay close attention to the language he uses: "a certain wonderful sunset," "radiating lines, ever so delicately traced," "the unobstructed splendor that was flowing from the sun," "I drank it in, in a speechless rapture." This kind of talk would give Huck Finn the fantods. Robert Frost would call it sunset-raving. In other words, Twain is using intentionally excessive language to indicate to us that his primitive naiveté left much to be desired. It was a relatively shallow romanticism. But did he ever break through his critical stage and rediscover the river's beauty in a more profound way? For that question also we have internal evidence: the entire book *Life on the Mississippi*, which shows conclusively that the critically knowledgeable Mark Twain appreciated the river far more than he did before he mastered it technically. He could see beyond the naiveté with which he approached the task of becoming a pilot in the first place. The passage with the glowing rhetoric exemplified what had to be thrown off before real vision was possible.

If I understand Ricoeur correctly, the breakthrough to second naiveté is never easy. Comfortable stopping places beckon all along the way. At the very outset of the pilgrimage of faith, one can refuse (or simply feel no need) to leave the warm security of the early uncritical devotion to religious belief and ideals; farther along on the journey, in the critical stage, one can settle down permanently in the increasingly complex intricacies of scholarship, which offer their own brand of security; and one can select or drift into gray areas of compromise where a partial commitment to modern learning leads not to a genuine postcritical restoration of sacred symbolism but to various amalgams of a limited critical perspective and a primitive naiveté.

However, even though a breakthrough to second naiveté is not easy, it is not impossible. Gird up the loins of your imagination and reflect briefly on the first ape that became a man. Ever since Darwin, the apes have not fared well at the hands of fundamentalists (monkey trials and all that). Even when post-fundamentalists have flirted with theistic evolution, they have often managed to do so without mentioning specific lower forms out of which humans presumably evolved. Carnell's brief discussion of evolution in *The Case for Orthodox Theology* is a classic instance. He acknowledges compelling evidence for the principle of evolution among plants and animals, but (not unexpectedly) he has trouble with human evolution. On that issue, orthodoxy does not find the scientific evidence compelling, although it *"is* sufficient to give pause."

When orthodoxy takes inventory of its knowledge, it admits that it does not know *how* God formed man from the dust of the ground. The Genesis account implies an act of immediate creation, but the same account also implies that God made the world in six literal days; and since orthodoxy has given up the literal-day theory out of respect for geology, it would certainly forfeit no principle if it gave up the immediate-creation theory out of respect for paleontology. The two seem to be quite parallel. Moreover, we must be very careful not to prejudice the counsels of God. (95)

Carnell, without actually mentioning the term, thus swings the door wide open to theistic evolution. But here is the rest of the paragraph:

If God was pleased to breathe his image into a creature that had previously come from the dust, so be it. Scripture only requires us to say that the physical antecedent of man was not denoted *man* until God performed the miraculous act of divine inbreathing. Thus, if science traces man's biological ancestry to dust, Scripture traces his spiritual ancestry to God: ". . . the son of Enos, the son of Seth, the son of Adam, the son of God" (Luke 3:38). (95)

While with these words he does not slam the door against theistic evolution, he surely tiptoes carefully around the issue. For the last two appearances of the word *dust,* substitute *ape* – which the sense of the paragraph clearly calls for – and observe the considerable change in tone and substance. If the issue in this passage is evidence from science, then the views of science should not be camouflaged by biblical terminology. The potentially inflammatory fact is not that "science traces man's biological ancestry to dust," but to lower animal forms. Carnell has the sense and the courage to acknowledge theistic evolution as a viable orthodox position, but he cannot bring himself either to use the term or to recognize the ape as ancestor on the human developmental tree. It is difficult to imagine a more apt illustration of compromise between a limited critical perspective and a primitive naiveté. That kind of internal braking system prevented Carnell, even in his most progressive period, from moving into post-critical second naiveté.

As a contrast, consider Chad Walsh. Unlike Carnell in that he is a poet, a critic, and a literary historian, Walsh resembles Carnell in that he is an ordained clergyman (Episcopalian) and has written a number of books that fall into the category of Christian apologetics, though from a considerably different perspective.[24] At this point I call your attention not to Walsh's intellectual defense of the Christian faith, but to one of his poems entitled "Ode on the First Ape that Became a Man."[25] As the poem begins, an ape is stumbling back to his nest in the gathering darkness with a dead rodent in his hand for his sick and starving mate, only to find that in his absence she has died. The darkness of the night parallels the darkness of his mind:

In double darkness he stood there while a life
Of pictures – if there were words they would be thoughts –
There were no thoughts but colors, sounds, and smells –
Tumbled disordered from that primal chaos
Where the bright trophies of two lives were housed.

He carries his mate's lifeless body to a little cave halfway up a cliff where once they had taken refuge from the lions. After laying her carefully on the ground, he piles stones to close the opening to the cave, gathers mud and fills the cracks, and shambles back to his nest. The rodent is still there, "fat and smelling of blood." At the point of starvation himself, the ape is about to tear into it when he suddenly stops. He runs to the cave, rodent in hand, grabs a stick, makes a hole in the cave opening, and pushes the rodent inside. Then he reseals the hole with mud and limps home hungry. Here is the poem's final stanza:

In the double darkness of his nest,
He listened to the sounds of the night. The roaring
Of lions, the whir of flying things, the wind
Dry and rough across the tattered grass.
A night bird's song came once, came twice to him.
Two tonic notes, the third a fifth above –
It sounded like Lo-nu-ha. She had been
A singing night. She had a name. "Lo-nu-ha,"
He wailed. In the word was the beginning.

It is sometimes argued that acceptance of the scientific perspective destroys the religious impulse, the sense of wonder as we contemplate the universe. Walsh's poem, an imaginative reenactment of a mythic moment, is a striking illustration of how faith can enter a full acceptance of the critical stance and then break through to the joyful freedom of a second naiveté. It is a liberation Carnell never achieved.

CHAPTER IX

The inerrancy issue

A. An ideological dead end

In 1976 Harold Lindsell – whom we have met in this book as one of Fuller Seminary's founding faculty members and Carnell's colleague for sixteen years – wrote a book that touched off within evangelicalism a new round of hostilities over an old issue. In *The Battle for the Bible*[1] he designated biblical inerrancy as "the crucial issue among evangelicals" (202) and declared that "once infallibility is abandoned, however good the intentions of those who do it and however good they feel their reasons for doing so, it always and ever opens the door to further departures from the faith." (25)

Evangelicalism's left wing quickly mounted a counterattack. *Biblical Authority*, a collection of essays edited by Jack Rogers of the Fuller Seminary faculty, although affirming whole-heartedly the authority of scripture as the infallible "rule of faith and practice," explicitly rejected Lindsell's notion of "total inerrancy" and cited both biblical and historical evidence in support of a broader, more flexible view.[2]

We might be tempted to ignore this fraternal struggle as irrelevant to the life and work of Edward Carnell who, after all, had been dead nine years when Lindsell's book appeared in 1976. However, we cannot deal responsibly with Edward Carnell and ignore the inerrancy question, for it never ceased being a basic issue in his own thought. Moreover, Lindsell introduced Carnell's name into the current discussion by including him in the dedication to *The Battle for the Bible*:

This book is gratefully dedicated to four of my teaching colleagues, all of whom stood or stand steadfastly for biblical inerrancy – Gleason L. Archer, Edward John Carnell, Carl F. H. Henry, and Wilbur Moorehead Smith

That Carnell's name should be included in the list of dedicatees carries considerable irony. We have seen how scathingly Carnell was criticized by certain segments of the fundamentalist public when he was perceived to be "soft on inspiration." We have also seen clear evidence that in some ways Carnell and Lindsell make strange allies. When Carnell assumed the presidency of Fuller in 1954, his chief motive was to preserve the academic integrity of the institution and keep it from coming under the control of the more conservative elements on the faculty, administration, and board of trustees, of which collection of people Lindsell was a leading figure. On the single issue of inerrancy, however, Lindsell has some solid evidence to support his use of Carnell's name, the most significant example of which is a letter from Carnell in the October 14, 1966, issue of *Christianity Today* (some six months before his death). Lindsell quotes almost the entire letter in his book:

"B. B. Warfield clearly perceived that a Christian has no more right to construct a doctrine of biblical authority out of deference to the (presumed) inductive difficulties in the Bible, than he has to construct a doctrine of salvation out of deference to the (actual) difficulties which arise whenever one tries to discover the hidden logic in such events as (a) the Son of God's assumption of human nature or (b) the Son of God's offering up of his human nature as a vicarious atonement for sin. This means that whether we happen to like it or not, we are closed up to the teaching of the Bible for our information about *all* doctrines in the Christian faith, and this includes the doctrine of the Bible's view of itself. We are free to reject the doctrine of the Bible's view of itself, of course, but if we do so we are demolishing the procedure by which we determine the substance of *any* Christian doctrine. If we pick and choose what we prefer to believe, rather than what is biblically taught, we merely exhibit once again the logical (and existential) fallacy of trying to have our cake and our penny, too."³

In response to my query about his rationale for including Carnell's name in the dedication (in view of his obvious struggles with the issue of inerrancy in *The Case for Orthodox Theology*), Lindsell wrote:

I am a historian. On page 32 of *The Battle for the Bible* you will find a quote from E. J. Carnell [the one included immediately above]. The quotation was placed there purposely because I anticipated exactly the question you have raised. A historian takes careful note of dates. The quotation comes from a letter printed in CT some years AFTER the book you mention was published. I am speaking about the Carnell two years before his death and after the book was long in print. At the end of his life he saw clearly what the issue was and was right back where he had started years before. The CASE book does open questions but it was an aberration which can be explained when one knows the full story on E.J.C.⁴

In the margin of the letter Lindsell added: "I call this a paper track."
    I have no inclination to contradict Lindsell's identification of Edward Carnell as a colleague who "stood steadfastly for biblical inerrancy." But

the case cannot be closed that easily. For one thing, we need to examine the "paper track" more extensively and more intensively. For another, as we follow that track we must always be looking for more than paper evidence. What about the evidence that has been left on the trail by a living human being? Can we be so confident that when the later Carnell reverted to an earlier position, he was seeing the issue more clearly? Or is it possible that other factors have to be taken into consideration? We may never know "the full story on E.J.C.," but the questions are worth exploring. If we can better understand the anxious zigzags in one man's lifelong effort to affirm credibly the authority of the Bible, we shall gain a better sense of the vulnerability of the evangelicalism he represented. More significantly, we can at least hope to discover some ways to move beyond the intellectually and existentially barren issue of inerrancy while at the same time affirming the transcendent value of the biblical literature.

Carnell tackled the inerrancy problem head-on in his first book, *An Introduction to Christian Apologetics,* published before he was graduated from Harvard Divinity School in 1948. He expressed misgivings about that youthful accomplishment in the last few years of his life. In a 1961 letter to an old Wheaton classmate, he acknowledged that "the book is full of literary crudities as well as ostentatious usages of technical terms and foreign phrases."[5] He regretted its excessive rationalism[6] and commented to one of his students that with every passing year it looked thinner and thinner.[7] But this list of shortcomings diverts attention from more serious problems. Nowhere are the book's fundamental deficiencies more evident than in a chapter entitled "The Problem of Biblical Criticism." Carnell's starting point is clear – the same all-or-nothing approach we have just seen in Lindsell's book: "when one leaves the conservative's position on textual inerrancy, there is no stopping point short of skepticism and irrationalism" (205). However, the book deserves to be criticized not so much for its point of view as for the manner in which it treats the issues. If a conservative apologist has decided that defending belief in inerrancy is worth the effort in the first place, then his case must be given its day in the court of enlightened reason and fair argument. That is Carnell's declared objective.[8]

Regrettably, the argument does not proceed on this level. Carnell caricatures higher criticism by holding up for ridicule extreme views no responsible critic would think of defending: For example, "the critic explains Christ's walking on the water by a series of submerged rafts" (204). Carnell takes refuge in the irretrievable "original documents" which, he says, have been purposely lost by God's decree, "even as He decreed the dissolution of Noah's ark, the brazen serpent, the tabernacle, the original temple, and the holy vessels" (198). He does away with the tough problems by declaring them solved: "The radicals of Christianity –

the Trinity, the deity of Christ, creation, the virgin birth, the atonement, the resurrection, the image of God in man, the fall, etc. – have not been successfully attacked by higher criticism" (206); and he acknowledges only that criticism has raised problems of a minor character related to the text: "it is not enough to show that Noah could not get all of the animals into the ark or that the genealogies of Christ in Matthew and Luke seem discrepant" (206). He uses flagrantly inappropriate analogies: "If there is a tree in the yard, for example, one does not succeed in explaining it by calling it a horse. Likewise, when the Bible claims to be an inerrant revelation, it is no explanation of it to call it a report of the religious experiences of certain men" (205).

To be fair, Carnell does point out repeatedly that the basic difference between the conservative Christian view (which in this book he equates with the fundamentalist view) and that of the critic is philosophical. The former is supernatural, the latter natural. Although this distinction contains an element of truth, it obscures the true nature of modern biblical criticism. In maintaining that "the higher critic starts with his hypothesis that there has been no revelation" (194), Carnell refuses – or is unable – to see higher criticism's historical and scientific stance as a useful and essential heuristic strategy. If the critic were to presuppose the reality of the supernatural and the fact of divine revelation, that commitment would go beyond the permissible boundaries of historical research. Higher criticism does not necessarily deny the supernatural but must rule it out of the investigatory process. Unable to acknowledge this neutrality, Carnell summarily dismisses the results of the critical enterprise. When the critic concludes that Isaiah 40–66 was written not by Isaiah of Jerusalem but by one or more anonymous postexilic prophets, Carnell does not even consider the various lines of evidence in support of that view but attributes it solely to the antisupernaturalistic bias of both the scholar and the discipline itself (203).

Reinhold Niebuhr was very much on Carnell's mind as he wrote *Apologetics*, for at that same time he was preparing his Th.D. dissertation under the direction of Professor Auer at Harvard: "The Concept of Dialectic in the Theology of Reinhold Niebuhr."[9] In the thesis, in his subsequent book *The Theology of Reinhold Niebuhr* (based in large part on the thesis), and in magazine articles of that period, he takes special pains not only to distinguish his own conservative views from Niebuhrian neo-orthodoxy but to focus attention on Niebuhr's acceptance of "destructive higher criticism" (TRN 119). And within that field of vision, at several points he narrows down the focus still farther to the historicity of the early chapters of Genesis. He calls Niebuhr's mythic interpretation of the fall an "obsequious devotion to science," an unconscious assumption possibly resulting from "presuppositions imbedded into his thinking while a liberal studying at Yale" (TRN 174). One looks in vain for even an implicit admission that a fundamentalist studying at Wheaton and Westminster might also have absorbed some presuppositions into his thinking. For Carnell, the question has no ambiguities: "The Scriptures assume without embarrassment that there *was* a real historical Adam and that this Adam was the literal federal head of the race" (TRN 137). The evangelical conclusion: "once the existential experiences of the race may veto Scriptural authority on such crucial doctrines as the historicity of the fall and the federal headship of the first Adam, it can likewise do the same with either the doctrine of the second Adam or that of God's taking our sins upon and into Himself" (TRN 132). The very fact that Jesus alludes to Noah and the flood constitutes an affirmation of their historicity also (CBC 54), and for Niebuhr or anyone to question that interpretation is to reject "the Bible's account of itself" (CBC 53).

At this stage, one of Carnell's chief mechanisms for dealing with those who differed from his position on inerrancy was to restate anticipated arguments in such a way as to minimize their importance and then to turn the charges back on the critics. The accusation most frequently leveled at fundamentalists has always been that they are "literalists" in their reading of the Bible. Given the insistence on a literal Adam and Eve and the Garden of Eden in which they first sinned, one might expect Carnell to exult in the accusation – or at least to recognize a measure of validity. Instead he discloses "the straw-man character of this sport."

When Isaiah says "the mountains and the hills shall break forth before you into singing; and all the trees of the field shall clap their hands" (55:12), no conservative is to be charged with teaching that the mountains and hills shall literally sing and the trees shall literally clap their hands. The Fundamentalist interprets Scripture *naturally;* when the natural is the literal, he is literal: and when the natural is not, he is not literal. In this passage we have the obvious use of poetic language to express that state of joy and exhilaration which will be enjoyed when the blessings of Jehovah are poured out upon all Israel. (ICA 194)

So the narrow-minded interpreters turn out to be not the fundamentalists but the liberal critics who muddy the distinction between the literal and the figurative. One wonders what Carnell's response would have been if he had discussed not singing hills and hand-clapping trees but, for example, a reluctant prophet who was swallowed by a great fish and then spewed out on dry land. Would it not be more "natural" to read that narrative nonhistorically? But of course the fundamentalist cannot entertain the literal–figurative question in the case of Jonah; that narrative has to be accepted as literal history because Jesus (allegedly) affirmed its historicity ("For as Jonah was three days and three nights in the belly of the whale . . .").

Carnell quotes from one of his major theological mentors, the nineteenth-century Princeton theologian Charles Hodge, to redirect the charge of nit-picking small-mindedness usually aimed at fundamentalists:

"The errors in matters of fact which skeptics search out bear no proportion to the whole. No sane man would deny that the Parthenon was built of marble, even if here and there a speck of sandstone should be detected in its structure. Not less unreasonable is it to deny the inspiration of such a book as the Bible, because one sacred writer says that on a given occasion twenty-four thousand, and another says that twenty-three thousand, men were slain. Surely a Christian may be allowed to tread such objections under his feet." (ICA 206, 207)

What this argument obscures is the fact that from the outset the critic has very little interest in searching out "errors" in the Bible. James Barr says:

It is only within the fundamentalist world-view that it seems as if critical scholars are primarily concerned with the imputation of "error" to scripture. It is the fundamentalist doctrine, and not any other, that insists on pressing the category of error to the forefront of the discussion.[10]

As Barr puts it, fundamentalists "do not in fact build a great deal of their living faith upon the talking powers of Balaam's ass, of which they probably do not think more than once in ten years. But the moment someone questions the story of Balaam's ass everything is different. Any doubt about this and the entire edifice of Christianity may tumble to the ground."[11] Furthermore, the alleged flexibility that Carnell finds in Hodge's Parthenon analogy would be more impressive if either Hodge or Carnell were to acknowledge even one speck of sandstone in the marble of the biblical edifice.

Lindsell is correct in maintaining that until 1959 the paper track yields no evidence that Carnell's views on biblical inerrancy departed in any significant way from his own. The disturbing questions Carnell raised in *The Case for Orthodox Theology*, however, deserve our close inspection. The new stance was in part a matter of rhetorical strategy. You will recall that Westminster Press selected three scholars to write books on three distinct Christian theological traditions: L. Harold DeWolf (liberal), William Hordern (neo-orthodox), and Carnell (conservative). So in writing this book for a non-evangelical publisher, Carnell was guaranteed a substantially different reading audience, and was operating under a rather different mandate. More to the point, since his book would appear simultaneously as part of a trilogy – along with those of two better known theologians – he could realistically hope for a broader range of serious critical response than his previous books had received. New conditions such as these can cause a writer to take a fresh look at himself and his material.

One of the most controversial chapters was entitled "Difficulties," all of which he reduced to one great difficulty: the nature and extent of the Bible's authority and reliability. Carnell acknowledged the difficulties but minimized their importance ("To confuse a system with its difficulties betrays a want of education."). The strategy was not a resounding success. He alienated the conservatives who held to biblical inerrancy without impressing the liberals with his grasp of the issues. Note, for example, his summary statement on the problem of biological evolution: "While orthodoxy does not think that the evidence for human evolution is compelling, the evidence *is* sufficient to give pause. The verdict of paleontology cannot be dismissed by pious ridicule" (COT 95). It is difficult to imagine a set of propositions, on the one hand, more transparently intended to please both groups but, on the other, more surely destined to satisfy neither. His own ambivalence on inerrancy breaks onto the surface in his use of earlier scholars: whereas he quotes the Princeton theologians Charles Hodge and B. B. Warfield, both defenders of inerrancy, and calls their work "possibly the finest theological and apologetical thrust in the history of American orthodoxy" (COT 100), he balances their input by quotations from the Scottish apologist James Orr, no less orthodox but critical of the Princeton position on inerrancy. Moreover, he affirms the value and the orthodoxy of both points of view.

Carnell then resurrects in some detail the debate between Warfield and the Old Testament critic Henry Preserved Smith, an interchange of the 1890s in which the Princetonians (whether they realized it or not, says Carnell) were forced to acknowledge that "inspiration, at times, ensures no more than an infallible account of error" (COT 102).

At first blush this may seem like a very desperate expedient, but it actually implies no more than a strained use of procedures already at work in orthodoxy. If Hodge and Warfield had honored this as a possibility, they might have avoided their lofty disregard for the inductive difficulties. And if Orr had done likewise, he might have avoided his perilous admission of historical errors in Scripture. (COT 111)

Once again Carnell alienates both liberal and conservative readers. The liberal hears him proclaim that to admit historical errors in the Bible is perilous. The zealous adherent of right-wing orthodoxy hears Hodge and Warfield accused of a lofty disregard for what Carnell apparently considers legitimate and difficult questions.

Carnell's own formula for preserving belief in the inspiration and authority of the Bible builds on the key hermeneutical concept of progressive revelation. According to this view, the entire Bible is inspired, but not all parts are equally normative. Since at each stage of divine revelation God took into account the spiritual and cultural level of the people being addressed, it follows that some parts of the Bible are subject to illumination by other parts. In his scheme, five rules govern interpretation: (1) the New Testament interprets the Old Testament; (2) the Epistles interpret the Gospels; (3) systematic passages interpret the incidental; (4) universal passages interpret the local; (5) didactic passages interpret the symbolic (COT 53). All five should be seen as variations on a theme. As developed by Carnell, they take for granted that the Bible is a "system" to which we must submit (COT 51) and that its ultimate objective is a didactic presentation, primarily in Paul's letters to the Romans and Galatians, of a set of propositions identified as "the gospel":

Christ is the federal head of a new and holy race; he invested human nature with perfection by loving God with all his heart and his neighbor as himself. The human nature was then offered on the cross to satisfy divine justice. Being propitious toward the world, God forgives all who repent. This is the gospel, and its nerve center is justification by faith. (COT 58)

So central is the content of these didactic epistles that "if the church teaches anything that offends the system of Romans and Galatians, it is cultic" (COT 59).

The hermeneutic of progressive revelation does enable Carnell to finesse some awkward passages. He can, for example, minimize the relative importance of Peter's instructions on how women should dress and Paul's acceptance of the institution of slavery. He gains a clear basis for rejecting the cultic fundamentalist practice of opening the Bible indiscriminately and claiming a "promise for the day." But the more serious "difficulties" remain just as difficult. Moreover, an additional one has crept on the scene: The tilt toward systematic and didactic passages has the dispiriting effect of reducing the Bible to a manual of directions for securing eternal salvation.

We have already noted that in the spring of 1962, Carnell joined with five other young American theologians in a dialogue with Karl Barth at the University of Chicago Divinity School. Actually, the term dialogue is something of a misnomer. Each of the six submitted questions weeks in advance. Then on successive nights, in two groups of three, they asked the questions of Barth, who delivered prepared answers. There was little opportunity for interchange. In Carnell's case there was virtually none. With each questioner being given, so to speak, a half-hour with Karl Barth, Carnell led off the second evening, asked his questions, and was given twenty-nine minutes of answers.[12] Not wanting to encroach on the time of his colleagues, he chose to relinquish the floor instead of pursuing the questions any further.

At this point we should not find it surprising (1) that one of Carnell's questions was on inerrancy, (2) that he was not fully satisfied with Barth's answer, and (3) that he was taken to task by inerrancy-watchers for not clearly saying so. Here is Carnell's inerrancy question, as reprinted in the transcribed text of the Thursday evening session: "How does Dr. Barth in this connection harmonize his appeal to Scripture, as the objective Word of God, with his admission that Scripture is, indeed, sullied by errors, theological as well as historical or factual? [This is a problem for me too, I cheerfully confess.]"[13]

The next few minutes became the object of some controversy within the evangelical camp. Carnell's philosophy professor from the Wheaton years, Gordon Haddon Clark (at this time chair of the Philosophy Department at Butler University in Indianapolis) covered the seminar for *Christianity Today*. His account of Barth's answer and Carnell's reaction puts neither in a favorable light:

Barth's answer does not seem to meet the question. He asserted that the Bible is a fitting instrument to point men to God, who alone is infallible. The Bible is a human document and not sinless as Christ was. Then a large part of the overflow audience – possibly 500 were standing in the aisles or sitting on the stone floor – applauded Barth's assertion that there are "contradictions and errors" in the Bible. After and possibly because of this expression of hostility, Carnell professed to be satisfied and did not press the matter of a nonbiblical criterion by which to judge what is a theological error in the Bible.[14]

The tape recording of that evening session gives a rather different picture.[15] Here is the full text of Barth's answer, with some interpolated comments concerning audience response:

I have always stressed, emphasized, the objective character of the inspiration of scripture, insofar as scripture is unique, the unique, for-good-and-all-given witness, for to that work of God whose content is the covenant, Jesus Christ, the reconciliation (or we can also say atonement) realized for all men. By objective character of inspiration, I understand the one work of the one Holy Spirit in which he evokes and instructs the prophets and the apostles to be witnesses to God's work and Word. And in which he discloses to hearers and readers of the Bible the meaning and the irresistible challenge of the testimony of the prophets and the apostles. That's what I understand speaking of the objective character of inspiration. This total work of the Holy Spirit, of God the Holy Spirit, as much as the reconciling work of Christ, has immediate bearing upon the existence of all men. So the biblical word is in its objective character an event of immediate bearing upon all men.

The Bible has proved and will prove itself as a true and fitting instrument to point men to God and his work and his Word, to God who alone is infallible. The Bible did and does so being a human instrument and document, bound and conditioned by temporal views of nature, of ideas, of values. Insofar the Bible is not sinless like Jesus Christ, and thus not infallible like God. No wonder that, seen from the viewpoint of the world views and the concepts of other ages, the question may arise whether we have not to reckon with the occurrence of certain, let us say, tensions, contradictions, and maybe (if you prefer the term) errors . . .

At this point a slight murmur ripples momentarily through the audience. It is not applause and it is not hostile. The crowd, I suggest, is responding here to Barth's good-natured irony as he uses the word "errors," which Carnell had used in the original question but is echoed here only to accommodate the questioner's point of view. Then Barth concludes his answer – very slowly, with a twinkle in his eye.

. . . on the level of its time-bound human statements.

Again there is a pause. The auditorium is silent. Barth has finished the substance of his answer, but he holds the moment in suspension. He has a question of his own to ask Carnell.

Is that enough to encourage you to continue to cheerfully confess that here is a problem also for you?

Now the audience does break out into general laughter, but it is not in the least hostile. And, contrary to Clark's account, the listeners do not applaud. They are responding, I think, in spontaneous appreciation of the captivating mix of honesty, perception, warmth, and gentle wit that characterized Barth's answer. The tape cuts off abruptly at that point. There may have been subsequent applause, but if so I should guess it was in reaction to a remark made by panel moderator Jaroslav Pelikan just after the break in the tape: "That is just another way of saying 'Welcome to the Club.'" Pelikan's comment obviously responds to the fact that Barth had picked up on Carnell's earlier statement ("This is a problem for me too, I cheerfully confess"). In any case, Clark's claim that the audience "applauded Barth's assertion that there are 'contradictions and errors' in the Bible" is simply not true. It is a gross distortion hard to understand and impossible to justify.

Carnell's acknowledgment of serious difficulties in the inerrancy position, both in *The Case for Orthodox Theology* and at the Barth seminar, inevitably involved Harold Lindsell, at that time still a member of the Fuller administration, in a sort of damage-control operation. He replied at length to criticism of Carnell's book made by evangelist John R. Rice, editor of the fundamentalist newspaper *The Sword of the Lord*.[16] In the Barth controversy Lindsell wrote a letter to *Christianity Today*, taking issue with Gordon Clark's portrayal of Carnell's Chicago performance, basing his defense on two main points in Carnell's May 15 report in the Fuller chapel: (1) his unequivocally declared belief in inerrancy; (2) his explanation of why he let Barth off the hook (i.e., not wanting to encroach on the designated time of his colleagues).[17] He might also have added a third point. Clark had charged that Carnell professed to be "satisfied" with Barth's answer on inerrancy. In his report, Carnell maintained that if by satisfaction one means a resolution of the objections that gave rise to the question in the first place, then of course he was not satisfied. He referred to Barth's "vague view of the authority of scripture" and added: "I was satisfied with the time and energy he had given to my questions."[18]

It is time, I suspect, to get back to the original question and try to work our way out of this less than edifying barrage of dogmatic affirmations, objections, and counterclaims. Where has the paper track led us? We have to agree with Lindsell, I think, when he calls Carnell's question-raising period an "aberration" – and not very much of an aberration at that. Carnell admits difficulties but insists one must not throw out a solidly based doctrine of inerrancy because of certain unanswered questions. He displays a charitable spirit to those who hold differing views – to the extent that he accepts Barth as an "inconsistent evangelical" (as opposed to an "inconsistent liberal") in spite of what he considers his inadequate stance on biblical authority. Carnell's ambivalence shows when he condescendingly pats Barth on the back for making "enormous progress" in conquering the presuppositions he imbibed as a student under Harnack at the University of Berlin, while at the same time regretting that he is still held back from "taking in scripture with the kind of abandon that you and I would consider normative for a theologian."[19]

Clearly we would be deceiving ourselves if we thought Carnell made some giant leap forward in his grasp of the inerrancy issue. But neither should we minimize how deeply troubling it was for a man of his theological outlook to live with questions for which he had no satisfactory answers. There is more to a theologian's life than a paper track. We must not forget that in 1959 Carnell had resigned from the Fuller presidency because his physical and psychological health was buckling under the responsibilities of administration and the pressure of adverse criticism. For five weeks immediately prior to the Barth seminar he had been hospitalized for a breakdown and had been receiving electroconvulsive therapy. And when he got to Chicago, as if just being in that pressure-packed situation were not enough to bear, he was renounced in a face-to-face meeting by his revered friend and teacher, Gordon Clark. The entire experience of opening the windows just a little bit and letting the fresh breezes of honest doubt blow through the musty dogma of biblical inerrancy had proved to be profoundly unsettling.

The ambivalence with which Carnell approached the inerrancy issue at this time was clearly evident in the role he played at what has come to be called Fuller Seminary's "Black Saturday" early in December 1962.[20] A faculty–trustee planning retreat held in Pasadena's Huntington Sheraton Hotel developed into a marathon session on the issue of biblical inerrancy, with special attention focused on the views of Dan Fuller, who had been studying at Basel under Karl Barth and had just returned to the seminary as newly appointed dean of the faculty. Fuller was convinced that any statement on inerrancy in the seminary's proposed new creed must take into serious consideration the discrepancies between certain biblical details and stubborn empirical facts. Carnell challenged him, arguing that since *all* worldviews confront empirical facts that do not fit their systems, evangelical Christianity should not jettison the doctrine of inerrancy just because of textual and historical difficulties in the biblical record. Fuller recalls that Carnell said to him: " 'My laundry list of difficulties that biblical Christianity has with empirical facts is longer than any other list in this room of 120 people, including yours, Dan Fuller, but this should not cause us to be disturbed, since my list is still the shortest of any world view.' "[21]

Nevertheless, disturbed he was. At some point in the mid-sixties Carnell accepted the invitation of Robert McAfee Brown to speak at Stanford University. Brown gives a chilling account of his behavior on that occasion:

I was very concerned about him. His speech was halting, with long pauses between words, and he was obviously under a very heavy tension and pressure. I think he was getting a very bad kind of pressure from his right-wing constituents during that period. One wanted to pull the words out of him, so great was the difficulty in articulation. What he said was good, but it was produced with tremendous effort. A student asked him some question that was particularly difficult to answer from an ultraconservative Biblical viewpoint, and he responded something like "That's . . . one . . . of those . . . questions . . . I . . . have . . . in a folder . . . marked 'Unsolved . . . Problems.' " He was clear that there were problems, and he was not trying to duck them. But the price of his intellectual honesty clearly took a heavy toll.[22]

I have delayed consideration of the inerrancy issue until this point in the book because I believe that it is the key to all the other issues – for both the man and the movement – though assuredly not on the grounds argued by Harold Lindsell. In the second and third parts of this chapter, I shall lift two phrases from Carnell's writings and pursue their implications for the evangelical belief in inerrancy – implications their author never acknowledged or fully explored. The next section will concentrate primarily on the Old Testament, the subsequent one on the New.

B. The "rights of language" in biblical literature

Two years before he died, Carnell wrote an article for *Christianity Today* arguing that "Conservatives and Liberals Do Not Need Each Other."[23] In it he breaks no new ground. In fact, his approach is substantially the same as that taken by J. Gresham Machen in *Christianity and Liberalism*, written in the 1920s.[24] Since conservatives are convinced that the Bible contains a divinely revealed system of truth, and since liberals subordinate the data of Scripture to data drawn from contemporary science and philosophy, "it is just about as meaningful to say that palm trees and icebergs need each other as it is to say that conservatives and liberals need each other" (CBC 39).

However, in his litany of dogmatic beliefs about the Bible, Carnell reintroduces a concept that made a brief appearance in his first book: "the rights of language." He uses it twice in the *Christianity Today* article:

Liberals are so dedicated to the vision of making the Christian religion relevant to the supposed needs of modern man that they consider it a handicap to be checked by the rights of language in Scripture. (CBC 37)

It is true that liberals sometimes claim to experience an encounter with God through the reading of Scripture, but this should never be confused with a whole-soul submission to the rights of language in Scripture. (CBC 37)

We can discern readily what he means by the phrase. It is another way of affirming what he also called the "natural" interpretation of the Bible. According to that view, the conservative is a literalist only when the "natural" reading is literal; when the reading is not "naturally" literal, the conservative is not a literalist. Scriptural language, says Carnell, has a *right* to be interpreted in this way. But if one tries to apply the principle, one discovers almost immediately that the crucial question has been swept aside: what is the definition of that slippery label "natural"? We could perhaps agree (at least tentatively) on the extreme ends of the figurative–literal continuum. If we read that "the trees of the field shall clap their hands," we know that this is a poetic metaphor. If we read that "David reigned over all Israel," we know that we should take the words at literal face value. But what of the expanse of territory in between? Carnell seems to have no problem. If there is the slightest whisper of a doubt, he opts for the literal as most natural. Consequently, he sees a whole range of widely differing biblical material as uniformly historical: from Adam and Eve's exit from the Garden of Eden to the entry of the children of Israel into Canaan; from the fall of the Philistine temple at Samson's hands to the fall of Jerusalem under the armies of Babylon; from the preservation of Daniel and his friends in the fiery furnace to the blinding conversion of Saul on the road to Damascus. This reluctance to differentiate among degrees of historicity – or, to put it another way, to rule out the categories of myth, saga, legend, fiction – stems from the same root-source as his Romans-Galatians principle. Carnell is unable to see the Bible as other than a divinely revealed "system" of propositional truths whose purpose is to convey accurately and unmistakably a set of directions for making peace with God. Scripture *demands* to be so interpreted.

That is what he *intends* the phrase "the rights of language in Scripture" to mean. However, if we take seriously the idea that the language of biblical literature has "rights" (and I suggest we must), we inevitably find ourselves in different territory, facing questions much more subtle and complex than are permitted by Carnell's principles of interpretation. The language of the Bible cannot be reduced to that of a guidebook through this life to the next. Even when it seems most direct, most didactic, there is a good deal more going on linguistically. As Northrop Frye puts it, "The Bible is far too deeply rooted in all the resources of language for any simplistic approach to its language to be adequate."[25] In the broadest sense, because the Bible is literature, its language has a "right" to be examined as literary. That is to say, we have an obligation to consider the means as well as the end, the medium as well as the message. Or to put it yet another way, if we conceive of the Bible's language as clear transparent glass through which we gaze at the objective content of divine revelation on the other side – totally unaware of the medium through which we are looking – we are not seeing as much or as clearly as we might think we are. The literary language of the Bible is a stained-glass window; we have to look *at* it, as well as *through* it.[26]

Obviously, no one would ever deny that the Bible is literature. Even an extreme right-wing fundamentalist – believing, let us say, that the Bible writers were glorified amanuenses who took dictation from the Holy Ghost – recognizes the difference between prose and poetry, between parable and epistle. But there is more at stake here than those elementary distinctions imply. Invariably, when one says, "The Bible should be read as literature," warning bells go off in the heads of theological conservatives. It is too easy to imagine the words "merely" or "nothing but" lurking in the underbrush, ready to leap out and plant themselves immovably in that sentence. To be sure, there is some reason for concern. Reading the Bible as literature can indeed be confined to an appreciation of the comforting cadences of the King James Version, archaic diction, and ornamental metaphor.

This seems to be what bothers Frederick Buechner in *Wishful Thinking: A Theological ABC*: "To read the Bible as literature is like reading *Moby Dick* as a whaling manual or *The Brothers Karamazov* for its punctuation."[27] Buechner's vividly phrased conviction provides a useful lens with which to focus this part of our discussion, for Buechner is no Carnell. Highly regarded author of ten novels, in addition to several nonfiction books, and artful prose stylist, he has solid credentials as a man of letters. Although he is an ordained Presbyterian clergyman, he does not classify himself as an evangelical. His view of the Bible is light-years away from Carnell's:

> In short, one way to describe the Bible, written by many different men over a period of three thousand years and more, would be to say that it is a disorderly collection of sixty-odd books which are often tedious, barbaric, obscure, and teem with contradictions and inconsistencies. It is a swarming compost of a book, an Irish stew of poetry and propaganda, law and legalism, myth and murk, history and hysteria. Over the centuries it has become hopelessly associated with tub-thumping evangelism and dreary piety, with superannuated superstition and blue-nosed moralizing, with ecclesiastical authoritarianism and crippling literalism.[28]

Moreover, Buechner's published sermons and *Peculiar Treasures*,[29] his delightful observations on a gallery of biblical characters, provide irrefutable evidence that he surveys the people, places, and events of the Bible with the sensitive eye of the novelist. If, then, he himself reads the Bible as literature, his whaling manual/punctuation analogy can mean only one thing: Buechner is insisting that the Bible be read as more than literature – "as the Word of God which speaks out of the depths of an almost unimaginable past into the depths of ourselves."[30] That is a legitimately arguable "overbelief" (to use William James's term for items of faith that elicit our personal commitment but for which we cannot give demonstrable proof), an overbelief in no way mutually exclusive with reading the Bible as literature. What is disturbing about Carnell's view of the Bible – a vulnerability that pervades evangelicalism still – is the sterile tendency to read the Bible as less than literature.

Why, we might ask, do we read literature? What do we get out of *Moby Dick* and *The Brothers Karamazov?* More, obviously, than cetological lore and lessons in correct punctuation. We can start on the level of pleasure – and if by pleasure we mean delight in how language is used to shape and share experience, we need never leave this level, but only deepen our capacity for being delighted. One of the components of that deeper pleasure is a broadening of our range of experience, not merely by vicariously treading the decks of the *Pequod*, on which we would never otherwise set foot, but by venturing out metaphorically with Melville on the heavy seas of metaphorical madness. Another component is the enrichment of our human understanding and empathy as Dostoevsky probes relentlessly into the hidden recesses of the Karamazovs, who compulsively lacerate themselves and others. We read literature, in other words, to grow, to increase our capacity to be human, to be more fully alive. Should we look for any *less* than this when we read the Bible as literature? Except for sounding like a truism, Buechner's statement might better have said: "To read the Bible as literature is like reading *Moby Dick* or *The Brothers Karamazov* as literature." If some feel compelled to read it as *more* than literature – to affirm it as divinely revealed scripture – that is a different and extremely complicated issue. We should in any case not read it as *less* than literature.

Whereas it would be folly to argue that the entire Bible is of equal literary value, it is remarkable how much of it holds up under close inspection: the intricate parallel structure of the Joseph story with its sophisticated symbolism; the brilliant rhetorical strategy of the prophet Amos, who wanders into town as a stranger, gathers an indifferent audience, cleverly manipulates them into certain tacit responses, and then springs his trap; the inverted strategy of the book of Jonah, a satirical comedy in which a reluctant prophet speaks unwillingly to foreigners, gets a wildly successful response in which even the animals don sackcloth and ashes, and then sinks into peevish despair because God's merciful forgiveness toward the repentant Ninevites has discredited him as a prophet; the composite structure of the Book of Job, in which the author of the poetic philosophical dialogues borrows a well known folktale, breaks it into two parts, and uses it as a prose prologue and epilogue to provide a setting for the interplay of ideas and a counterpoint to his real concerns.

It is no exaggeration to say that in his fearful tribulations on the ash heap, Job's stubborn refusal to bow to the conventional pieties mouthed by his friends rivals Ahab's monomaniacal obsession with the white whale. The extended narratives that center on David – some of them legend, some intimate court history – present a complex human being quite the equal of Ivan, Dmitri, and Alyosha: Brilliant statesman and petty tyrant, man of God and man of blood, David is the most fully developed character in the Old Testament.

Many of the minor characters too are deftly painted with just a few brush strokes: Michal, David's badly mistreated wife; Potiphar's seductive wife, who it seems had only one thing to say, "Come lie with me," and said it over and over, day after day; Reuben, who ostentatiously offered the lives of his two sons as surety if arrangements with Pharaoh's lieutenant governor went bad; and Judah, who under similar circumstances more convincingly offered his own life as a guarantee.

The literary qualities of the New Testament, though no less impressive than the Old Testament, are perhaps more difficult to appreciate as literature. Parables, gospels, epistles – we think we know them so well. But most readers – fundamentalists and liberals, clergy and laity, religious and secular, even nonreaders – think of them not as literature but as Scripture, whether or not they revere them as such. Commitment to the dogma of inerrancy only increases the height of the barrier.

Inasmuch as Carnell repeatedly brings up the early chapters of Genesis to reinforce his view of Scripture's inerrancy and literal historicity, he virtually invites using them as a test case. His own approach is clear in *Introduction to Christian Apologetics,* in the passage where he first uses the phrase "the rights of language":

> Christianity's problem at this point is organic evolution, for the Bible cannot sustain the view that man is genetically related to the lower animals. Only he who plays fast and loose with the rights of language can deny that Moses taught that man came from the dust, by a special act of God, not through an organic development from a lower animal. (ICA 112)

Carnell never significantly departed from this view. In *The Case for Orthodox Theology,* as we have seen, he opened the door to the possibility that orthodoxy might justifiably relinquish the immediate creation theory out of respect for paleontology, but that is a considerable distance from declaring his belief in organic evolution (which is what his critics accused him of doing) (COT 95).

In literary terms, what was missing from Carnell's engagement with the early chapters of Genesis was the concept of myth. In all his writings, the only references to "myth" are in *The Theology of Reinhold Niebuhr,* where he could not responsibly avoid the subject since it plays such a key role in Niebuhr's theology and biblical exegesis. He is reasonably fair in expounding Niebuhr's use of myth, pointing out that it is not equivalent to "fable" or "tale" (as most fundamentalists would interpret any use of the term). In Niebuhr's work, he says, myth and symbol mediate between the dialectical realms of time and eternity. Properly understood, they avoid on one side the literalism of orthodoxy and, on the other, liberalism's frivolous dismissal of biblical content. As Carnell interprets Niebuhr, "one must learn to take the myth earnestly, but not literally" (TRN 57, 112). But Carnell, of course, has no taste for this himself. He can discuss respectfully Niebuhr's sophisticated view of myth, but his mind simply does not operate on a mythic frequency. He cannot escape the dark suspicion that myth somehow denies something essential: that without a literal interpretation of a historical Adam and Eve in a Garden of Eden geographically located (however vaguely) on a map, Christianity would crumble as a system. With historicity as his main concern, he inevitably overlooks other things that are going on in Genesis one through eleven. Myth opens the door to these wider dimensions.

Paul Ricoeur, in his introduction to *The Symbolism of Evil,* sorts out what myth can and cannot do for modern readers. Acknowledging that modern historical-critical method has made it impossible for us to believe any longer in myth as explanation, he argues that we have gained something more important:

> But in losing its explanatory pretensions the myth reveals its exploratory significance and its contribution to understanding, which we shall later call its symbolic function – that is to say, its power of discovering and revealing the bond between man and what he considers sacred. Paradoxical as it may seem, the myth, when it is thus demythologized through contact with scientific history and elevated to the dignity of a symbol, is a dimension of modern thought.[31]

Milan Machovec, professor of philosophy at the University of Prague, points to a startling turnaround: "Twenty years ago when a Marxist opened the Bible, he said, 'mythology, fairytales, mythological cosmology.' When he opens the Bible nowadays, he finds also the question: 'Where is your brother Abel?' After all, that is the only ethical question of all times and all ages, and it is the question which the Marxists are tragically experiencing right now."[32] If Carnell were still alive, he would probably point out with some annoyance that he never doubted for a moment the eternally contemporary importance of the question "Where is your brother Abel?" And to a certain extent he would be right. Nevertheless, his hermeneutical straitjacket forced him to stress historicity so overwhelmingly that inevitably he shunted into the background the existential relevance of myth.

The evangelical refusal to acknowledge the presence of mythic elements in the Bible is undoubtedly due in part to the fear that the Holy Scripture will thereby be dragged down to the level of pagan mythology with its magical metamorphoses and less than lofty accounts of divine antics. However, a comparative analysis of the Genesis creation accounts with other creation myths should dispel that fear. To be sure, one is always susceptible to ethnocentric bias in making such comparisons, but there does seem to be a real and substantial difference between, say, the violent cosmic struggle in the Babylonian pantheon (in which the chaos monster was finally sliced in half, with the upper part forming the waters above the earth and the lower part the waters under the earth) and the majestic word of the deity in Genesis chapter one. Moreover, we must not lose sight of the fact that myth plays a relatively limited role in the biblical writings. Herbert Schneidau points out that although the Hebrews could neither avoid having mythology nor keep it out of the Bible, Hebrew mythology was inherently unstable. "Its forms had, as it were, short half-lives, because the Yahwist vision was always latent within them, ready to erode the comfortable assumption that they shared in Yahweh's sacredness."[33] Normally, in ancient times, myth affirmed the cultural status quo. Repeatedly we find the Old Testament literature struggling against the status quo in the name of a higher commitment to Israel's historical covenant with Yahweh. Brevard Childs puts it this way: "[Israel] could not tolerate the concept of reality found in the myth since it opposed that new reality of which they were a part."[34]

I have concentrated on the early chapters of Genesis because Carnell focused so much of his attention there. But much that has been said concerning the issue of historicity versus myth in these chapters applies as well to other parts of the Old Testament: to legendary material in the patriarchal narratives, to the saga of Israel's exodus from Egypt, to the more conscious fictional art of Jonah and Ruth. Herman Gunkel, one of the great Old Testament scholars whose long career bridged the nineteenth and twentieth centuries, was keenly aware that his views were controversial and sought to allay the fears of traditional biblicists without surrendering the conclusions of his research:

The senseless confusion of "legend" with "lying" has caused good people to hesitate to concede that there are legends in the Old Testament. But legends are not lies; on the contrary, they are a particular form of poetry. Why should not the lofty spirit of Old Testament religion, which employed so many varieties of poetry, indulge in this form also? For religion everywhere, the Israelite religion included, has especially cherished poetry and poetic narrative, since poetic narrative is much better qualified than prose to be the medium of religious thought.[35]

In our effort to widen the meaning of "the rights of language," we have confined our attention so far to the Old Testament. But for the defender of orthodoxy, however unshakable his faith that "all Scripture is given by inspiration of God," the truly important arena of conflict is the New Testament. One of Carnell's five hermeneutical principles, we recall, stated that "the New Testament interprets the Old." Carnell argued vociferously for the historicity of "the first Adam," but it is Christ, "the second Adam," who is Lord and Savior. Still holding on to the conviction that if we take seriously "the rights of language" in the biblical writings we shall be dealing with broad and complex literary questions, let us see where we are led when we direct some of those questions at Carnell's treatment of New Testament texts.

C. "We still have to *interpret* this interpretation": on using hermeneutical horse sense

In an argument, the appeal to "horse sense" is more often than not a verbal ploy on the order of "As any fool can plainly see," with the implied or stated conclusion never as obvious to the listeners as it is to the speaker. Carnell drags the horse into a review of William Hordern's *The Case for a New Reformation Theology* and L. Harold DeWolf's *The Case for Theology in a Liberal Perspective*, two-thirds of the Westminster Press trilogy on Protestant theology. Carnell, you will recall, wrote the third book, *The Case for Orthodox Theology*. When the three books were simultaneously published, *The Journal of Bible and Religion* invited the three authors (none of whom had been aware of each other's participation in the project) to review the books written by their colleagues.[36]

Starting with the conviction that "a Protestant has a sacred duty to test theology by Scripture and right reason," Carnell says that each author has done his best with regard to the latter criterion. As for the former, "I do not believe that an equal effort has been made to square theology with the claims of Scripture. It is here, not on the issue of right reason, that Protestant theology divides into such elements as orthodoxy, liberalism, and neo-orthodoxy" (CBC 171). And what are these claims? In this essay, Carnell does not argue explicitly for inerrancy; at least he does not use the term. However, everything he says adds up to the familiar appeal to an inerrant Bible. Here he builds his case on the primacy of the apostles, alluding to I Corinthians 12:28: "And God has appointed in the church first apostles . . ."

It is an exegetical fact, and no remonstrance against orthodoxy can change a line of it, that the apostles were appointed to render a normative interpretation of the redemptive events. . . . The apostles were chosen by Christ; they were first eyewitnesses, then preachers of Christ's resurrection; their gifts were excellent and extraordinary; they were endowed with the spirit of prophecy; and they enjoyed primacy over the entire church. (CBC 171)

He knows he will get feedback on this claim. Liberalism and neo-orthodoxy, he says, will hasten to point out that the apostles wrote many things that even the orthodox believer does not pay attention to any more – such historically conditioned concerns as "baptism for the dead, decorous female attire, and whether a man should give his virgin in marriage."
Enter the horse.

I do not think a genuine difficulty is here being raised, and the Reformation is proof of it. There is no cause to go beyond the apostles, provided we use a little horse sense when defining our rules of hermeneutics. The apostles supply a criterion by which we can distinguish between the permanent and temporary elements in the apostolic witness. Luther knew this, and so did the other Reformers. There are places in the New Testament where the apostles develop doctrine in systematic language. These places serve as a criterion by which the force of everything else in Scripture is decided. (CBC 172, 173)

Except for the unexamined assumption that any New Testament document with an apostle's name on it was in fact written by the apostle, Carnell does have a point in his emphasis on the importance of the apostolic tradition. The witness of the New Testament is indispensable to our knowledge and understanding of Jesus, the nature of his teaching, the events of his public ministry, and the life of the primitive church. Moreover, no one can dispute his statement that "we are separated from the redemptive events by nearly two thousand years." But when he sets up the systematic and didactic passages as the touchstone of the permanent elements in the apostolic witness, he is projecting onto the New Testament literature itself a whole set of extra-biblical assumptions. In his own terminology – repeated again and again in his various writings – the Bible is a consistent, unified system of propositional revelation; the most direct and systematic presentation of its plan of salvation is in Paul's letters to the Romans and Galatians.

This approach stirs up a nest of problems that can be narrowed down to two categories. First, it too easily bifurcates the didactic and the non-didactic. The parables of Jesus, for example, can hardly be called systematic, but are we to conclude that Jesus did not use them to teach? What about the sermons of Peter in Acts? One sees patterns of systematic organization and senses an underlying purpose that is in some sense didactic, but surely it is going too far to suggest that they "develop doctrine." The New Testament consists of a variety of literary forms, all of which have their own patterns of organization and their own didactic purposes. Carnell's oversimplified criterion appears more useful than it is in practice. Second, even if we could confidently sort out the passages in which "the apostles develop doctrine in systematic, didactic language," and thus feel able to distinguish between the permanent and the temporary, the problem would remain unsolved. What we discover when we apply Carnell's hermeneutical horse sense is that the permanent is no less in need of interpretation than the temporary. It simply will not do to brush aside the awkward references to "the baptism for the dead" as time-bound and enshrine "Christ died for our sins" as permanent doctrine needing no interpretation.

Carnell is not unaware of the problem. In this very essay, seeking to differentiate between the "free and open conversation" of Protestant theology and the Roman Catholic requirement that we submit to the truth rather than search for it, he stresses a "very stubborn fact":

Even though the apostles render a normative interpretation of the redemptive events, we still have to *interpret* this interpretation. Before we can submit to the apostles, we must use our own judgment to decide what the apostles said. (CBC 172)

"We still have to *interpret* this interpretation." One thinks back, perhaps, to the previous section of this chapter where Carnell's use of the phrase "the rights of language in Scripture" created a much wider opening than he intended. Here his purpose is to score points against Roman Catholicism's ecclesiastical control of interpretation. Once again, however, the door – having been unlatched and pushed open just a bit – swings freely on its hinges. In attempting to refute the Roman Catholic position, Carnell thereby raises serious questions about the meaning and extent of apostolic authority itself. If in reading the New Testament we have to *interpret* material that has already been *interpreted* by the apostles as they have engaged with the redemptive events, we are viewing those events through at least a double interpretive grid – which is two mighty leaps (at least) from the bumpersticker hermeneutics of "God said it, I believe it, that settles it."

Carnell himself is obviously uneasy with this position. His strategy is to lean heavily on the word *normative,* which he uses nine times in this section of the essay. Although the apostles rendered an *interpretation* of the redemptive events, their interpretation was divinely stamped as *normative.* Not content simply to declare that normative status, he attempts to buttress it in several ways. First he calls on the time-honored rule that "whenever a difference of opinion arises about the meaning of specific data, the novice should defer to the judgment of the expert." That unexceptionable generalization crumbles, however, when he tacks on an analogy: "When judging histology, a physician is more qualified than a shoemaker; and when judging theology, the apostles are more qualified than modern theologians." Even leaving aside the blatant bias in the particular terms that fill out the analogy, it confuses the issue. On-the-scene witnesses are essential as the source of data, but their interpretations of meaning and their evaluations of historical significance, though treated with profound respect, are something else again. The apostles are indeed more qualified as reporters of the redemptive events than those who lived generations or centuries later. But it is a red herring to say, as Carnell does, that they "knew a lot more about Christian theology than we do." It is not *theology* we get from the apostles. Christian theology was built on the foundation of their witness. We must not minimize the importance of that witness. We may even attribute a primacy to it. But insofar as it is interpretation with theological implications, we have to interpret it ourselves, struggle with it, weigh it, sift it.

Having swung the door open by acknowledging that the apostles' witness is itself an interpretation that we must in turn interpret, Carnell seems intent on immediately shutting it, or at least installing a three-inch safety chain. Evangelicals can peer into the next room but are not to enter. Anyone who offers an interpretation different from the apostles' is a "pompous egotist" who "would put his judgment on a par with that of Peter and Paul." Our only justifiable response to the normative apostolic interpretation, he says, is submission. But for all practical purposes this conclusion is identical to the Roman Catholic position he just finished rejecting. Ironically, at the beginning of this essay on the Westminster trilogy, Carnell recounted an experience of graduate school days when he "tried to enter into theological conversation with several Jesuit priests":

All went well until I challenged their exegesis. They answered, with flashing eyes, that they were under sacred vows not to consider the possibility of truth outside their own papal traditions. I told them, in parting, that I had a better chance of finding truth than they did, for unlike them I was free to consider both sides of a question. My remark made little impression. (CBC 170, 171)

Perhaps the remark made little impression because the priests recognized that this seemingly self-assured young man was not quite so free as he thought. If they were required to submit to an infallible church, he owed submission to an inerrant Bible and to a fundamentalist tradition that could be challenged only at great cost.

Facing the inerrancy issue in the New Testament calls our attention to the same kinds of problems confronted in the Old: narrative discrepancies throughout the synoptic gospels, certain instances of the miraculous and the supernatural, material of dubious historicity such as the claim in Matthew 27:51–53 that when Jesus was crucified there was a sort of earthquake that split rocks and opened tombs and that many of the believers were raised from the dead, walked around the city of Jerusalem, "and appeared to many." We can move our discussion ahead more significantly, however, if we get right to the heart of the matter. Keeping in mind Carnell's assertion that hermeneutical horse sense enables us to discern what is permanent as over against what is temporary in the apostles' witness, let us explore briefly what he unequivocally identifies as the permanent core of the gospel, which can be found, he says, in its purest form in Paul's letter to the Romans.

When Paul wrote Romans, not only was his apostolic authority fully established, but there were no local controversies to distract his mind from the grand task of reviewing the plan of salvation. The result was a perfect treatise in systematic theology. (COT 66)

The core of the core is found in Romans 3:20–26, which Carnell quotes in a key portion of *Christian Commitment:*

"For no human being will be justified in his sight by works of the law since through the law comes knowledge of sin. But now the righteousness of God has been manifested apart from the law, although the law and the prophets bear witness to it, the righteousness of God through faith in Jesus Christ for all who believe. For there is no distinction; since all have sinned and fall short of the glory of God, they are justified by his grace as a gift, through the redemption which is in Christ Jesus, whom God put forward as an expiation by his blood, to be received by faith . . . it was to prove at the present time that he himself is righteous and that he justifies him who has faith in Jesus." (CC 253)

Carnell's own comment on this passage is as unambiguous as can be imagined: "This *is* Christianity; let no one be deceived." We should pay special attention to the organizing legal metaphor he borrows from Paul and uses whenever he discusses the divine plan of salvation. "Christ propitiated the judicial sentiment in God, thus making it possible for God to offer pardon to sinners. *This* is the essence of the atonement" (CC 251). Or, as he puts it in a 1956 *Christian Century* article, "The line between the saved and the lost is drawn at the point of forensic justification" (CBC 88). Or yet again, in a 1950 book review: "The penal theory of Christ's death is so uncontrovertibly taught in the Bible that if the Scriptures do not mean what they say at this point, they do not mean anything at any point; for the whole covenant of grace points to, and is fulfilled by, the substitutionary atonement of the Lamb of God."[37] In other words, Carnell makes the New Testament passages that present this doctrine a litmus test for one's stance on the Bible as a whole and therefore on Christianity in general. Do the Scriptures mean what they say or do they not? It is that clear-cut.

And yet a small voice tells us to reserve judgment. It is Carnell's voice saying, "We still have to *interpret* this interpretation." However didactic Romans 3:20–26 may be, it is not the redemptive event itself; it is Paul's interpretation of the event. But then Carnell's more dogmatic voice insists that although an interpretation, it is normative and we must submit to it. But again that other voice: "We still have to *interpret* this interpretation." And so we do. We verbalize our own understanding of the gospel message in language and metaphors appropriate to our own time and place. If we hear only Carnell's dogmatic voice, we tend to treat Paul's words as if they were etched in stone. If it is the other voice that sounds in our inner ear, although we may treasure Paul's apostolic witness, we see him also as a first century Jewish rabbinical scholar with an inevitable propensity toward interpreting the redemptive events in forensic terms. Conceiving of God as a rigidly legalistic ruler whose "judicial sentiment" has been offended and who cannot forgive sinners until the sacrificial death of his own Son has balanced the books may be the Pauline way of trying to capture the Christ event in language. It is not the only way.

D. A few suggestions for which are made no claims of inerrancy

In an article entitled "Biblical Hermeneutics: The Academic Language of Evangelical Identity," Gerald T. Sheppard has put his finger on what in the inerrancy dogma is so damaging to evangelicals themselves. He points out first how all the denominations linked together by affiliation with the National Association of Evangelicals "have made a social contract on matters of biblical authority against the 'liberal' denominations":

> Although the function of this confession has changed, its linguistic expression still fluctuates within certain specific technical limits rarefied earlier through the Fundamentalist–Modernist debates. While the older apologetics of fundamentalism repeatedly defended the scriptural integrity of crucial doctrines – for example, the deity of Christ, the virgin birth, the bodily resurrection and the Second Coming – the newer evangelicalism has attempted to overcome this divided defense of separate doctrines by reducing the apologetics to a single more crucial issue, that of biblical hermeneutics.[38]

Theoretically, this strategy economically focuses apologetic energy on the one and only doctrine that needs to be defended in order to guarantee the perpetuation of orthodoxy. In actual practice, however, the strategy has exacerbated the threat.

The major weakness in this strategy, however, lies in the inflexibility of evangelical hermeneutics, since a question about these formulations is at once a challenge to the social contract at the heart of the evangelical identity.

Just how lethal a perceived challenge to that social contract can be was made clear by a series of events a few years ago at Gordon-Conwell Theological Seminary in Massachusetts. As the result of an internal debate that had been simmering for some time and finally boiled over, J. Ramsey Michaels, Professor of New Testament for twenty-five years, was forced to resign. The faculty senate, with evidence compiled during six months of interviews and study by faculty and trustee committees, ruled that although Michaels "personally holds fully to the GCTS statement of faith," his book *Servant and Son* raised doubts concerning his commitment to inerrancy. Michaels's response affirmed his belief in "the total inerrancy of Scripture" but noted that the faculty senate report "implies a greater restriction on certain historical and critical methods than I and some of my colleagues had previously thought." After being informed in the spring of 1983 by seminary president Robert E. Cooley that he was preparing "a letter of dismissal for cause which could result in termination of contract," Michaels submitted his resignation. In a subsequent letter explaining "Why I Resigned," Michaels cited "irreconcilable differences with the executive committee of the board of trustees" and pointed out that the faculty senate report will "in effect prohibit any use of the historical-critical method at Gordon-Conwell in the study of the Gospels." Then he mentioned a familiar name: "The decision commits the faculty essentially to the hermeneutic of Harold Lindsell, the chairman of our board of trustees."[39]

We can be sure that no one will ever prove to Harold Lindsell's satisfaction that there is a single error in the Bible. Whatever the weight of evidence, there will always be on hand an authority figure to explain away every apparent historical or scientific error, to harmonize every potential contradiction, and to invent an acceptable interpretation for every otherwise unacceptable passage.

If he had lived, would Carnell still be on the barricades alongside Lindsell, fighting the inerrancy battle? Whereas the inextricably intertwined evidence from paper track and personal life story are too ambiguous to say for sure, two hitherto unrevealed bits of documentary evidence shed more light on the question. The first is a manuscript entitled "The Inspiration and Authority of the Bible," which Carnell was working on at the time of his death. He completed only thirty-six pages of what appears to be the introduction to a book. It contains nothing new in substance. He stresses the Bible's view of its own inspiration and authority, argues that if we do not accept this doctrine we undercut "the divine doctrines of present salvation and the hope of eternal life," still leans heavily on Warfield and Hodge, repeats the five hermeneutical principles he had expounded in *The Case for Orthodox Theology,* and again takes refuge in progressive revelation. One passage, however, sounds a different note. He seems to be addressing himself to the problem of "tabloid-minded evangelical Christians" for whom these affirmations are not enough. One senses between the lines the scars left by years of hostile criticism from nervous evangelicals who would much prefer to believe there simply are no difficulties raised by the dogma of inerrancy. Carnell appreciates both the difficulties and the anxiety:

Whether we like it or not, we were created with the tendency as fallen sinners to compensate for the insecurity aroused through sin by resorting to convictions clothed about with the garments of absolute assurance. This means, of necessity, that a spelling out of the manifestations of truth which form Biblical inerrancy is somewhat frightening, and thus to avoid the fright the task itself is avoided.[40]

He himself is not immune.

All of us are frightened when absolutes are brought under the microscope for analysis and defense. I am uneasy as I explore the very question of the plurality of truth. How can I be certain that I am correct in my conclusions? How can I know for sure that I am not leading others astray? These questions, and a thousand more, haunt me as I attempt a system of Biblical inerrancy which, in my finite judgement, is correct. Whether we take pills to fight our fear (as I do), or whatever means we employ, the irresistible fact remains that we *must* tell in detail what we mean by Biblical inerrancy. There are more individuals than we would dare admit who forthrightly reject the concept of Biblical inerrancy because they suffer from lack of knowledge. Often they are experts in a certain field – perhaps the origin and the antiquity of man – and they seem forced to conclude that the Biblical genealogy is inaccurate. This might seem to be a trivial point, but it includes a rejection of the Gospel of salvation revealed in the Bible, and this is by no means a trivial point.[41]

The second bit of evidence is a part of Lindsell's "paper track" that he chose not to reveal and that calls into question his assertion that at the end of his life Carnell "saw clearly what the issue was and was right back where he had started years before." It is a letter from Carnell to Lindsell, dated September 26, 1966, less than a year before Carnell died. The spirit is consistently irenic, with not a hint of the tensions that colored their relationship while Carnell was president. The central paragraph in the letter contains these comments on the question of biblical interpretation and authority:

One of my difficulties is that I have sort of painted myself into a corner. I know perfectly well that the literalism of a century ago – both Catholic and Protestant – needs careful rethinking, but I also know perfectly well that our rethinking is all in vain unless we stay within the guideline provided by the Scripture's view of itself. The upshot is that I end up (so it seems) being a liberal in the eyes of the literalists, and a literalist in the eyes of those who have joined the mad race for relevance. Sometimes I wish I could go to the Isle of Patmos for about fifteen years and meditate, study, and pray – with your help an added blessing.[42]

In Chicago, Karl Barth, after responding to Carnell's question on inerrancy, asked him, "Is that enough to encourage you to continue to cheerfully confess that here is a problem also for you?" Whatever Carnell answered that evening in Chicago, the real answer is in this letter to Harold Lindsell and in the manuscript left behind at his desk when he left for Oakland that day in April 1967. Confess to problems? Yes. But cheerfully? No, unfortunately. We could hardly ask for more poignant and penetrating evidence of what an immense and crippling burden it was for Edward Carnell to carry around the doctrine of biblical inerrancy.

In a considerably lighter vein, Robert Frost describes a comparable struggle in "The Armful":

For every parcel I stoop down to seize,
I lose some other off my arms and knees,
And the whole pile is slipping, bottles, buns,
Extremes too hard to comprehend at once,
Yet nothing I should care to leave behind.
With all I have to hold with, hand and mind
And heart, if need be, I will do my best
To keep their building balanced at my breast.
I crouch down to prevent them as they fall;
Then sit down in the middle of them all.
I had to drop the armful in the road
And try to stack them in a better load.[43]

The fact that Carnell never (at least in his writings) seriously considered relinquishing his commitment to inerrancy provides all the credibility Harold Lindsell needs for including him among the dedicatees of *The Battle for the Bible*. But his phrase "stood or stand steadfastly for biblical inerrancy" conveys a far from accurate impression. Somehow I find Frost's image more true, more compelling, and more human: a man sitting in the road, with all those packages around him, suspecting deep inside how much easier it would be to get home with the whole load if it were not for that package labeled "Inerrancy," but unwilling and unable to leave it behind.

Part three

CHAPTER X

Figures in the carpet

In "The Figure in the Carpet," one of Henry James's late tales, three young worshipful readers of a particular author get deeply – one might say obsessively – involved in finding the basic underlying message or purpose that unifies all his novels and that he tantalizingly insists lies there quite obviously, waiting to be discovered. The story's narrator likens the object of their search to "a complex figure in a Persian carpet." He never finds it. His two friends supposedly learn the secret but die without divulging it to anyone else.[1]

So much for the story. It is the image itself that intrigues me, "the figure in the carpet," more particularly a variation of the image used by James's biographer, Leon Edel, in a brief essay on the art of writing biography: "The Figure under the Carpet."[2] The biographer, says Edel, must be concerned with both "figures." The figure *in* the carpet is traced in matters of record, in archival materials that often threaten to sink the project by their sheer volume. Coping somehow with the clutter of materials, the biographer goes to work like a portrait painter, "who reads only the lines in the face, the settled mouth, the color of the cheeks, the brush strokes and pencil marks of time. More often than not this offers us the revealing mask of life. The biographer must learn to know the mask – and in doing this he will have won half the battle." Then Edel goes on:

The other half is his real battle, the most difficult part of his task – his search for what I call the figure under the carpet, the evidence in the reverse of the tapestry, the life-myth of a given mask. In the archive, we wade simply and securely through paper and photocopies and related concrete materials. But in our quest for the life-myth we tread on dangerous speculative and inferential ground, ground that requires all of our attention, all of our accumulated resources. For we must read certain psychological signs that enable us to understand what people are really saying behind the faces they put on, behind the utterances they allow themselves to make before the world. (24, 25)

In Edel's scheme of things, then, the contrast between the figure *in* the carpet and the figure *under* the carpet parallels the contrast between mask and myth – that is to say, between "the revealing mask of life" (the public persona, the pattern of purpose that can be deduced in the written record and the concrete data of experience) and "the inner myth we all create in order to live, the myth that tells us we have some being, some selfhood, some goal, something to strive for beyond the fulfillments of food or sex or creature comforts" (30).

In the preceding chapters we have, for the most part, been examining the top surface of the carpet: tracing the public life of Edward Carnell and reflecting on the published words that constitute the face he turned to the world outside. Without presuming that we have discerned with absolute clarity the figure woven into that surface, I should like in this chapter to turn the carpet over, tug at some loose threads, and trace their connections to the surface design, risking in the process some educated guesses about both the mask and the life-myth beneath the mask. Here, as throughout this study of the making and unmaking of an evangelical mind, I shall press the claim that as an exemplar of evangelical Christianity, Carnell in his life and writings transcended the boundaries of an individual life, raising important questions about religious faith in the context of its encounter with modernity.

A. Christ or suicide

Of all the loose threads in Carnell's carpet, none dangles more obviously than the Alameda County Medical Examiner's inability to decide whether his death was an accident or suicide. In the absence of definitive evidence, he made the only possible decision. Medical examiners, however, operate within a radically limited frame of reference, in this case a body in an Oakland hotel room on a particular day in April 1967. Carnell's life in the forty-seven years that led up to the moment of his death contributed precisely nothing of relevance to the official report the coroner had to submit. But we know a good deal about that life as a whole. Consequently, whereas the report pronounces the last *official* word on Carnell's death, there is more of value that can be said.

The evidence in Carnell's early books suggests that he attached considerable importance to the subject of suicide, not as a permissible choice for a Christian but as the only logically defensible alternative to the world view of orthodox Christianity. In the first chapter of his first book, he laid out four possible paths one can take "through the labyrinth of human sorrow." The first is suicide, which people instinctively reject because it cuts across a basic urge to live. The second is the way of ignorance: "One can ignore the problem and go on living as if life had meaning, but goodness knows why!" The third is the path of stoic despair, along which one courageously makes the best of a bad situation. "On this view, however, no real reason can be advanced to dissuade people from committing suicide." The fourth path, of course, is the Christian interpretation of the universe which offers meaning in life and provides a basis for faith (ICA 24, 25). In other words, Carnell maintained that only Christianity gives one a logically defensible reason for not taking one's own life in despair over the tragedy of existence. Later in the same book, he went so far as to quote Revelation 20:15 ("If anyone's name was not found written in the book of life, he was thrown into the lake of fire") as support for his declaration that "To trifle with Christ is suicide" (220).

We do not have far to look for the fountainhead of this radical Christ-or-suicide dichotomy. In the book's preface, Carnell acknowledged an "incalculable indebtedness" to Dr. Gordon Haddon Clark, "whose spiritual kindness, fatherly interest, and academic patience made the convictions which stimulated the penning of this volume possible" (9). Clark stressed even more unequivocally in his books the two exclusive alternatives: either Christianity or suicide. A friend and former colleague told me that years ago, at a Christian Education Conference sponsored by Park Street Church in Boston, he attended a panel discussion involving a secular Jew, a Roman Catholic, and Clark. After a sharp exchange of views over questions of ultimate concern, the Jew somewhat frustratedly asked Clark: "What would you do if I could *prove* to you beyond all possible doubt that you were wrong?" Clark answered with not a moment's hesitation: "I'd shoot myself." Admittedly, if we had only this anecdotal evidence, we would be well-advised to leave Clark out of the discussion. In the heat of argument he might have said these words for rhetorical effect or with a mischievous twinkle in his eye. Written evidence, however, confirms that Clark meant precisely and literally what he said. The theme appears again and again in his books. His history of philosophy, *Thales to Dewey,* after having followed the whole philosophical enterprise full circle from ancient naturalism to modern naturalism, concludes by presenting the student an alternative:

Or, could it be that a choice must be made between skeptical futility and a word from God? To answer this question for himself, the student, since he cannot ride very fast into the future and discover what a new age will do, might begin by turning back to the first page and pondering the whole thing over again. This will at least stave off suicide for a few days more.[3]

In *A Christian Philosophy of Education* Clark flatly states that "the only reasonable reaction to humanism is suicide." In discussing the necessary fragmentation of any humanistic view – in which the fragments are valued without a realization that a life of detached fragments has no value at all – he asks, "Why not commit suicide and save so much bother?" Then, as if to pinch off the thought that he might be jesting, he adds, "Seriously, why not?"[4] In *Three Types of Religious Philosophy* he says: "Therefore to escape drug addiction, to escape irrationalism, to escape suicide, what else is there but dogmatism? At the least, if one can postpone suicide for five minutes, dogmatism deserves consideration as the only possible alternative to futility."[5]

I bring in these references from Clark's writings not to hang around his neck responsibility for what (in the coroner's official view) was only *possibly* a suicide. I do maintain that under Clark's tutelage at Wheaton College, Carnell drank deeply of this heady brew. Clark himself could live comfortably with the mutually exclusive alternatives of dogmatic Christianity or suicide because apparently never in his life did he have the slightest inclination to doubt his dogmas. Carnell was made differently.

Early in his career Carnell inherited the self-assurance of his mentor. He internalized the dogmatic rationalism of Gordon Clark, gave it the majority vote in his subliminal deliberations, and consciously chose it as his apologetical mask. What came naturally to Clark, however, became intolerable for Carnell. Whereas Clark had developed a monolithic belief system, totally impervious to the winds of change, Carnell at deep levels of his being could not ignore the ambiguities of experience, the sense of mystery at the heart of life, and the presence within him of an existential doubter every bit as strong as the dogmatic rationalist. Among that "anxious breed of younger men" about whom he had written in the *Christian Century*, no one was more unsettled by anxieties than Carnell himself. Most people who reflect on religious questions learn to live with cognitive uncertainties as a completely normal dimension of religious faith and life. The all-or-nothing approach – the arrogant insistence that the only logically defensible alternative to Christianity is suicide – seriously damaged Carnell's resiliency in matters of faith and doubt. For one as thoroughly indoctrinated as he (and as sensitive), it would not require specific crippling doubts concerning bedrock Christian beliefs to upset his equilibrium; it would take only a still small voice insinuating a suggestion now and then that he had overstated the certainty of his apologetical arguments and the confidence a thoughtful and intelligent believer should place in them.

Several years ago, the first member of Carnell's family whom I interviewed was his older brother Dr. Paul Carnell, for many years an administrator in the United States Office of Education. As we talked over lunch in a government cafeteria in Washington, D.C., I was stunned by his quiet matter-of-fact observation that his brother's breakdown resulted from building a whole career on something he did not really believe.

When I asked what led him to that conclusion, he answered, "It's what a brother knows about a brother." For some time I held that view at arm's length, attributing it to the inability of someone outside the fold to appreciate the life-changing power of an evangelical religious commitment. As time has gone by, as I have amassed more and more data of various kinds, I have had to reevaluate my skeptical response to Paul Carnell's theory. I think now that he made an important point, although it needs clarification and qualification. Edward Carnell was not living a lie all those years he wrote books, taught classes, and preached sermons. Nevertheless, we all wear masks, we all play roles. Erving Goffman, in *The Presentation of the Self in Everyday Life*, differentiates between the cynical and the sincere performer. He applies the term *cynical* to the individual who "has no belief in his own act and no ultimate concern with the beliefs of his audience." He reserves the term *sincere* "for individuals who believe in the impression fostered by their own performance."[6] Faced with these two possibilities, we must unequivocally acknowledge Carnell's basic sincerity. However, Goffman goes on to say that "to the degree that the individual maintains a show before others that he himself does not believe, he can come to experience a special kind of alienation from self and a special kind of wariness of others" (236). Religious belief cannot be reduced to the two alternatives of an off–on switch. Neither religious questions nor the people who wrestle with them are that uncomplicated. Goffman instead directs our attention to the extent to which the performance departs from inner conviction. If we apply the Goffman principle to the Carnell case, the question then becomes something like this: Does the defender of Christian orthodoxy claim a higher level of certainty than he himself feels? Paul Carnell, sensing the largely unacknowledged presence of the doubter in his brother's inner life, put his finger on an important partial truth. On certain issues at certain times, the doubter's voice in Edward Carnell was so insistent as to jeopardize his sense of his own identity and integrity. The disbelief (if it can be called that) was on the deeper level of being untrue to oneself, a subtle condition not always evident to the doubter because of various cultural and religious overlays.

One of Carnell's professors, D. Elton Trueblood, perceived Carnell's struggle with theological doubt during his first year of graduate study at Harvard. Robert McAfee Brown saw it during Carnell's visit to Stanford in his agonized admission that he kept a certain intellectual difficulty in a file marked "Unanswered Questions." The psychiatrist Dr. Philip Wells saw repeated evidence of the doubter's influence in Carnell's frustration with what he considered the creedal rigidity at Fuller. James Tompkins caught a brief revealing glimpse of Carnell's inner uncertainty when, at a crucial point in their correspondence, he acknowledged his fear of losing his faith.

Recognition of Carnell's susceptibility to the nagging presence of doubt sheds light on other dimensions of his life. Why, for example, was he so devastated by criticism leveled at him by the fundamentalists, even after he had predicted such negative reaction and declared, "I do not shrink from this threat" (COT 14)? One can easily understand his dismay at being rejected by Gordon Clark and sniped at by some of his own colleagues. But the spate of knee-jerk fundamentalist journalism that greeted the appearance of *The Case for Orthodox Theology* and the *Christian Century* articles on fundamentalism as "orthodoxy gone cultic" should have reassured him that he was doing something right. As he had said to Charles Fuller just three weeks before his final resignation from the presidency, "Criticism against the school, let us remember, is proof that our mission is being accomplished. If no attention were paid to us, I would be suspicious that we had failed to communicate the greatness of our distinctives." What was true for the institution was theoretically true for Carnell himself. But whereas in theory he understood and accepted the inevitability of this negative criticism, on a deeper level I suspect it set up sympathetic vibrations with his own doubts and uncertainties. He was profoundly troubled, in other words, because he knew that in a sense his critics, however self-righteous and uninformed, were right. Under these conditions, it would be surprising indeed if in his later years he never heard echoing in the corridors of his mind his own youthful warning: "To trifle with Christ is suicide."

I do not say that, however, in order to support the view that Carnell consciously intended to commit suicide. If that had been his purpose, he would have done a better job of it. Sleeping pill suicides are generally found comfortably ensconced in their beds, not lying on the floor after having pulled the towel rack from the bathroom wall in the act of falling. The 3.5 milligram-percent barbiturate level, while enough to kill him, was not an overwhelming dose. One study of 600 barbiturate poisoning cases found the average dosage of amylobarbitone and pentobarbitone to be 6.7 and 8.5 milligrams, respectively.[7] Moreover, if Carnell's main objective was to avoid the anxiety-producing obligations facing him the next day, he did not need to resort to the irreversible act of suicide. Psychosomatic illness, real or feigned, could have sent him to the hospital. Better still, he could have simply informed Duke Robinson (the Fuller alumnus who was a member of the conference committee and had suggested Carnell as a speaker) of his inability to go through with the commitment, checked out of the hotel, and taken a plane back to Los Angeles. At that point in his life, he did not have much left to lose from such a move.[8]

We know Carnell harbored apprehension concerning his coming speech, and his behavior after the Sunday evening banquet, as described by Robinson, betrayed a high level of tension (although Robinson's suspicion that something might have been seriously wrong *physically* was not borne out by the medical report). These bits and pieces of evidence, combined with Carnell's history of unreliability in doling out pills to himself, strongly suggest accidental death. To offer this hypothesis does not expunge from Carnell's record the stigma of possible suicide. Only solid evidence could do that, and the evidence does not exist. Furthermore, Carnell, I suggest, had been for several years what we might term passively suicidal. Over the same period during which he struggled with moderate success to cope with the daily personal and professional responsibilities of his life, he had been battling serious depression and had lost his ambition and his vibrant hope for the future. Carnell's own minister, Reverend Ray Ortland of the Lake Avenue Congregational Church, put it this way: "Carnell's death was certainly unfortunate, but it was not as shocking as it might have been. He was dying inside."[9]

B. The dark cloud of failure

In the spring of 1967, as Carnell looked back on his professional life, he saw little else but what he considered failure. The book he thought was his best work, *Christian Commitment,* had fallen into oblivion. He told a friend that with every passing year his earlier books looked thinner and thinner. Moderately favorable reviews of *The Case for Orthodox Theology* from some quarters hardly counterbalanced its harsh reception by many conservatives. He knew very well that *The Burden of Sören Kierkegaard* consisted largely of warmed-over material from a dissertation almost twenty years old. He considered himself not only to have been something less than a resounding success as president of Fuller Seminary but also to have been left behind in his primary field of scholarship as a result of his five-year tenure. The same man who fifteen years earlier had been known as evangelicalism's young triple-threat scholar – philosopher, apologist, theologian – now was no longer a force to be reckoned with either in evangelicalism at large or in his own seminary.

It is possible, of course, to look crassly at the Carnell story as a cautionary tale, derive from it certain counsels of prudent self-interest, and dismiss all questions about the ambiguities of faith and doubt as so much subterranean nonsense. From this point of view, anyone who knew Carnell could have essentially predicted what would happen when he accepted the presidency of Fuller Seminary. A man much more at home in the world of books and ideas found himself feeling his way through a maze of organizational charts and fund-raising statistics, soothing the ruffled feathers of squabbling colleagues, and pouring water on the fires of hostile criticism. Within a few years he suffered a severe case of burnout and broke under the various pressures. Shock treatments helped his depression intermittently but also drastically damaged his short-term memory. Although he made some progress toward a normal existence, he lost any sense of mastery in his field. On a three-day trip away from home, he accidentally took too many sleeping pills in a setting where he could not summon help. That is the end of it. To such an observer, the lessons are obvious: If you are faced with a significant career change in mid-life, carefully count the cost; know yourself and, if circumstances go bad, know when and how to get out.

On a certain limited practical level, that version of Carnell's failure contains irrefutable truth, but it leaves too much out. I should like in this section of the chapter to peel back the external layer of facts and explore under three headings some more subtle reasons behind the unmaking of Edward Carnell's mind: the inadequacy of his preparation, his incapacity for genuine dialogue, and his failure of imagination.

Carnell set for himself a life goal enormously difficult to attain. On one level, he aspired to be "a Harvard man," a respected member of the scholarly community. That much was well within his grasp. Simultaneously, however, he envisioned himself developing a rational defense of orthodox Christianity convincing to the modern mind. Whether any Christian apologist can ever reach this goal – or should even try – is debatable. I contend that, given the tools he brought to the task, Carnell was destined to fail right from the start.

In this regard we should not be deceived by his early success. He carved out a reputation not among secular unbelievers but within the evangelical community itself, confirming readers and students in their already adopted faith. He did not minimize the significance of such a ministry (nor should we), but he had his eye on something more significant and more subtle. Invariably, in describing the apologetic task, he stressed that it "must answer to the spirit of the times" (CC vii). "Each generation," he said in the preface to *Case*, "must formulate its own defensive strategies" (COT 13). The following paragraph from the preface to his first book sounds clearly the dominant note of the mandate he imposed on himself:

> Our defense of Fundamentalism is all the more challenging at this hour, because, *to the modern mind,* the vitality of Christianity's theology seems effete, and its basic doctrines appear, in the light of the scientific method, to be but figments of superstition and imagination, gratuitously assumed by timorous supernaturalists. Among the *contemporary intelligentsia,* therefore, the antecedent probability of conservative Christianity is very low. But the Fundamentalist is assured, however, that *the modern mind* succeeds in ridiculing conservative Christianity only because it assigns to the latter certain propositions which the system itself does not require. (ICA 8, italics added)

In other words, Carnell took on the stupendous task of answering any and all of the well-educated modern mind's objections to evangelical Christianity.

However, after spending his first seventeen years in a fundamentalist parsonage, the next four years in a fundamentalist liberal arts college only marginally broader culturally, and the next three in a staunchly conservative "Old Light" Presbyterian seminary, Carnell did not emerge on the Cambridge, Massachusetts, scene in 1944 as master of the sophisticated complexities of cultural and intellectual modernism. He had a lot of ground to make up. Furthermore, Harvard was not the answer to his serious deficiencies. Harvard Divinity School was certainly in touch with modern thought, but as a specialized graduate institution it was designed to build on a cultural foundation already established. Even in its own specialty, religious studies, it failed in one important way to provide Carnell with what he needed as a bridge-builder between evangelical Christianity and the modern mind. Like Wheaton and Westminster, Harvard saw orthodox Christianity and modernity as mutually exclusive alternatives separated by a great chasm.

The implicit understanding between Harvard and the cadre of fundamentalist students in the 1940s – namely, that they could remain as theologically orthodox as they pleased as long as they accomplished quality work in the institution's historically oriented, theologically neutral program of study – was ultimately no favor to a man with Carnell's objectives. In effect, Carnell faced only two competing alternatives at Harvard: the dogmatic rationalistic fundamentalism with which he entered and the historically and scientifically grounded humanism of the institution. Inasmuch as he believed the latter option inevitably led to nihilism, he faced no real choice. True, he read theologians representing points of view between these alternatives, but secondhand acquaintance is not the same as being confronted with live options, especially for a young man with so narrow an intellectual background. It was one thing for him to pore over *The Nature and Destiny of Man* late at night at his desk; it would have been quite another experience to sit in Reinhold Niebuhr's classes at Union Theological Seminary.

In later years, whatever Carnell thought of his own preparation for the work of apologetics, he left no doubt that he considered evangelicalism as a movement not yet qualified to confront modernity on even terms. In a 1957 *Christianity Today* article that by most criteria favorably contrasted Billy Graham with Reinhold Niebuhr, Carnell nonetheless acknowledged serious intellectual weaknesses in both Graham and orthodoxy:

After Billy Graham has reviewed the plan of salvation, he has very little to add. Billy Graham has not been to seminary. He has no criteria by which to measure the shades of better or worse in the complex systems that vie for the modern mind. And his weakness pretty well sums up the weakness of orthodoxy itself. Orthodoxy *tries* to relate Scripture to the more technical phases of science and philosophy, but its efforts are seldom very profound. Orthodoxy does not know enough about modern presuppositions to speak with authority. (CBC 171)

One would like to think that Carnell included himself in that indictment, but one suspects rather that he was quite willing to let stand the implicit but obvious contrast between himself and Billy Graham.

Carnell's failure can also be measured by his incapacity for genuine dialogue. To be sure, he gave lip service to the value of dialogue. "Free and open conversation," he said, "is the very lifeline of Protestant theology" (CBC 171). But he seldom grabbed that lifeline himself. He had little zest for the art of give and take, the kind of theological rough-and-tumble in which participants could argue vehemently, pick themselves up, dust themselves off, and continue to be good friends. Even within his own seminary faculty, he did not take advantage of collegial interchange. As a job applicant in 1947, he had cited the constant intellectual ferment within a community of scholars as a major reason for wanting to teach at Fuller. "I have no interest," he had said, "in being a lone-pebble-on-the-beach scholar." But that is exactly what he became. Carnell eventually came to believe that no one at Fuller qualified as a critic of his work. On one occasion, after the seminary had been criticized because of something a faculty member had written, a motion was made and seconded in a faculty meeting that none of them should publish anything without having three colleagues check it out. Carnell is reported to have icily stated that if the motion passed he would not comply. It did not pass.[10] On the one hand we are inclined to cheer his defiance of institutional timidity and his reluctance to submit manuscripts to the narrow ideological scrutiny of, say, Charles Woodbridge, Wilbur Smith, and Harold Lindsell. But if Carnell really thought he had nothing to learn from dialogue with Paul Jewett or Glenn Barker or Dan Fuller about theology and biblical interpretation, he was being pridefully short-sighted.

Carnell participated even less frequently in genuine dialogue with those outside the fold of evangelical orthodoxy. In his minimal experience of serious confrontation with competing theological perspectives (on a high-stakes personal level quite different from metaphysical mind-games), he suffers markedly in comparison with Frederick Buechner, another twentieth-century Christian apologist to whom I have referred several times. Buechner's apologetical weapons were tested in the crucible of battle at Exeter Academy, a prep school in New Hampshire where he preached and taught, counseled students, and chaired the Department of Religion from 1958 to 1967, nine years of hard experience in wide-ranging, intensive, uninhibited dialogue with some of secular modernity's most skeptical questioners. A young convert and a recent seminary graduate, he arrived at Exeter in the time of the *nego* ("in Exeter parlance . . . a student who was negative, against, anti just about everything"). As the new faculty member, introducing new controversial academic courses, he spent every day on the firing line, dodging bullets, trying to make Christianity compelling (as he put it, quoting Schleiermacher) to religion's "cultured despisers." Buechner realized, as a result of this continuing process, the absolute necessity of sharing honestly the ambiguities of his own faith.

Negos or straight arrows, religious or unreligious, sophisticated or unsophisticated, in one form or another we all of us share the same dark doubts, the same wild hopes, and what little by little I learned from those years at Exeter was that unless those who proclaim the Gospel acknowledge honestly that darkness and speak bravely to the wildness of those hopes, they might as well save their breath for all the lasting difference their proclaiming will make to anybody.[11]

Even more important, Buechner allowed the voices of those questioning young people to find a permanent place in his own thinking, to resonate there with his own doubting self. Years after he left Exeter, the voice of the nego remained a part of his inner dialogue. In *The Alphabet of Grace*, a book in which he invites the reader into the workings and wanderings of his mind on an average day in his life, an inner voice unexpectedly interrupts a period of silence with a pungent comment. Buechner explains:

My interlocutor is a student who under various names and in various transparent disguises has attended all the religion classes I have ever taught and listened to all my sermons and read every word I've ever written, published and unpublished, including diaries and letters. He is on the thin side, dark, brighter than I am and knows it. He is without guile or mercy.[12]

The voice speaks to him often. Sometimes it causes no little discomfort, but Buechner knows he is much richer for its presence.

Carnell, I suggest, also had an interlocutor, and I should like to hazard a guess that, whatever disguises he assumed, he looked and sounded something like James Tompkins. However, Carnell could not permit the sort of uneasy truce that Buechner reached with his young questioner. When the disembodied voice of Carnell's inner doubt took on the recognizable features of the closest of his old Wheaton friends, real dialogue became too much of a threat. He could initiate a correspondence with Tompkins on the level of academic debate, but when Tompkins suggested that they bypass their secretaries and get down to sharing the most personal commitments and convictions, Carnell's sleeping interlocutor woke up, threatened to undermine his hard-won status quo, and had to be silenced. The correspondence ended abruptly and Carnell made no attempt to resume it. The simplest way to deal with one's inner doubt is to keep it quiescent in the back room of one's mind. To that end, the fewer opportunities for genuine dialogue, the less likely that the voice of the doubter will find unsettling points of view with which to resonate.

Carnell's incapacity for dialogue intertwined with his natural inclination to play the role of a loner. We have observed that from his college years onward, with a few notable exceptions, he developed various strategies for keeping people at a distance. He could communicate to classes from behind a lectern and to congregations from behind a pulpit (although after his breakdown the prospect of even these formerly satisfying activities often made him physically sick). By all reports, however, he was ill at ease on social occasions and equally uncomfortable when circumstances forced him to deal with people on an individual basis. He armored himself in dark, formal clothes that discouraged easy camaraderie. His long walks functioned not just as opportunities for philosophical reflection but enabled him for a time to escape students, colleagues, and friends. He referred to the teaching profession ideally as "the obscurity of the monastery,"[13] remarking several times in letters to old friends that education would be a great profession if it were not for the students. He knew very well how tired that joke was, but it allowed him to reveal a partial truth without being taken seriously. In a talk on ethics and theology at an orientation retreat for new students, he acknowledged that such a simple act as driving back to Pasadena on the freeway underscored how much of a gap there was between Carnell as he was and Carnell as he ought to be: "Because, personally, people are a nuisance to me. And in my less sanctified self, the larger portion of me by the way, I would be just as pleased if about half of the people would somehow disappear, or commit suicide, or something."[14] Clearly that was the kind of statement that both conceals and reveals; the students probably accepted it as hyperbole (as indeed it was). But Carnell had managed thereby to tell them something true and important about himself.

The point is not that there is something inherently wrong with the solitary life. Henry David Thoreau, whose life at Walden Pond admittedly was not nearly so solitary as the book *Walden* implies, nevertheless left us an enduring American paradigm of creative aloneness. For Carnell the urge to draw apart from others produced guilt feelings, especially during his tenure as president. He wrote to Harold Ockenga in the spring of 1959, just before he resigned: "I am a misfit as president, that is the trouble. My temperament is monastic and academic; I have no natural desire to command, to assume authority."[15]

Carnell's problem, however, had much deeper roots than a distaste for crowds and the interpersonal demands of leadership. In 1942, two years before he arrived on campus as a graduate student, Harvard University finished selecting 268 of its most promising undergraduates as subjects of a continuing long-range study designed to examine the varying ways in which they would adapt to the changing experiences of their post-college lives. Thirty-five years later, an interim report declared, among other conclusions, that "it is not the isolated traumas of childhood that shape our future but the quality of sustained relationships with important people."[16] One does not find many such "sustained relationships" in Carnell's life, even within his immediate family. He was not close, that is to say, to his brothers and sister. He had a number of close friendships dating back to college and seminary days, but inevitably these few people were scattered around the country and could do no more than see each other occasionally. More revealing, perhaps, is the fact that even some of those friends, when they later became colleagues, were kept at a psychic distance.[17] Carnell's fraternizing with Fuller faculty was kept at a minimum, especially after he became president. After his resignation, the pattern of alienation only deepened. He found no sustaining relationships through the family's local church affiliation with the Lake Avenue Congregational Church where he regularly taught an adult class. A hyperconservative faction in the church generated so much negative criticism about him and the seminary that he felt very little rapport with the congregation. As for the church at large, he had cut himself off from the fundamentalists, would not make common cause with those theologically to his left, and with few exceptions stood aloof even from fellow evangelicals. The conclusion is inescapable: Virtually no one seemed to have the credentials to qualify for the kind of sustained relationships the Harvard study found so significant. Carnell resisted personal intimacy. Apart from occasional meetings with fellow theologian Bernard Ramm, who for a time became something of a confidant, or with his brother-in-law, Don Weber, who as his assistant during the presidential years enjoyed a limited sort of personal access, Carnell's true kindred spirits were Plato, Aristotle, Augustine, Kierkegaard. His real dialogue was with the philosophers of the past; it need hardly be said that this was not what the Harvard study meant by "sustained relationships with important people." There is a pathetic appropriateness to the fact that he died alone in a hotel room 400 miles from home.

In my effort to understand the making and the unmaking of Carnell's mind and to account for what I perceive to be his failure to build a sturdy apologetic bridge between evangelical Christianity and the modern mind, I should like now to grasp several threads at once and relate them to the common theme of the imagination's significance in religious thought. Richard Ellmann and Charles Feidelson, in the preface to their anthology

The Modern Tradition: Backgrounds of Modern Literature, shy away from any attempt to pin down definitely the concept of "the modern." They do, however, declare that the implications of "modern" transcend chronological boundaries: "The term designates a distinctive kind of imagination – themes and forms, conditions and modes of creation, that are interrelated and comprise an imaginative whole."[18] Although by the calendar Edward Carnell was a "modern man," growing up chronologically with "modern times" guarantees no particular stance toward modernity. To put it as succinctly as possible, if Ellmann and Feidelson are right in their judgment that the term *modern* designates a distinctive kind of imagination, then I suggest that Carnell failed to develop a modern apologetic because he lacked that kind of imagination.

To say that, however, does not make him a living relic of the premodern world. Knowing that evangelicals find the authority for their religious beliefs in the Bible, many modern observers too glibly classify their religious thought as premodern. From such a perspective, although evangelicals drive automobiles, watch television, and program computers, their religious beliefs deserve little attention because they have been taken intact from the ancient world. Of the innumerable ways in which evangelicalism can be misunderstood, this view may be the most misleading. In an effort to correct it, historian George Marsden argues that as a movement nineteenth-century evangelicalism was "early modern" in its origins, assumptions, and structures of thought as opposed to "late modern" or twentieth-century – champions, that is to say, of "common sense, empiricism, and scientific thinking."[19]

Specifically, the prevailing intellectual opinion in nineteenth-century America was enamored of the "Common Sense" ideals of the Scottish Enlightenment, which provided an intellectual base for an unshakable faith in the inductive scientific method associated with the seventeenth-century philosopher Francis Bacon.[20]

Truth was not only ascertainable by the common sense of ordinary human beings; it did not essentially change from era to era. Consequently, taking care to gather all relevant "facts" and then classifying them (the essence of the Baconian scientific method), one could confidently build a system of reliable knowledge. Furthermore, in those pre-Darwinian years, scientific examination of the book of nature tended to confirm the reliability of God's other book, the Bible. Between the mid-nineteenth century, when an earlier evangelicalism enjoyed a hegemony over American religious and cultural life, and the mid-twentieth century, when Carnell began writing his evangelical apologetics, the world profoundly changed. Darwinism imposed a new revolutionary way to read the book of nature, and German higher criticism suggested equally revolutionary new ways to understand the Bible. Historians studied the ebb and flow of causal relationships rather than the outworking of a divinely ordained plan. This complex set of interlocking radical changes clearly exemplifies Thomas Kuhn's concept of a paradigm shift.[21] Evangelicalism, however, sat tight on its philosophical foundation of rational common sense. For all the impact the paradigm shift had on Carnell, he might as well have been born in 1819 as 1919. His was an early modern imagination trying to develop a defense of traditional Christianity in late modern times. I am reminded of a striking analogy Clifford Geertz uses in *Islam Observed*. He points out that "the events through which we live are forever outrunning the power of our everyday moral, emotional, and intellectual concepts to construe them, leaving us, as a Javanese image has it, like a water buffalo listening to an orchestra."[22] Carnell's ears picked up the sound waves of modernity; his imagination never translated them into music. If his mind had ever really hummed along with the disturbing dissonance and atonalities of modernity, he would never have been able to buttress his allegedly up-to-date "case for orthodox theology" with seemingly endless passages quoted from a number of early modern theological authorities. Carnell's inability to build a bridge between the modern consciousness and evangelical Christianity was attributable in large part to a failure of the imagination.

There is another sense in which the imagination – or rather the lack of it – played a key role in the Carnellian apologetic. A 1927 entry in Reinhold Niebuhr's *Leaves from the Notebook of a Tamed Cynic* tells of having to deal with questions from the audience in a Sunday afternoon forum. At one extreme was an old gentleman who wanted to know when the Lord would come again; at the other was a young man who delivered a lecture in support of Communism and chided Niebuhr for not admitting that all religion is fantasy. "Between those two," said Niebuhr, "you have the tragic state of religion in the modern world." Advocates at both extremes fail to understand that the imagination can arrive at truth "by giving a clue to the total meaning of things without being in any sense an analytic description of detailed facts."[23] The lingering effect of this early modern bias toward an overly simple facticity appalled Niebuhr: "How can an age which is so devoid of poetic imagination as ours be truly religious?"

Since that time, religious thought has rediscovered the legitimate importance of the imagination.[24] Typical of more recent views is Amos Wilder's argument that religion can ill afford to disparage the value of the imagination as somehow inferior to reason. "It is at the level of the imagination," he says, "that any full engagement with life takes place."

Imagination is a necessary component of all profound knowing and celebration; all remembering, realizing, and anticipating; all faith, hope, and love. When imagination fails doctrines become ossified, witness and proclamation wooden, doxologies and litanies empty, consolations hollow, and ethics legalistic.[25]

Carnell at least acknowledged the validity and necessity of this dimension of human experience in his move toward inwardness, but he consciously and unconsciously imposed strict controls over what he allowed to enter his awareness from the noncognitive realm. Although he granted the presence of mystery, he was not comfortable with any data or experience that he could not process rationally. In this respect he was not unlike the rationalist schoolteacher Rayber in Flannery O'Connor's *The Violent Bear It Away*. According to Rayber's uncle, the fanatical old prophet Mason Tarwater, "every living thing that passed through the nephew's eyes into his head was turned by his brain into a book or a paper or a chart."[26] Furthermore, Rayber took special pains to stifle the influence of deeply buried psychic forces that threatened to gain control over him. To be sure, Rayber is a caricature and his rigorous rationalism served the cause of antireligion, but insofar as both men were dominated by strict rational controls, they are brothers under the skin. Dr. Philip Wells's brief summary of Carnell's experience in therapy lends support to this view. He mentioned that Carnell "was troubled during the years with severe and persistent thoughts and dreams which he could not prevent." Although without a detailed case history we can do no more than speculate, Wells's statement clearly implies that material long repressed was exacting its revenge. Even Carnell's insomnia may be related to this pervasive pattern. Since sleep is a state in which the sleeper is no longer in conscious control, certain insecure people "feel that, in order to maintain what is at best a precarious control, they must remain awake."[27]

Several years ago the poet John Ciardi delivered an address to a group of businessmen on the subject of the universal human need to nurture the creative life of the imagination. His intriguing title captures in a vivid image what I am trying to say: "An ulcer, gentlemen, is an unwritten poem." In Carnell's case, let the ulcer in that epigram represent not only the insomnia, guilt, depression, and various other anxieties that bedeviled him but also all the life that never got lived, not because he chronologically died in his middle age but because he never learned to trust and to draw on the imaginative depths of his own being. In more subtle ways, let the ulcer symbolize also his failure to achieve his apologetic goal. For in radically constricting the flow of the imaginative life, he was trapping himself in a biblical and theological hermeneutic foreign to the modern mind his apologetic effort was intended to convince. When he bypassed the more fundamental elements of the religious faith and life, manifested most significantly in myth and ritual, symbol and story, and moved directly to the secondary level of abstract philosophical theory and theological dogma, he thereby rejected the mythic consciousness that could have unshackled him from a sterile biblicism and the metaphoric imagination that could have liberated him to a fulfilling alternative.

Finally, then, what caused the unmaking of Edward Carnell's mind? What was responsible for his untimely death? There are, of course, no simple answers to these questions. But if there is one single circumstantial key that accounts for the dark cloud of failure that gathered over Carnell, it is his appointment to the presidency of Fuller Seminary. That key, however, opens only an outer door, giving us access to a foyer where we find other keys to other doors.

When Carnell told the Fuller faculty, shortly after taking over as president, that in assuming his new responsibilities he considered himself a sacrifice, he unknowingly foreshadowed a chain of personally destructive consequences. He meant only that for the time being he was voluntarily setting aside his own goals for the greater good of the institution. As a matter of fact, his vow to the faculty that he would continue to produce scholarship while in office suggests a confidence that he might not be making such a great sacrifice after all. Unfortunately, that is not how it turned out. Whereas it is no exaggeration to say that Fuller Seminary would not have become the institution it is today without Carnell's leadership in the crucial 1950s, it is no less true to suggest that in providing that leadership Carnell paid the supreme sacrifice. Two sets of circumstances conspired against him, one internal, the other external. If either had been different, he might have survived.

Externally, as we have seen, Fuller's peculiar financial situation and the insatiable need to find new sources of substantial income tyrannized his administration. We may think Carnell naive for accepting at face value the promise that while he supervised academic and administrative affairs the trustees would be responsible for raising money. But the fact is that he made sure there was no doubt in anyone's mind; he was not a fundraiser. Over and over again in his correspondence in those years, we hear the clear note of desperation: "I cannot raise money." But none of the solutions worked. The relentlessness of the demands wore him down. When to this situation was added the burden of hostile criticism, Carnell broke down and never fully recovered.

We have also seen considerable evidence of internal pressures. In his counseling sessions, Carnell uncovered what he felt were significant personality defects either inherited from his parents or carried with him from childhood family environment. Although I cannot fully discredit those personal insights, I have placed much more emphasis on the character tendencies of Carnell's maturity. What I am arguing here is that if the external circumstances had been different – specifically, if the catalytic influence of the presidential appointment had been kept out of the mixture – Carnell probably would have had the internal resources to survive. Conversely, if internally he had been a different person to start with – specifically, if he had been more uninhibitedly open to the infinite and mysterious ambiguities of the world outside his own mind – he could have transcended the troubles and demands of the presidency.

After Carnell stepped down from the presidency and returned to the professorial life, he wrote a rather testy note to his brother-in-law, Don Weber. In it he said, "Remember I lost five years as president. I also lost the field I had prepared for – systematic theology."[28] What Carnell failed to realize is that the loss of his "field," although it appeared to him as an irreparable disaster, could have been transformed into a magnificent stroke of good fortune. Erik Erikson maintains that "in some periods of history, and in some phases of his life cycle, man needs (until we invent something better) a new ideological orientation as surely and as sorely as he must have air and food."[29] Carnell was at precisely such a point in his own life. He had already moved a considerable distance away from his early embeddedness in the ideology of fundamentalism, but was still burdened with the dead weight of Clarkean rationalism and an anachronistic theology inextricably tied to an inerrant Bible. He needed to look at the recent five-year period in the presidency with a fresh eye. If he had, he could have seen it as a serendipitous liberation, what Erikson refers to as a "moratorium" – a means of marking time, an effective and permissible way of postponing for a while certain decisions that will permanently alter the shape of one's future.[30] In some ways, as Carnell shifted from the president's office back to the classroom, he was vocationally in an enviable position. He had a secure faculty appointment in a stable institution, receptive to change, with a strong administration (once David Hubbard became president) that could and would have absorbed whatever further changing he was likely to do. Admittedly his window of opportunity for taking advantage of this hypothetical new perspective opened for only a brief time. He resigned as president in April 1959. When his psychological distress became so acute in the summer of 1961 that he had to be hospitalized and given a series of shock treatments, his fate was sealed. But things could have been different. Unfortunately, he never saw the five-year presidency as a moratorium and thus did not take advantage of the regenerative possibilities it held out to him.

C. Walking

We have been tracing threads in the reverse side of Carnell's carpet. It is time to step back and try to discern the figure they form. Acknowledging that others may look at the same visual evidence and see something different, I see two figures that refuse to merge into a single image but unpredictably switch back and forth like an optical illusion.

In the first letter of his extended correspondence with James Tompkins, Carnell condescendingly prejudged the state of his friend's mind: "It is still my deepest conviction that you are merely passing through a phase change in your thinking and that the Lord will bring a complete adjustment between the head and the heart before long." What must surely have rankled Tompkins in that statement was the assumption that Carnell had already achieved the "complete adjustment" on which he placed so great a value. In truth he had not, and I suggest we get close to unraveling the mystery of Edward Carnell when we recognize not only that he never achieved the happy harmony of head and heart but that he found intolerable (unconsciously perhaps) his failure to do so. The two figures on the underside of the carpet that keep shifting back and forth and that he labels head and heart in his letter to Tompkins are the Clarkean rationalist and the Kierkegaardian existentialist. The images will not fuse because both represent sides of his character that rejected "complete adjustment." He was too imbued with the constraints of rationalism ever to be comfortable with Kierkegaardian existentialism and too inward ever to be content with Clarkean rationalism. He could not jettison one in favor of the other.

I am convinced, however, that Carnell's chief problem was not the mere continuing presence of conflicting inner myths, but rather his inability to accept such tension as normal. John Keats, more than a century and a half ago in a letter to his brothers, bequeathed to us an expression that identifies accurately the quality missing in Carnell's makeup. Puzzling one day over the essential character of greatness, Keats was struck quite suddenly with the answer – the "quality that went to form a Man of Achievement" (Shakespeare was the example he gave): "I mean *Negative Capability,* that is, when a man is capable of being in uncertainties, mysteries, doubts, without any irritable reaching after fact and reason."[31] The absence of this quality showed up early in Carnell. The incident during his years at Wheaton College that, with the gift of hindsight, we can identify as quintessentially Carnellian was his argument with David Roberts in the dining hall after a disturbing encounter with a questioner at a street meeting the previous night. Never again, he vowed, would he allow himself to be caught in such a trap – not, that is, *until he had all the answers.* Carnell never really transcended that need for certainty. He suffered, in Peter Berger's term, "the vertigo of relativity"[32] whenever he hearkened to the voice of his inner doubt. He never learned to accept and endorse the normality of perpetual tension between opposing views, an intellectual stance affirmed so confidently by Northrop Frye: "No idea is more than a half truth unless it contains its own opposite, and is expanded by its own denial or qualification."[33]

In the first chapter of this book, I commended Carnell for exposing himself to two kinds of risk in the encounter between religious orthodoxy and secular modernity: first, "the narrow ridge of total risk" between faith and nihilism; second, the less cataclysmic but just as dangerous risk of the cognitive bargain. I shall not contradict that judgment here, but I do think it needs modification. To his credit, Carnell insisted that the ultimate questions must not be stored in a dark corner of the evangelical basement and forgotten. He realized intuitively that, as an informed religious believer in modern times, he ought to shoulder his beliefs, questions, and doubts and walk with them out into the ambiguous wilderness of secular modernity. But a fundamental insecurity held him back. "It requires a direct dispensation from Heaven," said Thoreau, "to become a walker." Carnell, like Thoreau, was a walker all his life, but not in the added metaphorical sense that embodied Thoreau's deepest meaning. In his essay "Walking,"[34] which has been called his last will and testament, Thoreau expressed no interest in the kind of streets that Carnell walked in Pasadena – or, for that matter, in the streets he himself walked in Concord. "Roads," he said, "are made for horses and men of business. I do not travel in them much." He is drawn to the wilderness of the West and South-southwest. "The future lies that way to me, and the earth seems more unexhausted and richer on that side." *West*, as he uses the word, is a synonym for *wild*, and "in wildness is the preservation of the world."

For a moment the figure under the carpet stops shifting back and forth between rationalist and existentialist and holds still in a single image. It is an image we have seen before – a lone figure dressed in formal black clothes, complete with homburg hat and cane, walking the beach at Santa Barbara. However far west, the scene is hardly wild, but it *is* the natural world. The existentialist in Carnell has symbolically been drawn to the sea, sky, and sand, but the rationalist in him has selected the wardrobe. We might put it this way: Whenever Carnell – as a man who committed his life to an intellectual defense of evangelical Christianity in the face of all that threatened its very existence – walked out to do battle in the wilderness of mystery, uncertainty, and ambiguity, he always wore the protective armor of theoretical abstraction, fundamentalist dogma, and the haunting voice of conscience that reminded him that quite possibly thousands of people were depending on him to defend and preserve their Christian faith. To shed the armor would for him have been unthinkable, but the essential duplicity (for that is exactly what it was, even when it was only himself he was trying to convince) took its toll. The short poem by Emily Dickinson, quoted earlier in the book, takes on added relevance here:

Lad of Athens, faithful be
To Thyself,
And Mystery –
All the rest is Perjury –

This lad of Athens (by way of Antigo, Wisconsin, and Albion, Michigan) repressed the doubts and misgivings he held in common with others of his own time and instead opted for the certain sound of the polemical trumpet. In so doing he was unfaithful to the mystery of his own deepest self and to the mystery at the heart of existence.

There are those who would say he made the right choice: Better to choose faithfulness to Christ than to risk shipwreck on the rocks of unbelief. But to confine the alternatives to those two possibilities falls into the perennial trap of polarization to which all orthodoxies are susceptible: Ours is the one true religion; all others are false. Such cognitive intransigence will always work for some people. Whatever the pressures of modernity, there will always be fundamentalists and evangelicals who can accept such a gross oversimplification of the problems involved in faith and doubt. That evangelicalism in our day has won a sort of triumph and become an accepted part of the American cultural mainstream is largely irrelevant to the question at hand, which concerns cognitive and critical issues. Evangelicalism has succeeded so well in today's consumer-oriented society because it tells people what they want to hear, puts the official stamp of religious approval on their materialistic aspirations, and clears an easy path to narcissistic spirituality.[35] Nathan O. Hatch finds the beginnings of this trend in evangelicalism's nineteenth-century capitulation to the sovereignty of the audience, which "undercut the structure that could support critical theological thinking of the level of a Jonathan Edwards or a John Wesley." According to Hatch, "This meant that uncomfortable complexity would be flattened out, that issues would be resolved by a simple choice of alternatives, and that, in many cases, the fine distinctions from which truth alone can emerge were lost in the din of ideological battle."[36] Carnell could have done much more to counter this trend, to lead twentieth-century evangelical thought through criticism to a "second naiveté," to move (in the words of Paul Ricoeur) "beyond criticism by means of criticism, by a criticism that is no longer reductive but restorative." Unfortunately, Carnell lacked the will to commit himself to that uncharted terrain – and perhaps lacked also the emotional balance to survive if he had.

To make such a commitment would surely have purged what was left of his fundamentalism, but, as David Tracy has observed, "the collapse of religious fundamentalism is not the end of religion."[37] Because the kind of critical exploration we are talking about would also have threatened his *evangelical* orthodoxy, we might modify Tracy's statement to read, "the collapse of evangelicalism would not mean the end of a vital Christianity." Any religion, evangelical Christianity included, is "an imaginative statement about the truth of the totality of human experience,"[38] and thus its symbolism must be open to perpetual reinterpretation. If the Christian gospel must be understood finally as myth, it is not *merely* myth. It tells some truths about life and the world and ourselves – the most important truths there are – truths concerning which it is not possible for the most committed of believers to have more than a subjective certainty. Those of us who are at best unbelieving believers live in faith that this life does mean and mean intensely, that our human duty is to "let justice roll down like waters," that the Mystery that is the only ultimate reality we can affirm behind the God-language we cannot conscientiously use is in some fathomless way like the face of Jesus Christ.

Notes

Key to Books by Edward John Carnell

ICA *An Introduction to Christian Apologetics* (Grand Rapids: Eerdmans, 1948).

TSM *Television: Servant or Master?* (Grand Rapids: Eerdmans, 1950).

TRN *The Theology of Reinhold Niebuhr* (Grand Rapids: Eerdmans, 1951).

PCR *A Philosophy of the Christian Religion* (Grand Rapids: Eerdmans, 1952).

CC *Christian Commitment: An Apologetic* (New York: Macmillan, 1957).

COT *The Case for Orthodox Theology* (Philadelphia: Westminster Press, 1959; London: Marshall, Morgan and Scott, 1961). Page numbers throughout refer to the 1961 English edition.

KLPL *The Kingdom of Love and the Pride of Life* (Grand Rapids: Eerdmans, 1960).

BSK *The Burden of Sören Kierkegaard* (Grand Rapids: Eerdmans, 1965).

CBC *The Case for Biblical Christianity,* edited by Ronald N. Nash (Grand Rapids: Eerdmans, 1969).

Correspondence between Edward Carnell and Harold John Ockenga, from the files of the late Harold John Ockenga, Hamilton, Massachusetts, will be designated EJC to HJO or vice versa, along with the appropriate date.

Epigraphs

1 Edward Carnell, "Post-Fundamentalist Faith," *The Christian Century* (26 Aug. 1959).

2 Ernest G. Schachtel, *Metamorphosis: On the Development of Affect, Perception, Attention, and Memory* (New York: Basic Books, 1959), p. 53.

Preface

1 Geoffrey Wolff, "Minor Lives," in *Telling Lives: The Biographer's Art,* edited by Marc Pachter (Washington, D.C.: New Republic Books, 1979), p. 59.

2   George M. Marsden, *Reforming Fundamentalism: Fuller Seminary and the New Evangelicalism* (Grand Rapids: Eerdmans). Forthcoming in 1987.

I. The narrow ridge and the cognitive bargain

1   The best source on fundamentalism is George M. Marsden, *Fundamentalism and American Culture: The Shaping of Twentieth-Century Evangelicalism, 1870–1925* (New York: Oxford University Press, 1980).
2   See Joel A. Carpenter, "The Renewal of American Fundamentalism, 1930–1945" (Ph.D. diss., Johns Hopkins, 1984).
3   The "post-fundamentalist" label is more accurate in that it pinpoints the group's ancestry while at the same time differentiating it from both nineteenth-century evangelicalism (with which it shares some similarities but from which it significantly differs) and from a number of twentieth-century groups that justifiably claim the label evangelical but were relatively untouched by the fundamentalist–modernist controversy. See Donald W. Dayton, *Discovering an Evangelical Heritage* (San Francisco: Harper and Row, 1976), pp. 137–41.
4   Sydney E. Ahlstrom, *A Religious History of the American People* (New Haven, Conn.: Yale University Press, 1972; Garden City: Image Books, 1975), Vol. II, p. 599.
5   William G. McLoughlin, "Is There a Third Force in Christendom?" in *Religion in America*, ed. William G. McLoughlin and Robert N. Bellah (Boston: Beacon Press, 1968), p. 66.
6   Ahlstrom, *Religious History*, Vol. II, p. 600.
7   William G. McLoughlin, *Revivals, Awakenings, and Reform: An Essay on Religion and Social Change in America, 1607–1977* (Chicago: University of Chicago Press, 1978), p. 10.
8   Ibid., pp. 10–11.
9   William G. McLoughlin, "Introduction: How Is America Religious?" in *Religion in America*, edited by McLoughlin and Bellah, p. x.
10   Quoted by Clifford Geertz, "Religion as a Cultural System," in *The Interpretation of Cultures: Selected Essays* (New York: Basic Books, 1973), p. 99.
11   McLoughlin, *Revivals, Awakenings, and Reform*, pp. 12–13.
12   CBC, pp. 136–40.
13   Emil L. Fackenheim, "On the Self-Exposure of Faith to the Modern-Secular World: Philosophical Reflections in the Light of Jewish Experience," in *Religion in America*, edited by McLoughlin and Bellah, p. 221.
14   James Davison Hunter, *American Evangelicalism: Conservative Religion and the Quandary of Modernity* (New Brunswick, N.J.: Rutgers University Press, 1983), pp. 16–17.
15   J. Hillis Miller, *Poets of Reality: Six Twentieth Century Writers* (Cambridge, Mass.: Belknap Press of Harvard University Press, 1965), p. 5.
16   Paul Johnson, *Modern Times: The World from the Twenties to the Eighties* (New York: Harper and Row, 1983), p. 698.
17   Transcript of remarks made at Founders Day Banquet, 7 Apr. 1967. Fuller Theological Seminary files.
18   Richard L. Rubenstein, *Power Struggle* (New York: Scribners, 1974), p. 1.

Throughout the text, italics within quoted matter appeared in the original unless otherwise noted.

19 CC, p. 3.

20 Clifford Geertz, "Thick Description: Toward an Interpretive Theory of Culture" in *The Interpretation of Cultures*, p. 29.

21 See Gordon R. Lewis, *Testing Christianity's Truth Claims: Approaches to Christian Apologetics* (Chicago: Moody Press, 1976); John A. Sims, *Edward John Carnell: Defender of the Faith* (Washington, D.C.: University Press of America, 1979); Kenneth W. M. Wozniak, *Ethics in the Thought of Edward John Carnell* (Lanham, Md.: University Press of America, 1983).

II. The stigmata of fundamentalism

1 Herbert C. Carnell, "From Wooden Leg to Pulpit," unpublished typescript, used by permission of Paul Carnell.

2 Barrett John Mandel, "The Autobiographer's Art," *Journal of Aesthetics and Art Criticism,* vol. XXVII (Winter 1968), 220.

3 Ibid., p. 218.

4 Erving Goffman, *Stigma: Notes on the Management of Spoiled Identity* (Englewood Cliffs, N.J.: Prentice-Hall, 1963), p. 27.

5 CBC, pp. 45–7.

6 Personal interview with Don Weber, Dec. 1977. The chapter in question is in COT, pp. 113–26.

7 COT, p. 113.

8 Goffman, p. 129.

9 Ibid., p. 130.

10 Ibid. pp. 8–9.

11 George M. Marsden, *Fundamentalism and American Culture: The Shaping of Twentieth-Century Evangelicalism, 1870–1925* (New York: Oxford University Press, 1980), p. 191.

12 COT, pp. 113, 114; CBC, p. 46.

III. Wheaton

1 J. Wesley Ingles, *Silver Trumpet* (Philadelphia: Union Press, 1930), p. 25.

2 W. Wyeth Willard, *Fire on the Prairie: The Story of Wheaton College* (Wheaton, Ill.: Van Kampen Press, 1950), p. 114.

3 James Wesley Ingles, "The Silver Trumpet and How It Blew," *Christian Herald* (March 1970), 36–40.

4 Letter from Richard Weeks, 26 Feb. 1979.

5 I am indebted to many Wheaton College alumni especially from the late 1930s and early 1940s who have shared their memories with me. Most of these persons I have not named individually.

6 Letter, EJC to Jean Carnell, 11 Jan. 1966.

7 Marshall Frady, *Billy Graham: A Parable of American Righteousness* (Boston: Little, Brown, 1979).

8 Ibid., p. 133.

9 Ibid., p. 134.

10 Letter from James Tompkins, 17 Apr. 1978.

11 Carl F. H. Henry, "A Wide and Deep Swath," in *The Philosophy of Gordon H. Clark: A Festschrift*, edited by Ronald N. Nash (Philadelphia: Presbyterian and Reformed, 1968), p. 16.

12 Letter from James Tompkins, 17 Apr. 1978.

13 Letter from John Graybill, 15 Sept. 1977.

14 Ned B. Stonehouse, *J. Gresham Machen: A Biographical Memoir* (Grand Rapids: Eerdmans, 1954), p. 337.

15 Letter, EJC to Gordon H. Clark, 27 Jan. 1953.

16 Personal interview with David Roberts, Feb. 1978.

17 Letter, EJC to Paul Woolley, Registrar, 20 Apr. 1941.

18 Notes on Carnell's chapel talk taken by Wheaton College staff member Rana McDonald. Wheaton College files.

19 Letter, EJC to John Griffin, 17 Aug. 1962.

IV. Westminster

1 Ned B. Stonehouse, *J. Gresham Machen: A Biographical Memoir* (Grand Rapids: Eerdmans, 1954), pp. 61–2.

2 J. Gresham Machen, *Christianity and Liberalism* (Grand Rapids: Eerdmans, 1972).

3 See William R. Hutchison, *The Modernist Impulse in American Protestantism* (Cambridge, Mass.: Harvard University Press, 1976), pp. 272–4.

4 George M. Marsden, *Fundamentalism and American Culture: The Shaping of Twentieth-Century Evangelicalism, 1870–1925* (New York: Oxford University Press, 1980), p. 184.

5 Stonehouse, p. 448.

6 EJC to HJO, 24 Jan. 1948.

7 "Response by C. Van Til" in E. R. Geehan, editor, *Jerusalem and Athens: Critical Discussions on the Theology and Apologetics of Cornelius Van Til* (Nutley, N.J.: Presbyterian and Reformed, 1971), p. 368.

8 Letter, EJC to James Tompkins, 29 Apr. 1953.

9 Personal interview with Lloyd Dean, June 1978.

10 A description of the issues from a point of view sympathetic to Clark appears in *The Answer* to a Complaint against Several Actions and Decisions of the Presbytery of Philadelphia Taken in a Special Meeting Held on July 7, 1944. Proposed to the Presbytery of Philadelphia of the Orthodox Presbyterian Church by the Committee Elected by Presbytery to Prepare Such an Answer.

11 Personal interview with Glenn Barker, Dec. 1978.

12 Letter from James Tompkins, 6 May 1978.

13 Letter from Delbert Schowalter, 19 Oct. 1979.

14 Letter from James Tompkins, 17 Apr. 1978.

15 Reprinted in CBC, pp. 128–36.

16 CC, pp. 10–11.

17 CC, p. 11.

18 Letter from James Tompkins, 6 May 1978.

19 Letter, EJC to E. Dyrness, Wheaton Registrar, Aug. 1942.
20 Letter, EJC to David Lovik, no date.
21 Letter, EJC to David Lovik, 11 Feb. 1944.
22 Letter, EJC to Paul Woolley, Registrar, 20 Apr. 1941.
23 Letter, EJC to Office of the Dean, Harvard Divinity School, 31 Jan. 1944.

V. Fundamentalism-on-the-Charles

1 EJC to HJO, 24 Jan. 1948.
2 "Dean's Letter," *Harvard Divinity School Bulletin* (15 Mar. 1940), 42–3.
3 I am indebted for most of my general information about Harvard Divinity School to George Huntston Williams, editor, *The Harvard Divinity School: Its Place in Harvard University and in American Culture* (Boston: Beacon Press, 1954), especially the chapter "The Later Years (1880–1953)" by Levering Reynolds, Jr.
4 Ibid., p. 186.
5 Ibid., pp. 168, 186, 10.
6 Robert T. Handy, "The American Religious Depression, 1926–1935," *Church History* 29 (Mar. 1960), 3–16.
7 Material quoted or cited concerning the fundamentalist students at Harvard is based on either correspondence or personal interviews, in some cases both.
8 Theodore H. White, *In Search of History: A Personal Narrative* (New York: Harper and Row, 1978; Warner Books Edition, 1979), p. 43.
9 Roger Shinn, review of *Christian Commitment* by EJC, *Theology Today*, 15 (July 1958), p. 278.
10 Letter, EJC to Joseph Bayly, 31 May 1960.
11 Letter from Nancy Hodges Marshall, 6 Dec. 1977.
12 Personal interview with Mr. and Mrs. Dwight MacFarland, Oct. 1977.
13 Letter from David Chambers, 4 Oct. 1977.
14 Personal interview with Lloyd Dean, June 1978.
15 Unpublished notes for address, Fuller Theological Seminary files.
16 The theoretical differences in the apologetics of Carnell, Clark, and Van Til – and the approach taken by Carnell in ICA – will be discussed more fully in chapter seven.
17 Carl F. H. Henry, *The Uneasy Conscience of Modern Fundamentalism* (Grand Rapids: Eerdmans, 1947); F. Alton Everest, ed., *Modern Science and Christian Faith* (Wheaton, Ill.: Van Kampen Press, 1948).
18 Williams, p. 225.
19 Edward John Carnell, "The Concept of Dialectic in the Theology of Reinhold Niebuhr" (Th.D. diss., Harvard Divinity School, 1948), p. 417.
20 Ibid. p. 54.
21 "Report of the Commission to Study and Make Recommendations with respect to the Harvard Divinity School," July 1947, pp. 15–16. Used by permission of Andover-Harvard Theological Library.
22 The interview was with George Ladd, at that time (Dec. 1977) Professor of New Testament at Fuller. Ironically, my delayed interpretation of his remark is less applicable to him than to many others among the Harvard fundamentalists.

23   See Daniel P. Fuller, *Give the Winds a Mighty Voice: The Story of Charles E. Fuller* (Waco, Tex.: Word Books, 1972), pp. 189–210.
24   Personal interview with Shirley Carnell Duvall, Dec. 1977.
25   EJC to HJO, 24 Jan. 1948.
26   EJC to HJO, 12 Sept. 1947.
27   EJC to HJO, 24 Jan. 1948.
28   EJC to HJO, 24 Jan. 1948. Carnell is mistaken in saying he studied four years with Murray. He spent three years at Westminster – from Sept. 1941 to June 1944. Also, of course, the subject of his B.U. dissertation turned out to be Kierkegaard, not Brunner.
29   EJC to HJO, 21 Mar. 1948.

VI. Fuller Seminary

1   Daniel P. Fuller, *Give the Winds a Mighty Voice: The Story of Charles E. Fuller* (Waco, Tex.: Word Books, 1972), p. 208.
2   EJC to HJO, 3 May 1949. The dissertation's title was "The Problem of Verification in Sören Kierkegaard" (Ph.D. diss., Boston University, 1948).
3   EJC to HJO, 3 May 1949; 11 June 1949.
4   EJC to HJO, 11 Jan. 1949.
5   Personal interview with Shirley Carnell Duvall, Dec. 1977.
6   EJC to HJO, 3 May 1949.
7   Letter, EJC to Lloyd Dean, 23 Oct. 1950.
8   Personal interview with George Ladd, Dec. 1977.
9   EJC to HJO, 15 Dec. 1948. The brief stay of Bela Vasady, an outstanding leader of the Hungarian Reformed Church, precipitated one of the major crises of Fuller Seminary's early years. When Ockenga proposed that Vasady be offered a position on the Fuller faculty, Henry and Carnell were assigned the task of screening him theologically. Although some of his views made them uneasy, they gave him their stamp of approval. The differences in outlook, however, chiefly on ecumenism, biblical inerrancy, and neo-orthodoxy, soon led to Vasady's departure. See George M. Marsden's forthcoming history of Fuller Theological Seminary for a full account.
10   Personal interview with David Hubbard, Dec. 1977.
11   Personal interview with James Mignard, Aug. 1978.
12   Letter from Peg Lovik, 1 June 1978.
13   Personal interview with Lars Granberg, Feb. 1978.
14   Copies of the correspondence were made available to me by James Tompkins.
15   Telephone interview with Carl Henry, 4 Dec. 1982.
16   EJC to HJO, 12 Feb. 1954.
17   EJC to HJO, 8 Mar. 1954.
18   EJC to HJO, 15 Sept. 1954.
19   Fuller, p. 225.
20   EJC to HJO, 15 Sept. 1954.
21   In a telephone interview (4 Dec. 1982) Henry made an additional comment on his nomination of Woodbridge: "You've got to remember that Woodbridge then

was not quite the same person as Woodbridge now," a judgment one must question in view of how quickly Woodbridge became a serious thorn in Carnell's side.

22   Telephone interview with Carl Henry, 4 Dec. 1982. According to Henry, he gave five reasons but could not recall the fifth.

23   Personal interview with Shirley Carnell Duvall, Dec. 1977.

24   EJC to HJO, 14 Apr. 1955. Lindsell is on record as having had no interest in the Fuller presidency. "The Fuller people claim that I am disenchanted with the school because I was not chosen to become president. This canard has been repeated many times. It is interesting, in view of the fact that I have been offered five presidencies in the course of my career and turned all of them down." *The Bible in the Balance* (Grand Rapids: Zondervan, 1979), p. 242. The question that comes immediately to mind, of course, is whether he would have turned down the *Fuller* presidency if it had been offered to him in either 1954 or 1963.

25   Letter, EJC to Gordon Clark, 25 Oct. 1954.

26   Personal interview with Glenn Barker, Dec. 1977.

27   Personal interview with Ralph Lazzaro, May 1978.

28   EJC to HJO, 7 Oct. 1954.

29   EJC to HJO, 19 Nov. 1954.

30   EJC to HJO, 7 Dec. 1954.

31   EJC to HJO, 7 Dec. 1954.

32   EJC to HJO, 27 Jan. 1955.

33   Report to faculty, 16 Mar. 1955.

34   Letter from Dan Fuller, 9 Dec. 1980.

35   William Sanford LaSor, "Life under Tension: Fuller Seminary and 'The Battle for the Bible,'" *Theology, News and Notes,* published for the Fuller Theological Seminary Alumni, Special Issue (1976), p. 9.

36   Edward J. Carnell, "The Glory of a Theological Seminary," Fuller Theological Seminary Alumni Association, 135 North Oakland Ave., Pasadena, Cal. 91109.

37   LaSor, p. 9.

38   Letter from Carl Henry, 22 Nov. 1982.

39   Personal interview with Bernard Ramm, Jan. 1978.

40   I wish to thank Daniel P. Fuller for calling to my attention an error I made in an article covering some of this material: "Fundamentalism at Harvard: The Case of Edward John Carnell," *Quarterly Review: A Scholarly Journal for Reflection on Ministry,* II, 2 (Summer 1982), 79–98. I said there mistakenly that Charles Fuller ordered the impounding of the transcript. It was the 1947 Ockenga inaugural address that Dr. Fuller impounded. Carnell himself gave the order that no copies of his address be disseminated. When Carnell died in 1967, Professor George Ladd, a strong supporter of Carnell from the beginning, persuaded Shirley Carnell to allow Fuller Seminary to reproduce and distribute it.

41   Personal interview with David Hubbard, Dec. 1977.

42   Letter, EJC to Charles Fuller, 3 Apr. 1959.

43   EJC to HJO, 3 Jan. 1955.

44   EJC to HJO, 17 Mar. 1958.

45   Fuller, pp. 189–210.

46   Personal interview with Harold John Ockenga, Nov. 1977.

47 Letter, EJC to Don Weber, 17 Apr. 1956.
48 EJC to HJO, 22 Sept. 1955.
49 Telegram, EJC to HJO, 10 Oct. 1955.
50 EJC to HJO, 9 Jan. 1956.
51 EJC to HJO, 21 Dec. 1956. Carnell quoted the committee statement.
52 EJC to HJO, 20 Sept. 1956.
53 EJC to HJO, 23 Jan. 1957.
54 EJC to HJO, 16 Apr. 1957.
55 EJC to HJO, 23 May 1957.
56 Letter, Charles Fuller to HJO, undated.
57 EJC to HJO, 31 July 1957.
58 Telegram from Ockenga to Fuller Seminary, 10 Dec. 1957.
59 LaSor, p. 9.
60 Letter from Robert Rankin, 23 June 1978.
61 Personal interview with David Hubbard, Dec. 1977.
62 Personal interview with David Hubbard, Dec. 1977.
63 Letter, EJC to Don Weber, 25 Feb. 1956. Even asking for money became almost bearable with Weber as companion. Carnell's report of a fund-raising junket they went on together reflects with black humor on their discouraging trip. They "kissed babies, inspected turkey hatcheries, rode around vast ranches, listened to small talk, and sat hours in an unventilated room with children who were in the last stages of Asian flu." Report to Board of Trustees, 5 Nov. 1957.
64 Personal interview with Lars Granberg, Feb. 1978.
65 Letter from Daniel Fuller, 16 Oct. 1980.
66 Telephone interview with William Buehler, 30 Oct. 1976.
67 Letter from William Showalter, 20 Apr. 1978.
68 EJC to HJO, 26 Mar. 1959.
69 EJC to HJO, 2 Dec. 1954.
70 EJC to HJO, 28 Nov. 1955.
71 EJC to HJO, 1 Oct. 1956.
72 EJC to HJO, no date. Internal evidence suggests late 1956.
73 EJC to HJO, 1 Oct. 1956.
74 EJC to HJO, 5 Nov. 1956.
75 EJC to HJO, 17 Mar. 1958.
76 Memo, EJC to Don Weber, 11 Dec. 1958.
77 EJC to HJO, 6 Feb. 1959.
78 Day letter, HJO to EJC, 26 Apr. 1959.
79 Letter, EJC to Charles Fuller, 29 Apr. 1959.
80 EJC to HJO, 13 Sept. 1959.
81 The other two books in the trilogy: L. Harold DeWolf, *The Case for Theology in a Liberal Perspective,* and William Hordern, *The Case for a New Reformation Theology* (Philadelphia: Westminster, 1959). The apologetic approach in Carnell's book will be discussed in later chapters.
82 "Publisher's Note" in DeWolf, no page number.
83 Letter from Paul Meacham, 23 Sept. 1977.
84 ICA, p. 7.
85 Carnell, "Fundamentalism," in *A Handbook of Christian Theology,* ed. Marvin Halverson and Arthur A. Cohen (Cleveland: World, 1958), pp. 142–3.

86 COT, p. 111.
87 COT, p. 113.
88 Reprinted in CBC, pp. 45–7.
89 Reprinted in CBC, pp. 40–5.
90 CBC, p. 41.
91 CBC, p. 45.
92 *Sword of the Lord* (30 Oct. 1959).
93 COT, p. 14.
94 HJO to EJC, 9 Dec. 1958.
95 EJC to HJO, 11 Dec. 1958.
96 Harold John Ockenga, "The New Evangelicalism," *Park Street Spire* (Feb. 1958).
97 Action reported in EJC to HJO, 4 Dec. 1958.
98 Charles J. Woodbridge, *The New Evangelicalism* (Greenville, S.C.: Bob Jones University, 1969). Numbers in parentheses refer to pages from this edition.
99 HJO to EJC, 6 May 1960.
100 At 42, Carnell was the youngest of the six. The others were Bernard Cooke of Marquette University, Hans Frei of Yale, Shubert Ogden of Southern Methodist University, Jakob Petuchowski of Hebrew Union College, and lay theologian William Stringfellow, a New York attorney. Jaroslav Pelikan of Yale Divinity School acted as panel moderator. For a more detailed account of Carnell's participation, see chapter nine.
101 Tape recording of Fuller Theological Seminary report session, 15 May 1962.
102 EJC to HJO, 12 Jan. 1961.
103 EJC to HJO, 12 Jan. 1961.
104 EJC to HJO, 25 June 1961.
105 EJC to HJO, 25 June 1961.
106 See chapters seven and eight.
107 Letter, EJC to Don Weber, 19 Sept. 1962.
108 EJC to HJO, 31 July 1961.
109 EJC to HJO, 25 Mar. 1962.
110 Carnell made this point to Bernard Ramm, according to Ramm, personal interview, Jan. 1978.
111 Personal interview with Eric Lemmon, Nov. 1977.
112 Personal interview with Glenn Barker, Dec. 1977.
113 Letter from Gary W. Smith, 3 July 1978.
114 Letter from Richard Foster, 16 May 1978.
115 Letter from Fred Ivor-Campbell, 18 June 1978.
116 Letter from Richard Foster, 16 May 1978.
117 Reprinted in CBC, pp. 122–4.
118 Ibid., p. 123.
119 Ibid., p. 90.
120 Letter, EJC to John Griffin, 17 Aug. 1962.
121 As of summer 1986, Jean Carnell (Mrs. Warren Becker) and her husband work with United Evangelical Churches in Thomasville, Georgia. John Paul Carnell manages a store for the Alpha organization in Corona, California.
122 Letter from Dr. Philip Wells, 9 Aug. 1979.
123 Personal interview with Bernard Ramm, Jan. 1977.

124   Personal interview with David Hubbard, Dec. 1977.
125   Letter from Dr. Philip Wells, 3 Sept. 1979.
126   Personal interview with Don Weber, Dec. 1977.
127   Information about the arrangements for the Oakland Workshop comes from the Rev. Duke Robinson, letter, 23 Feb. 1979.
128   Personal interview with Shirley Carnell Duvall, Dec. 1977.
129   Letter from the Rev. Duke Robinson, 23 Feb. 1979.
130   Notes from telephone call, Rev. Duke Robinson to Fuller Seminary, 26 Apr. 1967.
131   Verdict of Coroner, State of California, County of Alameda, in the matter of the death of Edward John Carnell, May 24, 1967.
132   Edward J. Carnell, "The Conservative Protestant: Who Is He and What Is His Relation to the Ecumenical Movement?", unpublished typescript.

VII. Apologetics of the mind

1   Dan McCall, *Beecher* (New York: E. P. Dutton, 1979).
2   Frederick Buechner, *The Final Beast* (New York: Atheneum, 1965).
3   Carnell, ICA, 4th edition (Grand Rapids: Eerdmans, 1952), p. 8.
4   Bernard Ramm, *After Fundamentalism: The Future of Evangelical Theology* (San Francisco: Harper and Row, 1983), p. 59.
5   Leszek Kolakowski, *Religion: If There Is No God – On God, the Devil, Sin and Other Worries of the So-Called Philosophy of Religion* (New York: Oxford University Press, 1982), p. 16.
6   Quoted by Carnell in BSK, p. 116.
7   BSK, p. 117.
8   ICA, 4th edition, p. 7.
9   KLPL, pp. 5–6.
10   ICA, 4th edition, p. 7.
11   "Response by C. Van Til" in E. R. Geehan, editor, *Jerusalem and Athens: Critical Discussions on the Theology and Apologetics of Cornelius Van Til* (Nutley, N.J.: Presbyterian and Reformed, 1971), pp. 361–8.
12   "At the Beginning, God: An Interview with Cornelius Van Til," *Christianity Today* (30 Dec. 1977), p. 19.
13   Cornelius Van Til, "Introduction," Benjamin B. Warfield, *The Inspiration and Authority of the Bible*, ed. Samuel Craig (Philadelphia: Presbyterian and Reformed, 1948), p. 38.
14   Geehan, p. 368.
15   Reinhold Niebuhr, *The Nature and Destiny of Man*, Vol. II, *Human Destiny* (1943; reprint, New York: Scribner Library Edition), p. 125.
16   "Introduction to Theology," *Criterion*, II, 1 (Winter 1963), 18.
17   Personal interview with Don Weber, Dec. 1977.
18   Personal interview with Frederick Buechner, Oct. 1984.
19   Karl Barth, *The Word of God and the Word of Man* (London: Hodder and Stoughton, 1928), p. 107–8.
20   Ibid., p. 127.
21   Ibid., p. 206.
22   Ibid., pp. 206–7.

23   Stephen Toulmin, *The Uses of Argument* (London: Cambridge University Press, 1958), p. 7.
24   Robert N. Bellah, "The Historical Background of Unbelief," in *The Culture of Unbelief*, Studies and Proceedings from the First International Symposium on Belief Held at Rome, March 22–7, 1969, ed. Rocco Caporale and Antonio Grumelli (Berkeley: University of California Press, 1971), p. 40.
25   John Steward Collis, *The Vision of Glory: The Extraordinary Nature of the Ordinary* (New York: George Braziller, 1973), pp. 121–2.
26   Hal Lindsey with C. C. Carlson, *The Late Great Planet Earth* (Grand Rapids: Zondervan, 1970).
27   Van A. Harvey, "Is There an Ethics of Belief?" *Journal of Religion*, vol. 49, no. 1 (Jan. 1969), 43.
28   Van A. Harvey, *The Historian and the Believer* (1966; Toronto: Macmillan, 1969), p. 62.
29   Rudolf Otto, *The Idea of the Holy* (1917; reprint, New York: Oxford University Press, 1958).
30   Gabriel Marcel, *Being and Having: An Existentialist Diary* (1935; reprint, New York: Harper and Row, 1965).
31   Quoted by Paul W. Pruyser, *Between Belief and Unbelief* (New York: Harper and Row, 1974), p. 99.
32   Annie Dillard, *Pilgrim at Tinker Creek* (1974; reprint, New York: Bantam, 1975), p. 71.
33   Lewis Thomas, *Late Night Thoughts on Listening to Mahler's Ninth Symphony* (1983; reprint, New York: Bantam, 1984), p. 27.
34   Paul Van Buren, *The Secular Meaning of the Gospel* (New York: Macmillan, 1963). The other theologians to whom I refer and the books that first brought them to public attention: Richard L. Rubenstein, *After Auschwitz* (Indianapolis: Bobbs-Merrill, 1966); Harvey Cox, *The Secular City* (New York: Macmillan, 1965); Thomas Altizer and William Hamilton, *Radical Theology and the Death of God* (Indianapolis: Bobbs-Merrill, 1966); Sam Keen, *Apology for Wonder* (New York: Harper and Row, 1969).
35   Paul Van Buren, *The Edges of Language: An Essay in the Logic of a Religion* (New York: Macmillan, 1972).
36   Ernest Hemingway, "Big Two-Hearted River," in *The Short Stories of Ernest Hemingway* (New York: Scribner's, 1953), p. 231.
37   Peter Shaffer, *Amadeus* (London: Andre Deutsch, 1980), pp. 23, 66.
38   Karl Barth, *Church Dogmatics*, Vol. III, *The Doctrine of Creation*, Part 3 (Edinburgh: T. T. Clark, 1960), pp. 295–6.
39   Ibid., p. 299; CBC, p. 154.
40   Annie Dillard, *Living by Fiction* (New York: Harper and Row, 1982), p. 106.
41   Emily Dickinson, *The Complete Poems*, ed. Thomas H. Johnson (Boston: Little, Brown, 1960), p. 714.

VIII. Apologetics of the heart

1   E. M. Cioran, *The Temptation to Exist* (Chicago: Quadrangle Books, 1968), p. 167.

2 Carnell, PCR, "Preface," no page number.
3 Perry Miller, *Jonathan Edwards,* The American Men of Letters Series (New York: William Sloane Associates, 1949), p. 139.
4 EJC to HJO, 12 Sept. 1947.
5 Clifford Geertz, "Religion as a Cultural System," in *The Interpretation of Cultures: Selected Essays* (New York: Basic Books, 1973), p. 666.
6 Waldo Beach and H. Richard Neibuhr, eds., *Christian Ethics: Sources of the Living Tradition* (New York: Ronald Press, 1955), p. 34.
7 Clifford Geertz, *Islam Observed* (New Haven: Yale University Press, 1968), p. 97.
8 Clifford Geertz, "Thick Description," in *The Interpretation of Cultures,* p. 18.
9 Earl E. Zetterholm, review of *Christian Commitment* by Edward Carnell, *Westminster Theological Journal,* May 1958.
10 William Hordern, review of *Christian Commitment* by Edward Carnell, *The Christian Century,* 4 Sept. 1957.
11 EJC to HJO, 11 Dec. 1958.
12 Letter from Anne Kimber Beckon, 9 Feb. 1978.
13 Carnell, "The Glory of a Theological Seminary," Fuller Theological Seminary Alumni Association, 135 North Oakland Ave., Pasadena, Cal. 91109.
14 Carnell, unpublished notes for address, Fuller Seminary files.
15 Michael Cole, quoted by John Demos, "The Changing Faces of Fatherhood: A New Exploration in Family History," in *The Child and Other Cultural Inventions,* ed. Kessel and Siegel (New York: Praeger, 1983), p. 159.
16 Anne Tropp Trensky, "The Saintly Child in Nineteenth-Century American Fiction," *Prospects: An Annual Journal of American Cultural Studies,* Vol. I (1975), pp. 389–413.
17 Anne Frank, *The Diary of a Young Girl,* trans. from the Dutch by B. M. Mooyart-Doubleday (London: Valentine, Mitchell, 1952), pp. 174–5.
18 Mircea Eliade, *Cosmos and History: The Myth of the Eternal Return* (New York: Harper and Row, 1959), pp. 141–62.
19 EJC to HJO, 12 Jan. 1961, 25 June 1961; letters from Dr. Philip Wells, 9 Aug. 1979, 3 Sept. 1979.
20 Personal interview with Bernard Ramm, Jan. 1978.
21 Abraham Maslow, *Toward a Psychology of Being* (New York: Van Nostrand, 1968), p. 96.
22 Paul Ricoeur, *The Symbolism of Evil* (New York: Harper and Row, 1967), pp. 347–57.
23 Mark Twain, *Life on the Mississippi* (New York: Gabriel Wells, 1923), pp. 78–80.
24 See, e.g., Chad Walsh, *God at Large* (New York: Seabury, 1971).
25 Chad Walsh, *The End of Nature* (Chicago: Swallow Press, 1969), pp. 4–5.

IX. The inerrancy issue

1 Harold Lindsell, *The Battle for the Bible* (Grand Rapids: Zondervan, 1976).
2 Jack Rogers, ed., *Biblical Authority* (Waco, Tex.: Word Books, 1977).

3 Lindsell, p. 32.

4 Letter from Harold Lindsell, 8 Nov. 1982.

5 Letter, EJC to Philip Foxwell, 5 Jan. 1961.

6 See CBC, p. 48n.

7 Personal interview with James Malcolm, Feb. 1978.

8 Carnell, "Preface" to ICA, 4th edition (Grand Rapids: Eerdmans, 1952), pp. 7–9.

9 Carnell, "The Concept of Dialectic in the Theology of Reinhold Niebuhr" (Th.D. diss., Harvard Divinity School, 1948).

10 James Barr, *Fundamentalism* (Philadelphia: Westminster Press, 1978), p. 55.

11 Ibid., p. 69.

12 Tape recording of Fuller Theological Seminary report session, 15 May 1962.

13 "Introduction to Theology," in *Criterion: A Publication of the Divinity School of the University of Chicago*, II, 1 (Winter 1963), 11. The brackets around the last sentence in Carnell's question presumably indicate that it was a vocal comment appended to the written version of the question.

14 Gordon H. Clark, "Special Report: Encountering Barth in Chicago," *Christianity Today* (11 May 1962), p. 36.

15 The tape recordings and an accompanying study guide were produced by Creative Resources, a division of Word, Inc., Waco, Texas. ("Evangelical Theology," Karl Barth, CRC-0615, sides 9 and 10, Session 6, "Karl Barth Answers Questions"). Barth on tape is not always easy to decipher. Although fluent in English, he had a heavy accent that obscured some of the diction, and his frequent and sometimes lengthy pauses made punctuation and syntax uncertain. Rather than try to transcribe Barth's answers word for word from the tape, I have quoted from the *Criterion* transcript, which made a number of changes in the interest of syntactical clarity. The substance of Barth's answers was not changed in the editorial revisions made by *Criterion*.

16 *Sword of the Lord* (5 Feb. 1960).

17 *Christianity Today* (8 June 1962).

18 Tape recording of Fuller Seminary report session, 15 May 1962.

19 Tape recording of Fuller Seminary report session, 15 May 1962.

20 Letter from Daniel Fuller, 15 July 1986.

21 Harold Lindsell's account of "Black Saturday" is in his *The Battle for the Bible*, pp. 110–11. George Marsden also discusses "Black Saturday" in his forthcoming history of Fuller Seminary.

22 Letter from Robert McAfee Brown, 5 Mar. 1978.

23 Reprinted in CBC, pp. 33–9.

24 J. Gresham Machen, *Christianity and Liberalism* (Grand Rapids: Eerdmans, 1972).

25 Northrop Frye, *The Great Code: The Bible and Literature* (New York: Harcourt Brace Jovanovich, 1982), p. 29.

26 We have been conditioned to do otherwise. Richard A. Lanham says that deeply ingrained in our modern American culture is the questionable conviction that "prose ought to be maximally transparent and minimally self-conscious, never seen and never noticed." *Analyzing Prose* (New York: Charles Scribner's Sons, 1983), p. 2.

27 Frederick Buechner, *Wishful Thinking: A Theological ABC* (New York: Harper and Row, 1973), p. 6.
28 Ibid., p. 8.
29 Frederick Buechner, *Peculiar Treasures: A Biblical Who's Who* (San Francisco: Harper and Row, 1967).
30 Ibid., p. 12.
31 Paul Ricoeur, *The Symbolism of Evil* (New York: Harper and Row, 1967), p. 5.
32 "Variations in Perspective on Secularization and Unbelief," Round Table Discussion in *The Culture of Unbelief*, Studies and Proceedings from the First International Symposium on Belief Held at Rome, March 22–7, 1969, Rocco Caporale and Antonio Grumelli, editors, (Berkeley: University of California Press, 1971), p. 102.
33 Herbert N. Schneidau, *Sacred Discontent: The Bible and Western Tradition* (Berkeley: University of California Press, 1976), pp. 13–14.
34 Brevard Childs, *Biblical Theology in Crisis* (Philadelphia: Westminster, 1970), p. 98.
35 Herman Gunkel, *The Legends of Genesis: The Biblical Saga and History* (New York: Shocken Books, 1964), p. 3.
36 Edward Carnell, L. Harold DeWolf, and William Hordern, "A Trilogy on Protestant Theology," *Journal of Bible and Religion*, XXVII, 4 (Oct. 1959), pp. 311–19.
37 Carnell, review of *The Gospel and Modern Thought* by Alan Richardson, *Westminster Theological Journal* (Nov. 1950).
38 Gerald T. Sheppard, "Biblical Hermeneutics: The Academic Language of Evangelical Identity," *Union Seminary Quarterly Review*, XXXII, 2 (Winter 1977), p. 84.
39 "The Issue of Biblical Authority Brings a Scholar's Resignation," *Christianity Today* (15 July 1983), 35–8.
40 Edward Carnell, "The Inspiration and Authority of the Bible," unpublished typescript.
41 Ibid.
42 From the Archives of the Billy Graham Center at Wheaton College, Collection: Harold Lindsell, Box 9, Folder 5.
43 Robert Frost, *The Poetry of Robert Frost*, ed. Edward Connery Lathem, (New York: Holt, Rinehart and Winston, 1969), p. 266.

X. Figures in the carpet

1 Henry James, "The Figure in the Carpet," *The Complete Tales*, Vol. IX: 1892–1898, ed. Leon Edel (Philadelphia: J. B. Lippincott, 1964), pp. 273–315.
2 Leon Edel, "The Figure under the Carpet," in *Telling Lives: The Biographer's Art*, ed. Marc Pachter (Washington, D.C.: New Republic Books, 1979).
3 Gordon H. Clark, *Thales to Dewey: A History of Philosophy* (Boston: Houghton Mifflin, 1957), p. 534.
4 Gordon H. Clark, *A Christian Philosophy of Education* (Grand Rapids: Eerdmans, 1946), p. 62.

5   Gordon H. Clark, *Three Types of Religious Philosophy* (Nutley, N.J.: Craig Press, 1973), p. 110.
6   Erving Goffman, *The Presentation of the Self in Everyday Life* (New York: Anchor Books, 1959), p. 18.
7   Alan S. Curry, *Poison Detection in Human Organs* (Springfield: Charles S. Thomas, 1963), p. 89.
8   The medical report makes no mention of pill containers, a fact that surprised two medical examiners with whom I consulted. In reply to my query, Shirley Carnell Duvall had this to say: "In a list of the personal effects which were found with Ed mention is made of three containers – two with pills, one empty." She added, however, that the nature of the unused pills was not specified (Letters 20 July, 4 Aug. 1986). Why the containers were not mentioned in the medical report is not known. If the unused pills were sleeping pills, it seems likely that Carnell did not intend suicide; otherwise he probably would have ingested all of them.
9   Telephone interview with Ray Ortland, Jan. 1985.
10   Letter from Daniel Fuller, 16 Oct. 1980.
11   Frederick Buechner, *Now and Then* (San Francisco: Harper and Row, 1983), p. 46.
12   Frederick Buechner, *The Alphabet of Grace* (New York: Seabury, 1970), p. 46.
13   EJC to HJO, 22 Nov. 1957.
14   Carnell, unpublished notes for an address, Fuller Seminary files.
15   EJC to HJO, 2 Mar. 1959.
16   George E. Vaillant, ed., *Adaptation to Life* (Boston: Little, Brown, 1977), p. 29.
17   Personal interview with Glenn Barker, Dec. 1977.
18   Richard Ellmann and Charles Feidelson, Jr., eds., *The Modern Tradition: Backgrounds of Modern Literature* (New York: Oxford University Press, 1965), p. v.
19   George M. Marsden, "Evangelicals, History, and Modernity," in *Evangelicalism and Modern America*, ed. Marsden (Grand Rapids: Eerdmans, 1984), p. 98.
20   George M. Marsden, "Everyone One's Own Interpreter: The Bible, Science, and Authority in Mid-Nineteenth-Century America," in *The Bible in America: Essays in Cultural History*, ed. Nathan O. Hatch and Mark A. Noll (New York: Oxford University Press, 1982), p. 82.
21   Thomas S. Kuhn, *The Structure of Scientific Revolutions*, 2nd edition, enlarged (Chicago: University of Chicago Press, 1970).
22   Clifford Geertz, *Islam Observed* (New Haven: Yale University Press, 1968), p. 101.
23   Reinhold Niebuhr, *Leaves from the Notebook of a Tamed Cynic* (Hamden: Shoe String Press, 1956), pp. 141–2.
24   See, e.g., Kathleen R. Fischer, *The Inner Rainbow: The Imagination in Christian Life* (Ramsey: Paulist Press, 1983); Ray L. Hart, *Unfinished Man and the Imagination* (New York: Herder and Herder, 1968); William Lynch, *Christ and Apollo: The Dimensions of the Literary Imagination* (New York: New American Library, 1963); Sallie TeSelle, *Speaking in Parables: A Study in Metaphor and*

Theology (Philadelphia: Fortress Press, 1975); Amos N. Wilder, *Theopoetic: Theology and Religious Imagination* (Philadelphia: Fortress Press, 1976).

25 Wilder, p. 2.

26 Flannery O'Connor, *Three* (New York: New American Library, 1962), p. 314.

27 Hattie R. Rosenthal, "The Fear of Death as an Indispensable Factor in Psychotherapy" in *The Interpretation of Death*, ed. H. Ruitenbeek (New York: Jason Aronson, 1973), p. 176.

28 EJC to Don Weber, 19 Sept. 1962.

29 Erik H. Erikson, *Young Man Luther: A Study in Psychoanalysis and History* (New York: W. W. Norton, 1958), p. 22.

30 Ibid., p. 43.

31 Letter to George and Thomas Keats, 12 Dec. 1817, in *English Romantic Poetry and Prose*, ed. Russell Noyes (New York: Oxford University Press, 1956), p. 1211.

32 Peter Berger, *The Sacred Canopy: Elements of a Sociological Theory of Religion* (New York: Anchor Books, 1969), p. 183.

33 Northrop Frye, *The Modern Century*, The Whidden Lectures 1967 (Toronto: Oxford University Press, 1967), p. 116.

34 Henry David Thoreau, "Walking," in *The Portable Thoreau*, ed. Carl Bode (New York: Viking, 1947), pp. 592–630.

35 James Davison Hunter, *American Evangelicalism: Conservative Religion and the Quandary of Modernity* (New Brunswick, N.J.: Rutgers University Press, 1983), pp. 99–100.

36 Nathan O. Hatch, "Evangelicalism as a Democratic Movement," in *Evangelicalism and Modern America*, ed. George M. Marsden, p. 75.

37 David Tracy, *Blessed Rage for Order: The New Pluralism in Theology* (New York: Seabury, 1975), p. 135.

38 Robert N. Bellah, *Beyond Belief: Essays on Religion in a Post-Traditional Society* (New York: Harper and Row, 1970), p. 244.

Index